small voices & GREAT TRUMPETS

small voices

TRUMPETS

Minorities & The Media

Edited by
Bernard Rubin

PRAEGER

PRAEGER SPECIAL STUDIES • PRAEGER SCIENTIFIC

Library of Congress Cataloging in Publication Data
Main entry under title:

Small voices and great trumpets.

Includes index.
1. Mass media and minorities--United States--Addresses, essays, lectures. I. Rubin, Bernard.
HN90.M3S6 301.2'3 80-12427

ISBN 0-03-056973-7
ISBN 0-03-056972-9 (pbk.)

Published in 1980 by Praeger Publishers
CBS Educational and Professional Publishing
A Division of CBS, Inc.
521 Fifth Avenue, New York, New York 10017 U.S.A.

0123456789 145 987654321

Printed in the United States of America

For all whose ideas and works
enhance the First Amendment

CONTENTS

INTRODUCTION

Small Voices and Great Trumpets: Minorities and the Media is the third in the studies of major topics related to the First Amendment that have been undertaken by the Institute for Democratic Communication (IDC).* This book, like its predecessors, was designed to present original research to an audience composed of concerned citizens from the general public, media practitioners and critics, college and university students, and public- and private-sector leaders interested in public-policy opportunities and alternatives.

The objective of the IDC is to provide substantive research findings and professional critiques that clarify difficult issues pertaining to the goal of making public communication as free and responsible as possible. Since its founding in January of 1976, its programs of research and community-outreach efforts have been concentrated on priority topics as determined by much consultation with many individuals devoted to the cause of furthering democracy in both letter and spirit.

This book shows the results of contributors commissioned by the IDC to spend the better part of a year analyzing a topic which best reflects their personal experience, substantial research, and individual efforts to offer solutions to vexing problems. It emphasizes key issues and depicts key social political and economic situations, without pretending to encompass the entire area.

Small Voices and Great Trumpets aims at providing the readers with insightful rather than encyclopedic data. Analyses of the specific minority groups studied in this volume are meant to be indicative and illustrative of what other communities face. We endeavored to face up to major issues, without denying the need for additional and continuing research on a subject too sparsely considered by scholars. Other significant minorities such as Hispanics and Americans of Asian heritage, the abortion and right-to-life groups, homosexuals, and religious minorities need

*The first two were *Big Business and the Mass Media* (1977); *Questioning Media Ethics* (1978).

more attention. This volume provides important data as well as critical support for such research. We were selective in our topics, for good research-feasibility reasons. Our aim is to deal with salient data, as we are appreciative of that holy research grail—the fully comprehensive study.

Authors of these original explorations were drawn from a variety of professional backgrounds. A strong effort was made to include minority-group members who know first hand the aspirations and tribulations of people who rely on good media work. With a number of personally chosen approaches, they examine print and electronic-media claims to be, as democratic instruments, educative, instigative, representative, participatory, and generally responsible.

Other contributors provide professional knowledge of media law and communications theory as such information applies to minority-group access to, participation in, and ownership of, the mass media in this country.

A careful analysis of atypical advocacy-group work was also specially prepared for this study.

The range of subjects chosen to illustrate vital elements behind our endeavors to make media more democratic, thereby enhancing the First Amendment, is comparable to the range of a powerful telescope at a scientific astronomical observatory. What is brought into view makes all else more meaningful.

In that context, a revealing story of one woman's professional journalistic frustrations and triumphs is immediately connected to a crucial exploration by a black television producer of the media stereotyping that marks all periods of American history. A major television critic's critique of that medium's treatments of the aged in our society is no less socially important than the analysis of how immigrants are reported upon by their own and the general-circulation press. The latter was written by a professor of journalism who, fleeing persecution, immigrated about a decade ago. The theories of press roles are effectively in juxtaposition to a detailed survey of the imageries propounded by the press and the entertainment media to depict women.

The accounts of how blacks, Hispanics, Asians, Native Americans, the aged, women, and immigrants are treated provide much information that is deplorable and much that is constructive. All of the data really compound into basic ingredients for significant reform.

This study was, in part, made possible by a research grant from the Shell Oil Company, which had no participation or role whatever, other than providing a portion of the financial assistance needed to start the research phase. More corporations should take the lead and assist scholars with support for objective research.

The issues raised by *Small Voices and Great Trumpets* go far beyond the Fourth Estate's interests and activities. They are of paramount importance to every socially alert and responsible citizen. Our hope is to learn more about how to improve and perpetuate democracy.

I would like to extend my appreciation to Nolan Bowie of the Citizens Communications Center, for providing transcripts of important media advocacy-group testimony before the Federal Communications Commission and the Congress. Also, my appreciation goes to Norman Altstedter for his continued interest in the IDC. I thank all my colleagues for good work and for good cheer.

PART I

MEDIA REALITIES/MEDIA GOALS

ONE

"SEE US, HEAR US, KNOW ME"

Bernard Rubin

THE TIMES ARE CHANGING

A veteran reporter recently responded to a question of mine about the quality of minority-group coverage by the metropolitan press of Boston. He concluded that "we do a fairly good job. Whenever a minority person or group does something that's newsworthy, it gets in the papers." I found that answer to be fairly typical of the opinions held by newsmen with 20 or more years of experience. Only a small number of such long-service types feel that reportage of blacks, Chicanos, Native Americans, other Hispanics, and other communities is inadequate.

In part, his view is derived from experiences with a primarily white, male, and economically middle-class Fourth Estate. Ethnic minorities, women, and the poverty-level people of all backgrounds have never been well represented in the newsrooms he worked in. The publishers, editors, and reporters he has known have shared a series of life experiences and opportunities, and have been fortunate enough to miss others common to the ghettos. Women have never been wholeheartedly welcomed by the corps of veteran reporters, who are just now learning to accept and respect females as colleagues. In addition, many reporters, because of their own ethnic family trees, still find it hard to think of minorities except in terms of European immigrant families and their struggles.

The minority of experienced reporters who recognize that the reportage of minority-group affairs is unfair or inadequate is growing all the time, as professionals become more and more attuned to the changing responsibilities and roles of the mass media. Prompted by the emerging cadre of younger associates who have been trained to deal with social, economic, and political stories, from what is labeled an investigative-reporting approach, the most proficient of the veterans are grappling with all of the important stories of our time. The existing opportunities to work alongside women and persons from ethnic minorities also tend to produce positive results.

Keeping changing interests and job experiences of newspeople in mind, there is another important reason for inappropriate coverage of minority affairs. For most of our national history, the press has served better as a reflector of popular tastes and moods than as an educative system relaying messages about the range of alternatives on the issues it has surveyed. As an institution of society, the press has, by and large, catered to whims or enthusiasms. It has been more a powerful instrument of powerful people and organizations than an instrument for communication between the powerful and the powerless. Painting images of portions of the society, it has succeeded in blotting out knowledge of much that is on the canvas of our civilization.

Historically, the press has not been anxious, or in most cases even reluctantly willing, to take stands on social issues important to minorities, especially when those issues have been the hottest. Like the judiciary, the press has claimed to deal primarily in facts and only describe causes. Like the judiciary, it has been an ultimately reliable public protector, using its inherent and residual powers carefully. The press claims to record—its directors and managers do not want as a rule to lead society.

The veteran newsman referred to probably thought the press was doing a fairly good job of covering minorities because he didn't know what that job consisted of. He is little different than most people who don't realize that the nation was for a long, long time on a wrong path, and that we have never adequately told the minority stories. It would be inaccurate to place the blame for inadequate coverage of minority news and developments wholly on the shoulders of veteran reporters as a group, for two reasons. First, a minority of such professionals provide us with some of the best work we have today, going beyond the superficial happenings and delving into the complex backgrounds to the struggles of the distressed and oppressed. Probably, that minority is no less a percentage of the total group of news professionals than is to be found in other professional worlds, where lawyers or doctors or architects attempt to rise above median standards to excellence. The second reason is that the younger echelons are frequently hung up on the search for late news, rather than focusing on the stories behind the fast-breaking bulletins.

Old-timers and novices share a bad habit of pointing with pride to specific stories on minority problems to prove press interest. Steady readers of newspapers, or listeners to radio, or viewers of television would probably back up that claim, recalling how many times the news is about minorities. What is lost to the news professionals and their audiences is the fact that there is hardly any systematic reportage or analysis—hardly any followup on the most important stories, by way of looking into related events and circumstances over a long period of time. One can conclude generally that most stories convey news about the outbreaks of specific cases of disease, and a very few deal with basic virus-hunting research.

All too frequently, newspeople point to a story that was well done, as if they had discharged their general duty by specifically committing a story to paper or to the electronic circuitry of radio or television. "See," they seem to say, "we did a big story on Puerto Ricans only last month." Or, "don't forget our investigative report about conditions in the black-ghetto tenement houses." Or, "what a great job was done last spring on the insurance industry's redlining of minority-occupied sections of our city." Or, "we have a big story in the works on Indian rights."

The times are changing, and what is needed now and in the future is a more regular, systematic, and penetrating level of coverage. Ethnic minorities and generic minorities deserve more adequate reporting by those who claim to be informing the general public of what is going on.

TYPICAL COMPLAINTS

The mass media should be the nation's major conduits for news and views about minority interests, problems, and aspirations, given the substantial numbers of people in minority groups. However, there are many complaints about the quality of mass communications. Several examples follow.

Stereotyping of minorities is still all too prevalent. Three researchers in Native American media coverage recently concluded: "Stereotypical misrepresentation in United States media of

Native American peoples and cultures has been comprehensive and systematic since the 1880's. The methods of such stereotyping are known and the intent of their employment has been the effective dehumanization of the peoples depicted."[1]

Another worry is that media executives of the mass-circulation organizations catering to the affluent, white majority might consciously avoid placing stories about minorities. This is reportedly due to their fear of losing the attractiveness of their media products vis-à-vis "white readers coveted by advertisers." An analysis of the *Los Angeles Times* published in early 1979 suggests some of the background. It is pointed out that "a significant portion of the mostly white middle-class, the prime target of the *Times* advertisers, has left the city . . ."

Influenced by that movement, the *Times* created special editions in order to follow its readers—one for Orange County (launched in 1968) and one for San Diego (1978). About a million and one-half dollars has been so invested, and there is some talk of two more such editions.

With 36.3 percent of the municipal Los Angeles population being of Spanish heritage or black, according to the U.S. Bureau of the Census figures for July 1975, the new interests of the major newspaper have ominous overtones for minority groups complaining about inappropriate coverage. It is expected that blacks, Chicanos, and Asian-Americans will soon account for more than half of the Los Angeles residents.

Otis Chandler, the *Times* publisher, has opined that the paper had "a way to go" in covering minority news, and that it "would not make sense financially for us" to incline the *Times* toward low-income readers, considering that "that audience does not have the purchasing power and is not responsive to the kind of advertising we carry." In his view, the *Times*'s minority coverage has greatly improved since he took over as publisher in 1960. That judgment of better work was seconded by Anthony Day, his editor for the opinion and editorial pages, who offered as evidence a recent story on automobile insurance that told of a Chicano group's opposition to redlining, and editorial endorsements important to the black electorate. Day added: "We did a major series on the plight of inner cities in America and my mail shows the story didn't sit well with many in our primary target audience. But we felt the story had to be done."[2]

Complaints from leaders of the Hispanic community of Los Angeles, about poor coverage of their affairs by the major newspaper there, quite typically reflect what agitates Hispanic leaders in other metropolitan areas of the nation. Across the continent from Los Angeles, the press of Boston is similarly accused.

Boston has, according to one estimate, about 50,000 out of the 250,000 Hispanics in Massachusetts. They are approximately one-twelfth of Boston's urban population and include groups emanating from all of Latin America.

Above all, they resent invisibility in the media; however, it is not total. What little is related about the diverse community is considered by many to be irrelevant or misleading. One Puerto Rican leader was most critical: "And the little bit that's in the papers usually gives us a negative image. You know, the heroin arrests, and the violence, and things like that." An architect, Maurizio Gaston, considered it most important that the media "recognize the reality of Hispanic oppression in this city—and that it's not our fault!"

The picture painted of the media in Boston by Hispanic leaders is not entirely dismal. Some credit the *Boston Globe* for some management interest manifested in some important if limited coverage, but feel that there was a more pronounced effort a decade ago. It was reported that in late 1978, only one Hispanic was employed by the *Globe*, out of approximately 1,600 employees.

Anne Kirchheimer, according to some Hispanic observers, did a valiant if lonely job of reporting Hispanic matters with sensitivity. They were said to be angry when she was assigned to the *Globe*'s "Living" pages. Kirchheimer, in evaluating the indifference or prejudice she claims to have observed in middle-management story editors, said: "Half those people don't even realize they [Hispanics] exist. They consider Columbia Point like a war assignment." (Columbia Point is a vast low-rent apartment complex ridden with problems—with the residents being the victims of poor urban planning, and the recipients of inadequate services, e.g., police, sanitation, social. The housing development is a fine example of what should not be done for the poor, who so often are from the ethnic minorities.) She applauds the *Globe* owners and the editor, Thomas Winship, for past good deeds in the early 1970s: experimenting with a bilingual column authored by a Hispanic; doing a booklet on Hispanic life in the city; making possible and funding a Berlitz Spanish course for *Globe* personnel. For all those good deeds, she feels that at present, "they don't want to deal with the problems from the sixties. It's a bad time now for anything on the city or on poor people. They want no more social problems. It's all me-me-me now. You know, the leisure articles, the articles on food, the articles on taxes."[3]

Another major complaint deals with the lack of communications-media enterprises directed by minority-group members. On the premise that the stories of groups must in large part come from their own members, the dearth of minority owners and operators and editors is indeed a serious problem for all advocates of democracy. To illustrate, it was as late as 1949 that the first black-owned radio station came into being, when Jesse B. Blayton, a certified public accountant, bought WERD in Atlanta, Georgia. The first black-built radio station (WCHB in Inkster, Michigan) was created in 1956 by Dr. Haley Bell, a Detroit dentist. There has been, relatively speaking, a phenomenal growth of black-owned radio stations in the United States in the 1970s. From 1973 to 1978, more than 40 such stations appeared. For all that growth, nearly 500 percent since 1970, "only 57 of the country's 7,571 commercial radio stations are black-owned." A heartening development in an otherwise bleak picture of black radio-station ownership is seen in the collateral area of news services. The National Black Network, the first such black-owned service, was created in 1973. "It sells black-oriented news programs," from its headquarters in New York City, "to more than 8 affiliated radio stations. The network's programs are broadcast to about 17 million blacks a week."[4]

As another illustration of minority-media difficulties that affect us all, there are too few black publishers in the book-publishing business. Visibility and usefulness of such well-known black-oriented magazines as *Ebony* and *Jet* tend to blur visibility of the gaps blacks see in publishing. One researcher recently caught my attention with this statistic and followup: "In 1971 there were only two first novels published by blacks and even today there are few black writers who can claim success with a general white audience," Dudley Randall, called the doyen of black book publishers (he heads the Broadside Press in Detroit), lamented. "We are a nation of 22 million souls, larger than Athens in the Age of Pericles or England in the Elizabethan Age. There is no reason we should not support a literature that would be to our own nation what their literature was to theirs."[5] Randall's use of the word nation is in itself a reflection of how much we must all accomplish to convince traditionally oppressed minorities that we are allied cultures and interdependent persons, comprising one nation committed to the accomplishment of great democratic goals.

SIGNALS FROM ORGANIZED ETHNIC MINORITY GROUPS

Portuguese-Americans: Awakening

The Portuguese-American communities of New Bedford and Fall River, Massachusetts, constitute numerical majorities of those two cities. Historically, those communities have not been well known for protesting for rights or for vigor in seeking publicity. However, in the fall of 1978, two demonstrations—one in New Bedford over higher tax bills because of property reassessment (an estimated 400 participants), and one in Fall River over alleged local newspaper bias (an estimated 600 participants), showed that there was a new militancy.

To celebrate the 175th anniversary of Fall River, the *Fall River Herald-News* published a special-edition section on October 17, 1978. Articles related the contributions made by the city's "Polish, Italian, Lebanese, Greek, Chinese, Jewish, Irish and French populations but omitted the Portuguese community. Instead, the *Herald-News* printed a feature article, outside the section designated for ethnic news, about a successful Portuguese businessman." The newspaper's approach made many Portuguese ethnics angry, and hundreds marched from City Hall to the front of the newspaper's building. One report had it that a local radio station, WJFD, stimulated the demonstration. WJFD is a Portuguese-speaking station owned by a Portuguese-American, a former Bristol County district attorney, and is named for his father.

The newspaper's city editor, Charles Hewitt, said that there had been no intent to ignore the Portuguese community, and that only "a different approach" with the feature story was used. The news editor, Herman Mello, countering charges of discrimination in an article entitled "Portuguese-American Editor Replies," argued that "the concept of heritage must be broader than limiting it to a litany of accomplishment or a list of names."

Ten days after the initial special section was published, the newspaper provided a full page on Portuguese-American accomplishments.

The demonstration was a signal of a community striving for visibility, unity, and for a prominent role in civic decision making. It is especially interesting that one of this awakening ethnic group's leaders did not assert that the alleged omission by the newspaper was a conscious provocation. To the contrary, Onesimo

Almeida, of the Portuguese Youth Cultural Organization, one of the sponsors of the march, said: "We admit that this oversight may have been an unconscious act, but that is still a sign of their attitude. We are a majority in this city, but the paper remains a mouthpiece for Anglos only."

Hewitt of the *Herald-News* took a refreshingly constructive view of the protest against his organization, calling the response probably a "pretty good thing" showing some unity in the Portuguese-Americans of Fall River. He observed, "They've never really come together for anything before."[6]

Native Americans: Protesting Alleged Distortions and Asserting Community Views

It is the duty of a reporter, and the organization he works for, to present stories to media clients as honestly as humanly possible. That implies striving for objectivity while retaining the right to present personal insights into the meanings of what is learned. Obviously, the most sincere reporting is likely to foment controversy simply by antagonizing media clients who honestly see sensitive subjects differently than the reporters who analyzed those subjects did.

If protesters against the media can show obvious prejudice in any reports complained of, or better still can prove it, the media people involved ought to recant with a clearly apparent sense of regret. Should the newspeople concerned sincerely believe that their facts are defensible, or their opinions justifiable, they ought to boldly stand their ground against any single protest, or even a swarm of pressure-group demands for some admission of wrongdoing.

Such principles are sometimes put to the test. For example, *The Real Paper* of Boston found itself in a genuinely adversarial relationship with the Boston Indian Council (BIC) over two articles printed in November of 1978. Both were entitled "Native Americans." Part one dealt with "Paths of Survival—A Portrait of Three Brothers." The second was "Portrait of a Navajo Family."

The Boston Indian Council, Inc. was founded in 1970 to meet the "critical needs of Boston's growing Native American population," who "came looking for a better life." However, notes the BIC, "they found the urban environment hostile and demanding." BIC is a "multi-service, community-oriented organization" directed by a board of directors comprising seven persons annually elected. Its programs encompass efforts in such areas as health, legal aid, employment counseling and training, youth services, elderly affairs and adult education, emergency social services, child care, and some preschool efforts for its employees and students.[7]

The first article that triggered BIC pressure on *The Real Paper* dealt with three brothers, Alex, Robert, and William Thomas, who are Micmac Indians from the Cape Breton Island reserve in Canada. They came to the Boston area anxious to improve their situations. The Micmac tribe is unusual in one respect: Its members are rewarded with the right to dual residency in the United States and Canada, because their ancestors, and those of other tribes of the Wabanaki Confederacy (Micmac, Maliseet, Abenaki, Passamaquoddy, and Penobscot), aided the American revolutionary cause and opposed the British in the American Revolutionary period. British supplies and troops were stopped when passage to the colonies from Nova Scotia was attempted by the royal authorities. So, since the approval of the Treaty of Amity and Commerce of 1794 (the Jay Treaty), the Micmacs do not have to register as aliens, or pay duty. In addition, they can receive benefits that accrue to those holding U.S. citizenship.

The personal stories of these three brothers in the United States have not been bright or encouraging on the whole. Perhaps their stories are not dissimilar to those of many Indians in Boston. John Hubner, the author of the article, estimated: "Fifty-five percent of the Indians now living in Boston are unemployed. Seventy-five percent live below the poverty level. Seventy percent have not completed high school. One Indian out of every four is an alcoholic."

Hubner attempted to relate the situations of the Thomas brothers to the bigger problems of Native Americans who enter the worlds of the urban dwellers in our larger cities. He shows how, because of lack of training, education, and opportunity, they often fail and are psychologically devastated by their failures. He speaks of persecution and of Indians being ignored by the authorities. Hubner documents vast tragedies and demonstrates how general factors can be appreciated as leading to desperate personal histories. Alcoholism is one means of temporary escape for these victims of societal pressures in a complex technological environment: "Robert [Thomas] drinks because he is trapped between two cultures, neither of which he finds hospitable." After Alex had succeeded in graduating from high school and married (two children), only to have his marriage break up—"She was a city Indian and I was a reserve Indian"—he spent some time drinking in Dorchester and in the South End of Boston. William has had periods when he drank heavily, but according to Hubner, he did start an apprentice program as a pipe fitter.[8]

Are these matters of general background and personal lives, gone into in detail by Hubner, treated systematically or in a derogatory fashion? As a critical reader, I was much taken by the plight of the subjects, and did not conclude that Hubner was spelling out his own biases.

The BIC took the view that the article represented a "betrayal." In a three-page open letter "to the editor, staff and readers of *The Real Paper*," it accused Hubner of gaining the confidence of BIC people and others and then writing two articles. The first was not printed, they say, even though it was read by "some of us" and "our reaction was favorable." It did not gloss over problems, and dealt with a chain of problems like "alcoholism, poor housing and personal frustration." The BIC open letter claims that a second article, which it considered distorted, one-sided, and not inclusive of "women, elders, young people and members of different tribes,"[9] was the one published by *The Real Paper*.

The published article is described, in addition, as offering simpleminded and unqualified explanations leading to the maintenance of negative stereotypes. The BIC also complained about "Portrait of a Navajo Family," by Peter R. Melnick, which was the second part of the series. It is about the Yazzie family, which lives in White Horse, Arizona. That reservation area and surrounding region is home to 150,000 Navajos. It is described as "dry and infertile, a barren wilderness." The Yazzie family lives under the most difficult conditions, sustained by general assistance money and by what its members can make from sheep raising and odd jobs. There are many children, and hope for a better future usually seems dim. The federal government's Bureau of Indian Affairs is roundly criticized in the article for inadequacies and "fragmented attempts at helping the Navajo people." The article delves into new assertions of independence and self-reliance by Indian tribes and into much social and political background, explaining how the Yazzie family and many, many others like it came to be in such an economic, social, and political straitjacket.

Melnick strikes a chord hit in the Hubner article, detailing how alcohol has been a tormenting alternative to vicissitudes which distressed Indian people must face daily:

> Of Pete Yazzie's nine children, two have died in drunk-related car accidents. One was drunk, and died when he flipped his car on the way home from a Holbrook bar. . . . Annie Gray Goats still walks

> with a stooped back from the time a few years ago when Martha struck her with a frying pan in a fit of alcoholic rage.
>
> For more than thirty years Pete too was a drinker. A heavy, pour-it-down-with-a-vengeance drinker.[10]

According to the BIC's open letter: "*The Real Paper* has chosen to offer its readers only the most damaging, negative view of Native American life. It has isolated a small part of Indian life and presented it as a whole. There is no balance to these articles, no look beyond the problems to the solutions." Also, "this perspective on Indian people is a racist perspective."[11]

BIC's director, Clif Saunders (a Sioux), went with a delegation to see *The Real Paper*'s editor, Martin Linsky, after the first of the two articles was published. Saunders, two BIC associates, and a lawyer talked to Linsky, with about 100 members of the community present, at the paper's premises. Linsky stood by the article, but offered space on the letters-to-the-editor page in a future edition, for rebuttals. That was considered a minimal response by the BIC delegation. After the second story appeared, "again, the reaction of the Indian community was one of outraged disbelief." A community meeting of protest was said to have been attended by "100 Native people." The BIC claimed wide support for its protest by similar groups in the Boston area.[12] The December 2, 1978 edition of *The Real Paper* published five letters of complaint about the two articles.

Two weeks later, in his "Behind the Lines" column, Linsky said:

> The pieces are sound, both in their reportage and in their representation of life as seen through the eyes of some (although not all) Native Americans . . . I agree with the Boston Indian Council that the articles did not improve the image of the Native Americans. They were not intended to. Nor were they written to tell the whole story of the Native American community. But they were stories of real Native Americans dealing in different ways (some successful and some not) with similar problems of discrimination and cultural conflict. The portraits were explanatory, if not positive.
>
> Finally, I agree with the BIC that the articles would have existed in a different context if *The Real Paper* had been providing regular coverage, good and bad, of Boston's Native American community. That has not happened so far, and it is a situation that should be corrected.
>
> The stories were good stories . . . I did my job in editing and

> publishing them. The BIC did theirs in protesting and getting publicity for their complaints. I probably would have done the same thing in their place.[13]

Was *The Real Paper* guilty, as charged, of publishing distortions of Indian life? Truth, it has been said, can be in the eye of the beholder. The articles were harsh and presented unfavorable pictures. One honest reader might conclude that if we are ever to do better by our distressed peoples, such stories will act as catalysts to get people to see what has to be done. Another equally honest reader, especially one who felt that the group he belongs to is too frequently maligned, might be more taken with the depiction of distress than with the possible opportunities to alert our citizenry through the depiction. I could not read the story as an Indian would. However, it did make me anxious to grapple with the basic problem behind the local confrontation. Although I honestly conclude that the BIC was more sensitive than absolutely correct in this case, while deserving of more credit than criticism for taking the opportunity to acquaint the rest of the community with the views of aroused Native Americans, there is more behind the confrontation than can be revealed by the actual circumstances and the present participants.

Whether data or background or analysis presented in any media story does or does not satisfy minority critics who discern something capricious or sinister, in content or context, is almost irrelevant in one regard. Reporters, editors, and media owners should almost expect that, barring the exceptions to prove the rule, man-built mountains of injustice will normally produce deep rumbles of discontent, or great crashes as parts of those mountains give way. For Indians of all tribes, the army massacre of Indians at Wounded Knee, South Dakota, in 1890 and the 70-day confrontation between Indian militants and federal officers there in 1973, are two events tied to the same umbilical cord. Blacks, Hispanics, Native Americans, and Asian-Americans tend to be supersensitive when it comes to rights, to access and participation, and to matters of social acceptance, and it would be unnatural if it were otherwise. Each group recalls its version of Wounded Knee vividly.

The Real Paper-versus-BIC confrontation made me seek more background to the poor record of the press as a public service carrier of news about minorities. I began to wonder if the majority of mass media managers have ever decided to represent the powerless adequately. Is it a question of will?

Out of our history we trace prejudices which still must be

overcome. In my view, the BIC was protesting not so much the particulars as the whole context of attitudes about minorities that are still prevalent in the media and evident in hiring practices, ownership data, and directorial opportunities and training programs, as well as in sparse coverage of minority affairs.*

FOR THE RECORD: SIGNIFICANT ETHNIC AND CLASSIFIED MINORITIES

Excluding, for the moment, minorities based upon national background and culture, representing European nationalistic history, almost a quarter of the U.S. population has minority back-

*There is no shortage of reporting opportunities for a press interested in covering Native American affairs adequately. Any careful review of the literature enforces that view. To illustrate with media-related subjects, more work is needed on the history and current practices of those in the media who describe Indian life accurately or inaccurately, so shaping public opinion. Are they collectively to be accused of creating and perpetuating colonialism? In Gerald Wilkinson's judgment, "through these media, a picture of Indian people is painted which serves the interest of the white public, and not necessarily the interest of truth and morality." It is usually a negative image of the drunken, dumb, helpless savage, or the other extreme of the noble savage so detached from reality that he achieves fairy tale proportions. (see Wilkinson, "Colonialism Through the Media," *The Indian Historian* 7, no. 3 [Summer 1974]: 29-32). Are films a major weapon, used since the motion picture industry began, against Native Americans? What about American Indian Movement complaints against: whites portraying Indians, depictions of Indians as poor warriors, "the overemphasis of drunken Indians", dialogue and customs condemned as inauthentic, "non-portrayal of Indian accomplishments" and the "non-showing of Indians as personalities and entities"? (see Hedy Hartman, "A Brief Review of the Native American in American Cinema," *The Indian Historian* 9, no. 3 [Summer 1976]: 27-29).

What are the effects of radio on traditional Native American cultures? Is it true that the radio station established on the Ramah Navajo Indian reservation of northwestern New Mexico in 1972 has backfired on Indian culture? "The radio station [KTDB-FM], an institution partly created and entrusted with the responsibility of preserving and perpetuating the Ramah Navajo culture, has instead, provided the Anglo culture with the means to hasten the acculturation and assimilation of the Ramah Navajo into the greater Anglo society." (see Stephen E. Rada, "Ramah Navajo Radio and Cultural Preservation," *Journal of Broadcasting* 22, no. 3 [Summer 1978]: 361-71).

What can be accomplished to provide adequate media training for Native-Americans? How can such projects help to reverse a pattern of failure by the press to serve, thus producing "an alienated society deprived of the resources with which to understand educational opportunities, knowledge of health benefits, awareness of social possibilities or even the location of job opportunities." (See, Timothy Feder, "Native American Media Training Projects Fill Communications Vacuum," *Access*, No. 52, June, 1977, pp. 4-5).

grounds. When one includes the European-origin and European-ancestry citizens who cherish the old traditions, it is probable that half of our citizens might consider themselves members of minorities. Add to that percentage those of varied heritages who share the grinding-down environment imposed on those who are below the government-cited levels of adequate income, and one wonders if there is a genuine majority in this country.

The U.S. population in 1979 was approximately 220 million. The black citizenry, as of July 1975, was estimated to number 24,426,796. An estimate of the Spanish-origin population in 1976 was 11,117,000 (Mexicans—6,590,000; Puerto Ricans—1,753,000; Cubans—687,000; Central or South Americans—752,000; other Spanish—1,335,000). In 1970 it was calculated that there were 591,290 Japanese-ancestry persons and 435,062 of Chinese ancestry. Native Americans or Indians were estimated at 792,730; "all other" persons were estimated at 17,063,580.

"Persons below the poverty level by race and Spanish origin, 1966 to 1974 . . ." added up to 16,290,000 whites; 7,467,000 blacks; 2,601,000 of Spanish origin. While the median American family income in 1976 was $14,960, about 12 percent, or 25 million people, lived in poverty (according to government-set standards defining poverty levels), about the same population as in 1969.

By August of 1978, "9.3 percent of all U.S. families lived below the poverty level; . . . other rates were Mexican-American, 18.9 percent; Puerto Rican, 38.9 percent; and Cuban, 15.1 percent." Between 1970 and 1977, average black family income decreased from 61 percent to 57 percent of white family income. Also, it was reported that as of June 1978, "median weekly income of full-time women workers was 73 percent of men's pay in professional-technical jobs, 64 percent in clerical jobs and 45 percent in sales jobs." Highlighting how little power, in the economic areas, women and minority-group members have, those owning businesses from these two classifications do "just 2 percent of the nation's gross business."[14]

Women are not a minority on the economic front alone. They are usually undervalued, underestimated, underrepresented, and poorly reported about when grave social or political questions are in debate. Today there is more confused or misleading reporting about the proposed Equal Rights Amendment and about the so-called "right-to-life"-versus-abortion rights issue than is justifiable, even if emotions are high.

Women and men who wish to sanely and constructively protect battered wives and children from further abuse find it very difficult to drum up general interest, as against flash interest in terrible instances, which signals on and off. Protectors of our elderly citizens, and those who would look after the interests of institutionalized children, also are forced to accept minority status, vis-à-vis reasonable or steady press interest. What majority has really been educated to be concerned about the elderly that are without rights, or safeguards in some nursing homes, or about orphans who are literally imprisoned in giant cribs for years after infancy, to make it easy for those who have charge over them? What about the minority of those assigned to mental institutions and left to rot, kept placid by drugs? All of these minorities are representative of those which the media, as educational agencies, should make important to the majority, in mind and heart.

HARSH REALITY: MINORITY EMPLOYMENT IN THE MASS MEDIA

Newspapers

In 1978, a decade after the National Advisory Commission on Civil Disorders (the Kerner Commission) had reported to President Johnson that "the nation is rapidly moving toward two separate Americas," divided between a white society living in the suburbs and "smaller central cities," and a "Negro society largely concentrated within large central cities," the frustrations which had led to black (and other) rioting were only moderately impacting the mass media.[15] Reforms affecting minority employment were modest indeed.*

---

*A recent survey of newspaper-group executives, newspaper editors, and reporters, based on interviews conducted by Nick Kotz, shows how modest are the gains in minority employment. Preparing his article ("The Minority Struggle for a Place in the Newsroom," *Columbia Journalism Review* 7, no. 6 [March/April 1979]: 26), he collected statistics on newspapers and chains, revealing in each instance the number of journalists (NJ), the minority journalists (MJ), and the percentage of minority journalists (PMJ) employed. Here follow some illustrative employment situations taken from the Kotz survey (assisted by Jim Dawson): *Albuquerque Journal*, NJ—70, MJ—3, PMJ—4.3 percent; *Atlanta Constitution*, NJ—110, MJ—9, PMJ—8.2 percent; *Atlanta Journal*, NJ—156, MJ—5, PMJ—3.2 percent; *Boston Globe*, NJ—330, MJ—16, PMJ—4.8 percent; *Chicago Tribune*, NJ—430, MJ—19, PMJ—4.4 percent; *Gannett Newspapers*, NJ—2715, MJ—147, PMJ—5.4 percent; *Knight-Ridder Newspapers*, (including "some managerial and professional personnel outside the news departments"), NJ—4762, MJ—287, PMJ—6.0 percent; *Los Angeles Times*, NJ—572, MJ—28, PMJ—4.9 percent; *Minneapolis Tribune*, NJ—135, MJ—5, PMJ—3.7 percent; *New York Times*, NJ—670, MJ—40, PMJ—6.0

Seventy-five percent of the newspapers of this country had no minority employees. A scarce 4 percent of reporters and editors on dailies (approximately 1,700 individuals) were of minority origins. In ten years this last percentage had risen by 3 percent, significant only if you close your mind to the report of the Committee on Minorities of the American Society of Newspaper Editors (ANSE), which pointed out in 1978, it would be the year 2000, at the present rate of growth, before minority employment by the nation's newspapers equaled the minority proportion of the general population (estimated at 17 percent of the general population, through a misunderstanding of how many of us are minority-group members in real life). That committee was reporting on a Medill School of Journalism (Northwestern University) survey of 1,762 daily newspapers, of which 1,038 had responded.

Other shocking data include: a mere 11 top-management editors were classified as minority-group members, of the thousands holding such positions; only 12 percent of newspapers with circulations of under 10,000 copies employed minority-group members; newspaper funding aimed at encouraging more minority-origin reporters through scholarships and training programs had sunk from an embarrassing total of $225,000 (approximately) in 1972 to an incredible $115,000 (approximately) in 1977.[16] Not much need be said about the industry's high sense of civic responsibility vis-à-vis this employment and training-support pattern.*

Jesse Jackson, the well-known national leader whose Operation Push has had a positive impact on black and other minority youth, told ASNE editors at their April 1978 meeting: "The news media have the knack of keeping us busy looking at everybody else's sins but their own—Watergate, Koreagate, the sexual escapades and preferences of Congressmen—when they've got a news-media-gate in their own ranks when it comes to race." William Wong, a reporter for the *Wall Street Journal*, advised the newspaper industry leaders that "race relations in America are not a black and white issue anymore; . . . there are other ethnic minorities who have been maligned and do need coverage." Jose M. Ferrer III, *Nuestro* magazine's managing editor, concluded that

*Training programs for minorities are few and far between. One heartening indication of what is possible when media and university leaders get together, in order to further professional training for minority-group persons, is seen in the

percent; *Philadelphia Bulletin*, NJ—274, MJ—14, PMJ—5.1 percent; *Philadelphia Inquirer*, NJ—250, MJ—17, PMJ—6.8 percent; *United Press International*, NJ—857, MJ—52, PMJ—6.0 percent; *Washington Post*, NJ—353, MJ—35, PMJ—9.9 percent; *Washington Star*, NJ—186, MJ—10, PMJ—5.4 percent.

"there's a lot of talk in the press about affirmative action but there's not much affirmative action in the news budget." Domingo Nick Reyes, the director of the Hispanic American News Service, asked that minimal standards of accuracy be maintained and, in pithy comments, suggested that "the name Chicanos" not be used to describe Puerto Ricans. "We have not," he observed, "really gotten away from our perception of Latinos as fiery little folks, rustic and with mustachios."[17]

WCCO Scholarship Program at the University of Minnesota, which was begun in 1973. Formally titled the WCCO-University of Minnesota Minorities in Broadcasting Scholarship Program, this initiative between Midwest Radio and Television, Inc. (owner of the three WCCO broadcast stations—television, AM and FM radio) and the School of Journalism of the University of Minnesota is designed to principally serve the black, Chicano, Native American, and Asian-American communities. Most of its student participants have been drawn from Minnesota and the upper Midwest area. Between 1973 and 1978, Midwest Radio and Television gave or pledged $185,983 to the scholarship program. In the period 1973 to 1979, 27 scholarships were awarded: blacks, 14; Chicano or Spanish surname, 3; Native American, 7; Oriental, 2; East Indian, 1. Of that number 13 were (or are) undergraduates. The Scholarship Committee filters "several hundred requests for information" to "about 20 to 30 partially-completed applications each year." It looks for academic achievers, especially for the graduate program but has been willing to "accept some students who can accurately be described as 'marginal.'" An effort was made in the beginning years to take a risk with a few marginal Native Americans, because so few applied. The recruitment for that group was stepped up. The risk-taking is described as "partially successful." WCCO scholars have been able to secure jobs in broadcasting, industry, and education. Most have gone into broadcasting. Graduates have joined CBS News in Atlanta, WTOP-TV in Washington, D.C., WLS-TV in Chicago, WOTO-TV in Grand Rapids, WCCO-TV in Minneapolis, WCCO-AM in Minneapolis, "Sixty Minutes" of CBS, and KSJN-FM in St. Paul (as of 1978 report on the program).

The author thanks Professor Everette E. Dennis of the School of Journalism, University of Minnesota, for a copy of his report, as the scholarship coordinator: "The WCCO Scholarship Program for Minorities in Broadcasting: The First Five Years, 1973-78" xeroxed; also, a letter from Professor Dennis to the author, February 9, 1979.

Support for minority training for the print media has been very weak. In 1978, the Ford Foundation cancelled a graduate program in journalism education for minorities that had been supported with a fund of $60,000. Also, the American Newspaper Publishers Association ended a minority training fund provided by its Foundation. It has been reported that there were, in early 1979, only about 100 minority journalism scholarships in the nation. Also, in 1978 there were 64,500 (plus) journalism-degree candidates in the United States of which only 4.1 percent were from minorities. (See, Nick Kotz, "The Minority Struggle for a Place in the Newsroom", *Columbia Journalism Review*, Vol. XVII, No. 6 March/April 1979, p. 31). The prestigious Columbia University Graduate School of Journalism developed a program in 1968 for minority-group training, supported by the Ford Foundation, local stations, and newspapers. It was funded at approximately $12,000 per student, provided for a stipend of living expenses, and assured job placement upon graduation from the 11-week course. It ended in August of 1974, after 225 minority-group

Of the approximately 1,700 minority individuals working on daily newspapers in 1978 in the United States, 62 percent were blacks. Others included: 12 percent Latino, 12 percent Chicano, and 4 percent Native American. In the Medill School of Journalism survey, only 1,357 minority employees were actually accounted for. With such a small number on the job, be it 1,700 or 1,357, it is significant not to lose sight of particulars such as the fact that about 50 minority persons were employees of the two dailies in Honolulu. What would total minority employment in the United States be if Honolulu was ever to become typical insofar as minority participation in the print media was evident? What would be the social effect on this country and the world? What if minority-origin deskpersons rose from the 1978 level of 16 percent, and minority-origin news executives were to exceed the 4 percent of 1978? One can reasonably assume that the social consequences of each increase in percentage, if the true span between increases reflected honest and sincere affirmative action moves by the industry and society, would have to be measured geometrically rather than arithmetically.

The Committee on Minorities of the American Society of Newspaper Editors, after much review of the employment patterns described above, agreed that "the commitment to recruit, train and hire minorities needs urgently to be rekindled. This is simply the

---

journalists had been trained. When the program ended its director Robert Maynard said,

"Now that there are no riots, we can't get any action." Also, "If this program doesn't continue, then we go back to the old system in which minorities simply weren't hired and it will mean that a lot of brilliant people simply won't get in." (See, Bernard Rubin, *Media, Politics and Democracy*, N.Y.: Oxford University Press, 1977, p. 38).

Since June, 1976 there has been a *Summer Program for Minority Journalists* at the School of Journalism of the University of California (Berkeley). It is the current manifestation of the Columbia University efforts which had placed about 70 persons with media organizations. The present eleven week course, for fifteen minority group persons each summer, is supported "primarily from newspaper-related companies and foundations." Included are, "The Gannett Foundation, the Philip Graham Fund of the Washington Post Co., John and Mary Markle Foundation, Ford Foundation, Capital Cities Communications, Inc., the Times Mirror Foundation, William Randolph Hearst Foundation, Dow Jones and Co., Inc., TRW, Inc., New York Times Foundation, Forbes Magazine, National Urban League, The Boston Globe Newspaper Co., the Scripps-Howard Foundation." (See, brochure on the program, *The Summer Program for Minority Journalists*, n.d., School of Journalism, University of California), Robert Maynard is the chairperson of the Institute for Journalism Education, a non-profit educational corporation, which runs the summer training program as a major project.

right thing to do. It is also in the newspaper industry's economic self-interest."

Paul Poorman, editor of the *Akron Beacon Journal* and a member of the Committee on Minorities, has analyzed the story behind the statistics in a terse, inclusive, and analytical manner—as a good reporter is obliged to do:

> In a quarter-century in the newspaper business, I've encountered some racism, some sexism, some moneyism and every other/ism; . . . a more accurate name for the thing I've observed is simple prejudice.
>
> . . . newspapermen were putting out newspapers their publishers and their readers wanted, or at least thought they were.
>
> And those newspapers were white. The black population of cities like Philadelphia and Detroit were invisible, except for certain ministers, the cotillion and, to an extent, crime.
>
> . . . most of those big city newspapermen changed direction after the civil disturbances of 1967—not because of the Kerner Report, but because right here in Newark, Philadelphia, Los Angeles, Detroit, things had changed.
>
> . . . in the rash of efforts to understand what happened, and why, we learned there were as many reasons as there were blacks. So much for the "black community." Lots of blacks out there, but goddam, they seemed to be individuals.
>
> . . . we learned that blacks were concerned about police protection, about crime in their neighborhoods, about trash collection. And once we began reflecting this, we learned that blacks also like to read newspapers. We might even convince them to read ours.
>
> So I think that big-city newspapers, and I'd like to include Akron, gradually evolved a policy of treating news as news, with no color involved.[18]

Robert C. Maynard* is a distinguished newspaperman, and a former editorial board member at the *Washington Post.* He now heads the Institute for Journalism Education, which runs the Summer Program for Minority Journalists at the University of California, Berkeley. He offered a cryptic insight into the employment statistics: "The 1,700 nonwhite journalists . . . are employed by only 32 percent of the newspapers."

---

*In 1979 Mr. Maynard became the editor of the Oakland, California *Tribune.*

One result of the employment situation is clear, in the opinion of Charlayne Hunter Gault* of the *New York Times*: "As black reporters, we know where the errors of omission occurred; know that if we had been given the chance all along to write what we knew, no one would have been surprised at Harlem, 1964; Watts, 1965; Newark and Detroit, 1967; Washington, 1968, and hundreds of other ignited cities. . . ."[19]

What are the employment-related indications that minorities will be given chances to forewarn the newspapers that employ them of social problems, with the objective of heading off the worst possibilities? S. J. Micciche, Managing Editor, administration, of the *Boston Globe*, which dominates the Boston metropolitan area in influence and circulation, calculated, in an early 1978 response to a request for information on minority recruitment in the editorial echelons of that newspaper from *The Bulletin* (published by the American Society of Newspaper Editors), that "we still have a way to go." He went on: "As of December 1, 1977, out of a total editorial department staff of 328 permanent employees we had 256 males, or 78 percent, and 72 females, or 22 percent. The number of black employees was 17, or 5.1 percent; orientals numbered two, or less than 1 percent." Micciche noted that since the previous December, replacements for personnel who had resigned or died, and additions to staff were all white (eight women and four men). He continued: "We are concerned with our inability to find experienced blacks, orientals or Spanish-speaking staff people. Though we do not advertise, we have been in touch with other newspapers and with journalism schools; we have also sent our editors on recruiting trips." What are the jobs minorities were sought out for? "Primarily," said Micciche, "our problem is that current openings are for copydesk editors. We have been unsuccessful in finding minorities who would be interested in working on the News, Sports and Living/Arts copydesks. We do have minority applicants for reportorial positions but we have not had those openings." What jobs did minorities hold on the editorial side of the *Boston Globe* as of early 1978? According to Micciche: "A black is an editorial writer, another is an assistant metropolitan editor, an oriental is an assistant librarian. Most of our blacks are reporters and they cover a variety of beats—including one at the State House and another at the Supreme Court."

It is difficult to secure specific minority employment data for the noneditorial departments of the *Boston Globe*. My request for

---

*Charlayne Hunter Gault is now with the McNeil-Lehrer Report on National Public Television.

that information was made to the personnel manager, who responded that she "was named Affirmative Action Director in 1974 and moved to Personnel in 1977 to insure the success of this program in all phases of hiring." Adeline M. Callan wrote to me on February 1, 1979, and outlined the general scope of that newspaper's efforts since the formal affirmative action program was initiated in 1974:

> The *Globe*'s ultimate objective is to achieve a level of minority and female employment in parity with the labor force of the Boston S.M.S.A. [standard metropolitan statistical area]. We recognize that the degrees of success in attainment of these objectives are influenced by a number of constraining factors.
> 1. Low turn-over rate.
> 2. Projected zero employee population growth.
> 3. Creativity and specialized knowledge and skills required in many positions.
>
> We also have an Equal Employment Council here at the *Globe* that meets quarterly with management to review the progress of our Affirmative Action Program.

An effort to obtain more specific employment data failed.* William O. Taylor, the *Globe*'s publisher, wrote the author on February 26, 1979: "We feel that we do not wish to share data from non-editorial departments for you to use in your study of minorities and the media."[20]

Television

The record of the electronic mass media is not more positive than that of the daily newspapers cited. The report of the U.S.

---

*The complete text of Mr. Wm. O. Taylor's letter of February 26, 1979 follows: "Dear Mr. Rubin: Thank you for your letter of February 21. We feel that we do not wish to share data from noneditorial departments for you to use in your study of minorities and the media. I appreciate your getting in touch with us. Best Wishes." The author can only speculate on why the publisher of one of the nation's outstanding newspapers refused to make the requested information available. After all, the *Boston Globe* is a major source used by individuals and broad publics interested in democratic progress in all industries and enterprises, including the Fourth Estate's institutions. A colleague of mine, experienced in the day-to-day work of the newspaper business, may or may not be correct in his opinions. He suggested to me that sometimes publishers might prefer to disappoint a professor rather than to provide data which might cause confrontations with such groups as the trucking or printing unions connected with the newspapers. *The Boston Globe* is a distinguished American newspaper. The ethnic and classific minorities interested in the data should be as disappointed as this researcher by what superficially appears to be a cavalier response to a reasonable request.

Commission on Civil Rights, entitled *Window Dressing on the Set: Women and Minorities in Television* (August 1977), bears that fact out.

As background, bear in mind the slow-paced work of the Federal Communications Commission (FCC) in dealing with discrimination. Research, agitation, and legal work by many concerned groups—such as the Office of Communications and the Committee for Racial Justice Now of the United Church of Christ; the Chicano Coalition (Los Angeles); the National Organization for Women; Asian Americans for Fair Media; the National Black Media Coalition; the National Latino Media Coalition; the American Indian Press Association; the Puerto Rican Media Action and Educational Council; and the National Association for the Advancement of Colored People—have pushed the FCC to do what was required. In the 1960s civil rights leaders deplored and denounced the virtual denial of meaningful access to, and fair portrayals by, the television industry. They demanded that the FCC prohibit such discrimination and begin work to ensure affirmative employment and an environment conducive to programming reflective of democratic goals.

The FCC was sluggish and reluctant, to the extreme, to take action, even in flagrant situations of discrimination against minorities. WLBT-TV, located in Jackson, Mississippi, lost its license when a Federal District Court ordered the FCC to revoke it.[21] WLBT served an area in Mississippi and Louisiana with some 900,000 viewers, and approximately half were black. It had been strong on presentations of the segregationist credos, had excluded blacks from locally produced programs, and had featured derogatory appellations to describe blacks.

The Alabama Educational Television Commission's (AETC) loss of its right to operate eight educational-television stations (albeit under provisos of the FCC allowing it full equality of consideration in future petitions for licenses involving other potential applicants, as well as continued operational control pending reassignment of licenses) is considered another landmark, this time, of 1975.[22] It took a decade of public-interest group work to accomplish the result. On examination of the contents of over 10,000 sample-period hours of programming between October 1967 and January 1970, the license term, the FCC found only 0.5 percent of that time span that could be characterized as "integrated programming"—46 hours and 45 minutes, by the clock. One should not be carried away by the phrase "integrated programming" as used by the FCC in this case. It only means that there was the appearance of one black person per program. Considering that about 30 percent of the citizens of Alabama are black, it is also interesting to ponder the employment-production patterns of the AETC the FCC found:

> There were no black A.E.T.C. announcers, no black A.E.T.C. professional staff, and no blacks on the Program Board during the license period. The production centers were located at predominately white institutions and the record establishes that there was no significant black involvement in the preparation of programming; . . . no blacks on the Curriculum Committee; . . . no integrated in-school programming was produced locally.[23]

Does it not seem incredible that it was as late as June 4, 1969, that the FCC adopted a nondiscrimination rule? We ought not forget that the classic education breakthrough came with *Brown v. Topeka et al.*, announced on June 17, 1954. The great educational system of electronic mass media was given a 15-year reprieve from any regulation equally as forceful as that judicial ruling.

In 1969, discrimination based on race, color, religion, or national origin was prohibited. In addition, all licensees were ordered to "establish, maintain and carry out a positive continuing program of specific practices designed to assure equal opportunity in every aspect of station employment policy and practices." It wasn't until May 1971 that the FCC published an amendment assuring women equal employment opportunity under its Equal Employment Opportunity rules. Women, it decided, "constitute over 50% of the population, and the history of employment discrimination . . . is amply demonstrated. . . . It is fully appropriate . . . for the attention of broadcasters to be drawn to the task of providing equal employment opportunity for women, as well as Negroes, Orientals, American Indians and Spanish-surnamed Americans."[24]

The extension of guarantees to women, as just described, or by any other order, regulation, or decision, properly opens our minds to a key consideration for all who oppose improper denials to, or impositions on, minorities. If each one of us is or can be a minority member because of perceived status or imposed sanctions, or by entrance into a situation or environment (accidentally or deliberately), then the range of basic minority groups goes beyond race, religion, color, and national origin, and must include sex. That basic group must also include the aged, who are subject to crucial discrimination, being dependent, imposed on, or ignored in far too many cases. Children whose rights or protections are inadequately defended by government and the private organizations of our society are another of the basic minorities. Obviously, children, the aged, the institutionalized infirm, the welfare-system population, and those needful of help because of mental handicaps, are all interested parties in the struggle to get fair employment for ethnic minorities and women. The security and well-being of all such minorities are absolutely linked. When ethnics and women take their rightful places, the concern to enhance the human condition should replace unnatural interest in commerce as the only critical factor in mass-media enterprise. As ethnics and women assume responsibility, we must watch to see that those who lead are not merely like old wine in new bottles. As a colleague of mine said to me recently—please bear in mind that he is an extremely talented television producer who is black—"I am not as interested in whether my boss at the station is black or white as I am in whether I have to deal with one of those minority-group token administrators who uses a responsible position to stymie or stop my creative ideas or projects. I want democracy, not a game of seeing who has the name on the door."

Minority Employment Data for the FCC: Some Skepticism

Forty local television stations were surveyed by the FCC to determine the effectiveness of the Equal Employment Opportunity rule. The period of time covered was from 1971 through 1975. The criteria for selection of the stations included: location of stations in large cities with high viewership and sizable minority groups; stations to show developments in every geographic region of the nation; inclusion of commercial- and public-television stations; representation of stations owned and operated by the networks.*

Results of that survey indicate that there is a distinction to be made between the appearance of progress and actual progress in the hiring of minorities and women. While the numbers of such employees increased, there were reasons why compliance by the 40 stations was not up to expectations of civil rights advocates. First, the FCC rules on affirmative employment action were not mandates that specifically corrective action be taken. Apart from the

*Fifteen network-owned stations of ABC, CBS, and NBC in New York City, Los Angeles, Chicago, Detroit, Philadelphia, Cleveland, St. Louis, and Washington, D.C. were surveyed; also, 15 network affiliates in Philadelphia, San Francisco, St. Louis, Cleveland, Detroit, Washington, D.C. and Atlanta. The ten public-television stations are located in Philadelphia, St. Louis, Los Angeles, New York, Cleveland, Detroit, Washington, D.C., Atlanta, and Chicago.

requirements of the FCC that the stations keep data banks on interests and skills about minority employees and provide counseling and assistance to help such employees to prepare for upgrading in positions, the rules lend themselves to much flexibility of application by management and owners. There were some training-program, job-counseling, and tuition-reimbursement activities in combination at 31 of the 40 stations surveyed.

However, from the management-ownership side, there were statements which gave the impressions that expansion plans at some stations were either not possible or very limited, and that promotions from within the organizations were the policy. General managers in some instances questioned whether women who entered the industry in clerical work can benefit from "clearly-defined career paths by which women can move up from such positions."[25]

It was a conclusion of the *Window Dressing On the Set* report that in determining why equal employment opportunities are not realized, "the real deterrent is the lack of genuine commitment by licensees, which was conveyed in their attitudes towards minorities and women."[26]

In respect to reported improvements in minority-women utilization in "upper-level" jobs at the stations, there is much skepticism over the remarkable and sometimes unbelievable reports. To illustrate, women working in the top four categories (officials and managers, professionals, technicians, sales workers)* rose in percentage, between 1971 and 1975, from 19.6 percent to 38.5 percent. Minorities rose in the same period of time from 41.1 percent to 60.5 percent.

To look at the increases noted in the report and to contrast actual numbers with percentages, we find this situation in 1975:

> In 1975 the 40 stations employed 1,093 officials and managers, of whom 68.3 percent were white males, 20.4 percent were white females, 6.5 percent were minority males, and 4.8 percent were minority females.
>
> ... many public interest groups have asserted that in actuality, minority and female employees are not playing a major decisionmaking role at television stations. They claim that frequently minorities and women are classified as officials and managers, but the positions they hold call primarily for routine administrative or even clerical tasks.

---

*The categories classified as "higher-pay" categories also include craftsmen. "Lower-pay" categories include office and clerical workers, operatives, laborers, and service workers.

Is there better indication than this of misutilization of minorities and women? The report noted, "Interestingly, over one-fourth (26.1 percent) of all minority male and female professionals were on-the-air personnel." This and other statistics "support the notion of minority and female 'presence without power,' i.e., that minorities and females are being placed in a few highly visible positions while being excluded from the decision-making process."

Window Dressing on the Set: An Update was published by the U.S. Commission on Civil Rights in January 1979. It deals with more recent data than utilized in the original report, which primarily concentrated on research on the years 1969 through 1975. The latest information carries the assessment into the period 1975 through 1977. Much attention was given to reappraising images presented of minorities and employment opportunities.

The employment picture had not brightened. Among the findings are those dealing with employees of television-news departments and management:

> White males continue to constitute the great majority of all correspondents, 82.2 percent. . . .
>
> The proportion of minority and female newsmakers declined in 1977, while the proportion of male newsmakers increased significantly, from 78.7 percent to 88.4 percent. . . .
>
> No significant increase in the percentages of minorities and women employed as officials and managers in the 40 station sample occurred between 1975 and 1977. . . . White males continue to hold the vast majority of the official and manager positions.

In addition, in the updated report the U.S. Commission on Civil Rights found much new evidence of warped images of minorities.

Stereotyping remains one of the most important problems. Television drama is cited as a vehicle for such projections:

> Television drama continues in its failure to reflect the gender and racial/ethnic composition of the American population. . . .
>
> Minority males are disproportionally seen in comic roles. . . . Minorities, regardless of sex, are disproportionally cast in teenage roles; in contrast, white male characters are disproportionally cast in adult roles. . . .
>
> Minorities, regardless of sex, are less frequently portrayed in an identifiable occupation than majority characters. . . . When minority characters are seen in occupations, they are typically in jobs with lower status than those of majority characters. . . .

> Although violence in the form of killing has decreased, significantly more characters are now seen hurting others. This is particularly true among minority characters.[28]

Public-Broadcasting's Record

The Corporation for Public Broadcasting (CPB), which exists as a private, nonprofit entity to formulate policy and to channel government monies to public-broadcast organizations, has been much criticized for its work by minority-group activists. To its credit, it funded an investigation with $186,000, to look into the facts relative to minority participation in public broadcasting. The researchers were headed by Gloria Anderson, chairman of CPB's Board of Directors Committee on Human Resources Development. Anderson is also the chairperson of the Chemistry Department of Morris Brown College in Atlanta.

The research report, *A Formula For Change*, was made public in late November 1978. CPB's Board of Directors ordered its management leaders to evaluate the findings and submit recommendations for action by May 1, 1979. In the 496-page report are the findings of the 28 multiethnic members of the task force.

First, we look at the numbers of minority-origin persons working in public broadcasting: 1,539, or 14.1 percent. Of that total, the public-television employees were 1,178, out of a work force of 8,486 (14 percent). Employed in public radio were minority-origin persons totaling 233, out of the 1,855 employees (13 percent).

The task force declared that "the public broadcast system is asleep at the transmitter," and that programming about minorities "is seriously deficient." Since 1974, only 18 (7 percent) of the 147 programs selected, by the CPB's Station Program Cooperative (SPC), for telecasting were minority programs. As of the issuance of the report, "only one SPC-funded minority program series—'Black Perspective on the News' is carried by public television, and that show was purchased by only 77 of a possible 276 stations."

Referring to a dismal record on the radio side, the researchers concluded:

> National Public Radio's (NPR) track record . . . is just as appalling as that of PBS [Public Broadcasting System]. In fiscal 1975, NPR distributed 61.4 hours of original minority program hours, the production costs of which were approximately $65,098, or only 4.2 percent of the total NPR programming budget for that year. Two years later. . . , only 70 hours of programming distributed by NPR (or 4.7 percent) were devoted to programs by or about racial and ethnic minorities. The scarcity of minority programs can be

directly attributed to the insufficient number of minorities employed in public broadcasting, particularly in decision-making positions.

In the decision-making categories of positions, i.e., officials, managers, and professionals, 108 of the 184 public-radio stations, and 52 of the 160 public-television stations, reported "no minority staff at these levels." The picture is much brighter for minorities in the office-clerical categories of public radio and television, with such jobs representing about 40 percent of that work group. Only one public-television program manager and five of the public-radio managers came from minority groups.

Money talks, as we all know. With all of the statistical data to support the contention that public broadcasting needs some basic reforms to bring it into greater compatibility with the American ambitions for democratic participation in public affairs, I would be negligent if I didn't cite the report's findings on spending for "national minority programming." Almost half of the public-television station managers responding to the management questionnaire sent out reported annual spending of less than $5,000. About the same proportion of responses from radio-station managers showed such annual spending at less than $1,000.[29]

To focus on females, minority women had the lowest salaries (averaging between $7,000 and $9,000 a year, and nearly half of them were in clerical positions—45.4 percent). Of the total group of women employed, about a third were in clerical positions.

Average salaries for minority males were approximately $2,000 a year less than for nonminority males (nonminorities averaged $15,000 to $17,000 annually).[30]

MINORITY OWNERSHIP OF MASS-MEDIA ORGANIZATIONS: TRENDS

Radio and Television

As has been noted, there is a very slow but persistent movement toward minority entrepreneurs becoming owners of media organizations. In the radio world, new developments are somewhat encouraging. The Federal Communications Commission, in December 1978 announced a plan to create as many as 125 new AM stations. To accomplish that goal, it intends to end the "clear-channel" superstations that have had access to national audiences at night. Originally these "clear channels" were allowed to give service to many small communities that would have had no other broadcasting programming available at night. When the new policy was announced, there were about 25 such radio stations, each beaming its signals with 50,000 watts of electrical power. By 1978 there were only about 4 million people who were outside the range of radio, television, or cable services at night.

The new plan will establish new opportunities for minority ownership.[31] There are many needs already registered with the FCC. For instance, a church-group/American Indian-group coalition asked the FCC, in November of 1978, to set aside a minimum of one FM and one AM frequency for every Indian reservation (54) with more than 1,000 inhabitants. For every reservation (19) with more than 3,000 inhabitants, they asked that a television channel "in perpetuity" be allocated.

In October of 1978 the Oglala Sioux of Pine Ridge, South Dakota, formed a broadcasting company and filed with the FCC to operate a television station, which could be the first Indian-owned station. They number 14,000, and there are 2,000 non-Indian residents at Pine Ridge. Their plan called for a station to cost about $6 million.[32]

As of this writing in early 1979, of the approximately 8,000 radio stations in the nation (AM and FM), only 70 are minority owned.

In the world of television, only three television stations are black owned, and they are located in Detroit (UHF) and the Virgin Islands (two stations—VHF). In Boston, the New England Television Corporation recently purchased WNAC-TV, a CBS affiliate. The minority shareholders—eight blacks, out of the 51 shareholders—own approximately 13 percent of the company.[33]

An 18-year-long battle to win control over WLBT, Mississippi's biggest television station, began with charges of discrimination against blacks in the community. The challenged licensee lost the station in 1969, through a process initiated by the United Church of Christ. It culminated in a withdrawal-of-license order from the U.S. Court of Appeals, Judge Warren E. Burger presiding. The next year, the FCC, which had been laggard in action, gave temporary control to a nonprofit, biracial group. That group appointed the first black person to serve as general manager of a VHF television station. At the end of 1978, it looked fairly certain that a coalition of four organizations, with a total of 51 percent black members, would be permitted to purchase the station, under an order given by the FCC administrative-law judge who was overseeing the reorganization.[34]

The road to ownership by minorities will not be easy in the broadcasting-media area. Among the more important reasons are the lack of licensees available to be awarded licenses, the huge amounts of money that must be raised to operate and meet FCC requirements,* the difficulty in challenging any license holder, and the reluctance of the FCC to take action transferring licenses. The FCC sees some hope for minorities through spectrum reallocation or modification.

However, the financial problems are perhaps the greatest for minority groups. Financial institutions are reluctant to lend to what they consider to be high-risk borrowers with limited or no broadcast managerial experience. Such institutions do not relish lending when "the principal asset . . . is a license subject to revocation by a federal agency." While there is some money available from the federal government itself (the Small Business Administration and other agencies), the amounts available are not sufficient to allow borrowers to secure "attractive broadcast stations" in the top markets.

Under the capitalistic system, advertising revenue provides the necessary income. Would-be minority-group owners have problems of a special nature. The advertising agencies and services tend to give minority groups unfair treatment, say many observers. Among the commentators reporting before the FCC, there are those who "believe that there is a preconceived notion on the part of some

---

*For more specific detail on how much financing is required to close the deal on a television-station sale, the proposed sale in early 1979 of WHEC-TV (Rochester, New York) by the Gannett Company to Broadcast Enterprises Network, Inc., of Philadelphia, was said to be at the asking price of $27 million. Bank financing of all but $3 million was being arranged at a floating rate of nearly 14 percent interest; the annual interest exceeds $3 million dollars. See "The Boom in Media Financing," *Business Week*, January 22, 1979, p. 90. The WHEC-TV situation is an unusual case study because the station is being sold to a black-owned company, and because a public-interest group based in Washington, D.C., the influential National Black Media Coalition (NBMC), was instrumental in acting as an instigator of the change. It appears that when the Gannett Company, which owns 78 newspapers, wanted to merge with the Combined Communications Corporation, which owns seven television and 12 radio stations, the NBMC stepped in with certain questions and certain ideas as to whether the merger was or was not in the public interest, as the FCC would determine public interest by its regulations. James McCuller of the NBMC joined the parties for *private* talks over a six month period. Without government intervention, Gannett will sell its television station in Rochester to the black-owned company, Broadcast Enterprises Network, Inc., and agreed to take on other work, such as aiding minority entrepreneurs by providing information about future possibilities for media acquisition; helping to finance training seminars for minority businessmen; giving greater priority to affirmative action programs; offering minority representation on its board and executive group; promising access programming. See "Issues and People," *Access*, no. 62 (December 4, 1978), p.4.

advertisers that minority consumers are unimportant. As a result they are less inclined to purchase time on minority owned stations."[35]

The FCC is taking limited action to somehow overcome the financial difficulties for minorities who aim at broadcast-station ownership. On August 2, 1978, it changed certain financial-qualification standards for radio-broadcast stations. "The new standard requires that applicants demonstrate the ability to construct the station and operate the facility for three months, without relying on advertising or other revenue to meet these costs." It was stipulated that "the Commission's decision here is based, in large part, on the finding in its *Minority Ownership Task Force Report* [May 17, 1978], that station financing has been a principal barrier to minority broadcast ownership." Perhaps this will aid those who apply for new radio-broadcast stations and "those assignors and transferees of 'bare' radio construction permits."[36]

While he was a commissioner of the FCC, Benjamin L. Hooks was tireless in his criticism of the electronic media, for failures toward minorities. Often he disagreed with his fellow commissioners. In the *Mid-Florida Case* of 1972, involving applications for a new television station in Orlando, he agreed for some sort of "a preference to be computed along with other criteria." There were two black stockholders involved in an application which proved unsuccessful. Together they held 14.17 percent "of the unsuccessful corporate applicant." An "Administrative Law Judge and the Review Board found that they could not award a preference to an applicant proposing substantial minority ownership." Hooks disagreed:

> If this Commission—and this government—are sincere (and I believe they are) in their espousal of hopes of addressing past injustices, then I projected one simple, painless step to turn this polarized society around. I am asking only for a "preference" to be computed along with various other criteria; nowhere have I suggested that black ownership, standing alone, [be] dispositive. If this device is being criticized as racist and artificial, it should be remembered that Blacks have been, for so many years, oppressed by racist and artificial devices that it may take other "artificial" measures to offset the prevailing conditions.[37]

The Black-Owned Printing Press: Operating In A World of Conglomerates

There are less than 200 black-owned newspapers in the United States; the majority of that number publish weekly. Again, the story is one of ethnic-minority difficulties in dealing with business conditions in the industry in such a manner as to successfully compete with the established, primarily white-owned newspapers. White-owned newspapers have more attraction for advertisers aiming their messages to the majority of the affluent in the nation. We may be on the verge of a modest breakthrough on that problem, because of the respectably sized and growing black middle class. More than a half million black families had income of $25,000 or more in 1977. Also, some 32,000 black households earned more than $50,000 each in that year. Such higher-income black families had doubled in a span of a decade.[38]

An increased number of relatively affluent minority families will not in itself be the key factor in regard to ownership of important organs of the press. Any minority group seeking to acquire a single property in this field of communications is counter to the trend of chain ownership. Ben H. Bagdikian, the press critic, reported in 1978 that "the 10 biggest chains control 20 percent of all daily newspapers."[39]

One result of minority-owned business difficulties is the short lifespan of many black newspapers. It was reported in 1973 that although some 3,000 black-owned newspapers have come on the scene since the first appeared (*Freedom's Journal*, 1827), the average life span of a black newspaper was nine years. In 1972 there were 203 such black-owned newspapers in operation, with a total circulation of about 4 million readers. Three were dailies. The largest-circulation newspapers in 1972 were New York's *Amsterdam News* (about 83,000 copies), and the *Los Angeles Sentinel*. The weekly voice of the nation of Islam, *Muhammad Speaks*, claimed a circulation of over 600,000 copies. Among other important black journals in 1973 were the *Baltimore Afro-American*, the *Philadelphia Tribune*, the *Chicago Defender*, the *Pittsburgh Courier*, and the *Norfolk Journal and Guide*.

Magazines representing black life have been more successful than newspapers. *Ebony* (founded in 1945 with a format similar to the *Life* magazine of the time) achieved a circulation of approximately 1,250,000 by 1972. The publisher and founder of *Ebony*, John H. Johnson, also published *Jet*, *Tan*, and *Black World*.[40]

Giants of the black press were dwarfed, as of 1977, by the giants of the white, majority press. Several examples will show the tremendous variance in sizes and influences. The Times-Mirror Company (232d on the Fortune 500 listing of the biggest U.S. companies) owned the *Los Angeles Times*, *Newsday*, the *Dallas Times Herald*, and the Los Angeles Times-Washington Post News

Service (joint). That company also controlled the following magazine and book-publishing organs: New American Library; Signet, Mentor, and Meridian paperbacks; Abrams art books, Matthew Bender law books; Year Book medical books; C.V. Mosby medical, dental, and nursing journals and books; *Popular Science, Outdoor Life, Golf, Ski, The Sporting News, Ski Business, How to*, and *The Sporting Goods Dealer.* The Times-Mirror Company also owned two television stations in Texas (KDFW-TV and KTBC-TV in Dallas and Austin, respectively). That conglomerate, in addition, owned two newsprint mills, ten wood-product mills, 320,000 acres of timber, and three companies in the information-services, cable-communications and directory-printing areas.

Similar pictures of giants could be traced from the holdings of other conglomerates dominating the communications industries, such as the New York Times Company (394th on the Fortune list), Time, Inc. (217th), Gannett (426th), and Knight-Ridder (295th).[41]

What are the results of the big-versus-tiny situation, in the publishing business, that apply to all minorities? Kevin Phillips put it this way in a recent *Harper's* article entitled "Busting the Media Trusts":

> . . . Intellectual diversity suffers, too, because the conglomerates are more purely profit oriented. They go for what is: 1) safe and established; 2) inflammatory, but profitable; or 3) safe, established, *and* profitable. Rough-edged ideas that are neither very marketable commercially nor respectably established may be necessary for diversity and balance in the world of liberal First Amendment theory. But that is not the world of information-conglomerate practice.[42]

Small Newspapers With Important Roles

The small-circulation minority-centered newspaper has several primary functions in any community it serves. First and foremost, it is an available reminder that there is a community in existence, with important social, political, economic, educational, and entertainment needs and concerns. Second, it is a message-exchange medium, which may be the most efficient such medium available to the community. Third, the newspaper serves as an historical record keeper. Fourth, it has protest as a principal raison d'etre. Fifth, it is the essential relief for the community from the distortions, the omissions, and the warped images about the community that are so widely and constantly circulated by the white-owned mass media. Sixth, it is the carrier of two kinds of advertising: the aimed-at-minorities messages of dominant white-owned commercial and industrial corporations, and the commercial advertising that is essentially intracommunity in content. The latter represents one of the few opportunities open to and affordable to small entrepreneurs who own or rent small shops and own service companies. Lastly, the small community newspaper is a light, a signal showing the way to new hopes and expectations for every member of the community. The small community journal is a newspaper in the broadest sense of that word. As Ralph Ellison phrased it, speaking on behalf of blacks and all minorities more than a quarter-century ago: "For this is a world in which the major energy of the imagination goes not into creating works of art, but to overcome the frustrations of social discrimination."[43]

One Illustration: the Bay State Banner

A case in point is Boston's *Bay State Banner*, the leading newspaper for the black community of Boston. Founded in 1968 by a young and creative black entrepreneur, Melvin B. Miller, it has become a weekly necessity for many of its readers. With a circulation of approximately 10,000, the *Banner* is a key means for the residents of the Dorchester, Mattapan, and Roxbury sections of the city to learn information of direct community interest. Through years of racial turmoil and political incompetence over desegregation of the schools, the newspaper has championed democratic good sense while conveying vital information. It has had more than enough to cover in routine as well as fast-breaking stories about housing, employment, politics, youth, the elderly.

A review of the stories carried in a typical issue reveals the scope of its work. From the August 3, 1978 edition, here are front-page headlines: "Local Clinics Enter Fight for Abortions"; "Sen. Brooke is Cleared of Perjury"; "A Poor People's Drive to Save Historic Church"; "Why Do Haitians Flee Haiti—Economics, Politics or Both?"; "Paige Academy Holds Talks on How to Survive Pollution" (Paige is an alternative school for preschoolers and elementary-level students). On the inside pages there were such stories as those on "New Detoxification Center Set to Open Pending Local Appeal"; "Looking at Candidates Vying for Local Seats"; "Boston's Black History, Roxbury Mansions"; "U.S. Well-Being is Tied to Third World"; "Black is Beautiful in China"; "CLEO [Council on Legal Education Opportunities—a federally funded program] Offers Minorities Aid with Law School Application"; "8-yr. Fund-raising Effort Nets $500,000 for Black Colleges"; "Changes Make a Difference in Film on Blacks in Britain."

The stories are all well written. The *Banner*'s format reflects editorial concern for good style and design.

Regular columns in the August 3 issue included "Who's News", the featured editorials; "News Digest"; and columns on books, the theater, art, films, recordings, sports, church news, and obituaries. They were offered along with full sections for classified advertising (nine pages of the 32-page edition), the "Community Calendar," and "Letters to the Editor."

Advertising offered the products of large corporations (Ken-L ration, Carlton cigarettes, the Jordan Marsh department store of Boston), and a number of local advertisers—supermarkets, a pharmacy, a black-owned bank, the Boston Public School system (a notice advising parents on kindergarten registration), a law firm (emphasizing uncontested divorce and personal injury-connected legal services), a local university, movie houses, legitimate theaters, a restaurant, and the *Boston Globe.*

The editorial of that day and the editorial-page cartoon were on the problem of racially motivated physical attacks on blacks. The editorial began: "Attacks on hapless blacks trapped in white neighborhoods is a common occurrence in Boston. The public is not really aware of the frequency of the incidents because they are not all reported in the press." It ended on a semihopeful or pessimistic note (it depends upon the reader): "Only sound economic prosperity can change white attitudes. In the meantime, city officials must be willing to crack down on each incident as severely as they would if it were a case of blacks harassing whites." The cartoon depicted a black family, a father, mother and child, looking somewhat baleful as they prepare for a ride in an armored truck. The caption: "A Sunday drive ain't what it used to be."[44]

Caught in the Middle: Black-Owned Media

Seeking an appropriate magazine for advertising aimed at black teenagers, the Burrell Advertising Agency of Chicago had difficulties. "There wasn't any strong national magazine reaching just that audience. The major black magazines (*Ebony, Jet, Essence*) appealed to a mass audience or to young women."[45] In that particular case, a solution was found, and the material was placed with a new black magazine, *Right On,* which Sarah Bozeman, the senior vice president and marketing director at Burrell, characterized as a "black oriented *People*"-type publication. It happened that the advertiser was a black-owned company willing to take the chance. However, the problems of reaching specific black audiences comprising the estimated "$70-billion black market" are, usually, not easily resolved.

Apart from the few high-circulation black magazines and newspapers, there are virtually no commercially important print outlets for reaching any major black audience. Therefore, some advertisers, faced with what is called the Catch-22 black-media situation (an expanding market and extremely limited opportunities to make contact) are interested in black-owned radio stations. But, most advertisers like to "buy by the numbers" and place their enticements with those radio stations that lead the field in metropolitan areas. That commercially sensible approach is also taken by some black-owned advertising agencies who place their clients' work with the major radio stations in any city. One black agency executive has said, "If we have money left over, we go into a black-owned station."

Even when the desire to place an account with a black-owned radio station is clear, it is often necessary to reach black radio audiences via white-owned radio stations featuring so-called black-oriented programming. Reportedly, "of the 200-plus black radio stations (it fluctuates with programming decisions at stations) about 57 are black-owned."

There is another catch-22 problem for the black-owned radio stations. When they try to create programming which will attract a crossover audience of all races and interests, their ratings can improve while their importance to advertisers decreases. Big companies tend to approach general audiences through specific advertising contracts, arranging for utilization of dominant media organizations. Specific black audiences are targeted for marketing purposes via advertising placed with black-owned or black-aimed media. Consequently, the black-directed radio station, magazine, or newspaper that tries to reach audiences beyond the black community falls between the cracks of the tested advertising structures and finds crossover advertising economically perilous.

GRIEVANCES FROM TWO THIRD WORLDS

This discussion has concentrated on minority groups in the United States, sometimes said to be incorporated into a global Third World, by critics who are very disappointed in, or very disillusioned with, democracy as practiced here. Using the labels favored by internationalist students of politics and government, such commentators conclude that the first world (nations at a high state of technological development) and the second world (nations of the Communist blocs) are not meeting problems of minorities realistically. The Third World (developing nations characterized by presently low levels of technological prowess), it is argued, constitutes an abused minority as measured against the great powers of the day.

Any knowledgeable student of foreign affairs will quickly point out that the foregoing definitions are inadequate. As corrected by additions, the first world consists of those nations committed to some form of liberal democracy, and the second world is so identified because of autocratic or dictatorial government and little respect for civil or human rights i.e., the Communist countries, as perceived in the West. The third world is harder to define according to an acceptance of democratic forms or processes. Its member-states run the gamut from the democracies of India or Malaysia to the overall tyranny previously imposed on the people of Uganda by an irrational dictator and his henchmen.

So, a country can be at a high stage of technology and be the absolute opposite of what true democrats approve of. Similarly, a low-technology state can be seen to be either the mirror image or the antimatter of democracy. What counts is human freedom in all its manifestations.

Where peoples struggle to secure democratic dignities against terrible odds in the low-technology nations of the third world, there is usually acute sensitivity on the subject of how well or poorly the professed liberal democracies of the first world assist them. There are two principal bases for such assistance: fellowship and material aid.

The United States, the more-or-less accepted leader of the first world, has provided both forms of assistance, as have its primary associates and competitors, Great Britain, West Germany, and France. Vast amounts of material assistance have poured forth since 1945, with the overall American policy attuned to the desire to raise standards of living in underdeveloped countries and to encourage the growth of democratic systems. That great effort has been generally successful, with two extremely important exceptions. First, the United States has too often kept its official eyes upon technological goals or short-range security concerns, and kept an official blind eye to the rise of autocracies made possible by the flow of material benefits to the few at the expense of the multitudes. Second, the United States has underestimated the needs in developing lands for human uplifting to be paced by technological changes.

American commercial and industrial corporations have had even more impact than the government in pushing the secular religion of materialism. Goods and services, a la the American models, have been perceived by many hopeful peoples as the great indications of progress. The giant American corporations have not been notably concerned with emphasizing our social themes and aspirations.

We have all heard and learned much about the waves of unfulfilled expectations, triggered by the mass media, that tend to uproot and then resettle cultures according to a generally unplanned cycle. What has taken centuries in the West has unfurled in decades and portions of decades in the developing world—the third world.

Faced with changes that no person can wholly understand, whole populations have galloped into the technology race of the twentieth century. One result is that many of the mistakes of their technological tutors are made over and over again by leaders who haven't had the time to assess or distill.

It is natural, then, that there should have developed a psychological dependency of the tutored on their tutors. The initiates have asked questions, and have hoped to receive answers, as to how the technological puzzles fit together, still allowing for cultural protection and enhancement.

Culturally, we have been very laggard in providing answers. Most of our replies have come indirectly and as a by-product of the technology we have pushed—governmentally or commercially—via our giant corporate entrepreneurs.

On the information fronts, we have dominated international news with our international press agencies. When we add to the American press agencies and newspaper and television giants, with overseas activities, those of all the other powers, we see how completely swamped the third world has been with views and news and ideas from outside.

The third world is complaining very loudly now about sharply perceived cultural neglect. Its complaints are fortified by new clout, as exemplified by the natural resources possessed by some of its member-states and crucially necessary to the physical and political well-being of the major technocracies. Another cause of turmoil is the collapse of some of the West's most depended-upon major power schemes for maintaining alliances based upon provisions, goods, and services. The fall of the Iranian structures that the United States had influenced and supported is one example.

A specific outcry against media domination or alleged media

domination was made in 1976 at a conference in Nairobi, at which members of UNESCO debated world communications issues. At that conference a resolution was passed with the support of Soviet-bloc sponsors and the support of third-world nations anxious to express their frustrations.

The U.S. delegates and delegates of other Western governments were particularly disturbed by this phrase in the resolution: "states are responsible for the activities in the international sphere of all mass media under their jurisdiction." They attempted to head off what was considered a basis for a new antidemocratic order in the third world. However, there was more emotion than support for a choking of international communications at that conference. A better indication of the real desires of the third-world delegates is in the following section of Resolution 23: ". . . the importance of a free and balanced circulation of information and the need vigorously to intensify efforts to put an end to the imbalance which, as regards capacity to send out and receive information, typifies the relationship between developed and developing countries." In the approved medium-term plan for UNESCO activities for 1977-82, the conference asked for "promotion of policies, infrastructures and training in the field of communications and encouragement of a better use of the media for social ends."[46]

One is struck by the similar chords struck by representatives of minorities at home and of those abroad who perceive third-world peoples to be relegated to minority status in every way by the Western authorities. At home and abroad, they are railing against being deluged with information by those who ignore them. They have lost patience with those who sell everything and buy little to nothing, be the products physically tangible or intellectually intangible.

I have studied the arguments of such protestors at home and abroad, in pursuit of my research data. In general, I conclude that they have valid arguments adding up to a good cause. Recently, as a member of the American delegation (government officials and private-citizen gatekeepers of the media or from the universities)* to the April 1978 conference on "International News Media and the Developing World" in Cairo, I was able to update my knowledge about position taking on news matters. That conference was sponsored by the Fletcher School of Law and Diplomacy and the

*Including Boston University, the Massachusetts Institute of Technology, University of Washington, University of Minnesota, Tufts University among others.

Middle East News Agency. It is important to note that at the 30-nation conference, with delegates representing governments, news services, UNESCO, and institutions of learning, there were no third world clamorers for attention for its own sake. Indeed the search for mutual understanding was so real, and the debates were so constructive, that it may have been one of the most unemotional meetings ever convened at the site—the headquarters of the Arab League.

When we examine what was claimed by third-world delegates at the Cairo conference and at similar international meetings held between 1976 and 1979, in such places as New Delhi, Colombo, San Jose (Costa Rica), Nairobi, New York City, and Paris, the statements of commonly held third-world opinions seem moderate. It is pointed out that developing nations are usually passive recipients of information, including information considered biased, distorted, or inadequate; they are supplied with information which supports cultural goals of the West (sometimes tagged as cultural imperialism); they are receivers of substantial news at the cost of what they really need—fundamental national development material.

As is true on the domestic scene in the United States, the rejoinders to the complaints are also reasonable. In general, gatekeepers of the media (owners, publishers, editors, reporters) of the West admit past shortcomings and promise to deliver more useful information and, above all, to encourage more and better third-world news supplied by third-world media gatekeepers. Through new attempts at systematic reportage, and by aiding the upgrading of media technology of the third world, beneficial mutual work is promised. The West's media leaders are worried that the third world is becoming so mindful of past problems that not enough concern is shown for protecting freedom of the press. Attempts to regulate news coverage in developing countries, with officially imposed restrictions on reporters and their employers, are especially troublesome.

In recent years, national and international news services have been organized to reflect third-world interests. In 1975, a non-aligned press agency was established by 58 developing countries to counter and supplement such services as the Associated Press, Agence France-Presse, Reuters, and United Press International.

Rudiments of organized Western responses to now-accepted third-world complaints are beginning to appear in the forms of special journalism training programs, grants for technology, and new opportunities for coverage of third-world affairs, with the objective of bringing the emerging reports to the vast audiences of the first world as well as to the peoples of the developing states. Cultural imagery will more frequently go two ways.[47]

Demands by ethnic and classified minorities for fair treatment from the media have one theme at home and abroad. What is wanted are the minimal standards for full minority participation acceptable to advocates of democracy. If the responses by those in power or authority are prompt and equitable, we are on the verge of a splendid renaissance of culture, which might just divert us from the martial solutions to problems so frequently resorted to in the past. If the remedies are half-hearted or dishonest, then the unsatiable desires of minorities for places in the sun will violently disturb all organized societies and endanger every community. The basic plea must be answered: "See us, hear us, know me!"

NOTES

1. Ward Churchill, Norbert Hill, and Mary Ann Hill, "Media Stereotyping and Native Responses: An Historical Overview," *The Indian Historian* 2, no. 4 (December 1978): 45-56. See comments on p. 55.

2. For July 1, 1975, demographic data on Los Angeles, see "Cities," in Bureau of the Census, *County and City Data Book 1977* (Washington, D.C.: Government Printing Office, 1978), p. 615. For Otis Chandler's and Anthony Day's comments, see Felix Gutierrez and Clint C. Wilson II, "The Demographic Dilemma," *Columbia Journalism Review* 17, no. 5 (January-February, 1979), pp. 53-56.

3. See Alan Berger, "The Globe: Ignoring Hispanics," *The Real Paper* (Cambridge, Mass.) 7, no. 44 (November 4, 1978): 5, 10, 14.

4. Roland Alston, "Black-owned Radio Taking to the Airwaves in a Hurry," *Black Enterprise* 8, no. 12 (July 1978): 20-25.

5. See Sheila Smith-Hobson, "Black Book Publishing: Protest, Pride and Little Profit," *Black Enterprise* 8, no. 10 (May 1978): 39 (especially), 40, 42, 47.

6. See the following news accounts: Kay Longoope, "Push for Portuguese Power Underway in New Bedford"; Patricia Gatto, "Portuguese in Fall River Protest Edition of Paper," in *Boston Sunday Globe*, October 29, 1978, Metro and Region Section, pp. 29, 34, 35.

7. See Boston Indian Council statement on its history and programs mimeographed (Boston, n.d.), 2 pp.

8. See John Hubner, "Native Americans/Part One. Paths of Survival, A Portrait of Three Brothers," *The Real Paper* 7, no. 46 (November 18, 1978):17-19, 22-23.

9. See Boston Indian Council, "The Fight of the Urban Indian: Native Americans Respond to *Real Paper* stories," open letter, mimeographed (Boston, n.d.), 3 pp.

10. See Peter R. Melnick, "Native Americans/Part Two. Portrait of a Navajo Family." *The Real Paper* 7, no. 47 (Nov, 25, 1978):22-23, 26-27, 30.

11. See "The Fight of the Urban Indian," op. cit.

12. See Boston Indian Council, "Area Indians Confront The Real Paper," Wednesday, November 29th, News Release (Boston, November 24, 1978).

13. See Letters page, *The Real Paper,* 7, no. 48 (December 2, 1978). Also, Martin Linsky, "Behind the Lines," *The Real Paper* 7, no. 50 (December 16, 1978).

14. For population estimates, see Manuel D. Plotkin, "United States Population," *The World Almanac, 1979* (New York: Newspaper Enterprise Associates, 1979), pp. 205, 218. Also, Bureau of the Census, *Consumer Characteristics of the Population Below the Poverty Level, 1974 Income* (Washington, D.C.: Government Printing Office, January 1976), p. 3; "Distribution of U.S. Population by Race, 1850-1970" *Information Please Almanac and Yearbook, 1978,* 32d ed. (New York: Viking Press, 1978), pp. 761-62. For other data on women, Hispanics and blacks, see Richard T. Pienciak, "Progress of Blacks, Women Doubted," *Boston Sunday Globe,* January 21, 1979.

15. See *Report of the National Advisory Commission on Civil Disorders* (New York: Bantam Books, 1968), pp. 407-8.

16. Dierdre Carmody, "Survey Found No Minority Employees at Two-Thirds of Nation's Newspapers, Editors Are Told," *New York Times,* April 13, 1978.

17. See Walter Stovall, "Desegregation of Press by Year 2000 is Urged," *Editor and Publisher,* April 15, 1978, pp. 7, 13.

18. See "Minorities Comprise 4% of Newsroom Employees," *Editor and Publisher,* April 15, 1978, pp. 9, 30. For the 1978 data of the Committee on Minorities of the American Society of Newspaper Editors, see *Committee on Minorities Report* (Easton, Penna.: ASNE, 1978), especially pp. 402-7, and ASNE, *Minorities Supplement* (Easton: ASNE, 1978), pp. 408-11. The author thanks Gene Giancarlo, executive secretary of the ASNE, for sending him a copy, and copies of documents on the subject dealing with statements issued in 1971 and 1972. *American Society of Newspaper Editors,* 1350 Sullivan Trail, Box 551, Easton, Pa., especially pp. 402-407 and the *Minorities Supplement* with Mr. Poorman's remarks pp. 408-411 with attention to p. 409.

19. See Robert C. Maynard, "Media's Integration Record—'This Far by Fear'," *Boston Globe,* April 15, 1978.

20. For the specific data on the editorial segment of the *Boston Globe,* see response to ASNE inquiry provided by S. J. Micciche, managing editor, administration for that newspaper in *The Bulletin* (ASNE) no. 614 (April 1978), p. 5. The noneditorial work-force information was provided by a letter to the author from Callan, February 1, 1979. Also, letter to author from Taylor, February 26, 1979.

21. See *Office of Communication of the United Church of Christ v. F.C.C.,* 425 F.2d 543 (D.C. Cir. 1969).

22. See Federal Communications Commission, In Re Applications of Alabama Educational Television Commission, FCC 74-1385, 29210 (decision adopted December 17, 1974), (Washington, D.C.: FCC, January 8, 1975), 39 pp.

23. Ibid.; for details, see pp. 2-4, 8-10, and 25-27, especially.

24. See U.S. Commission on Civil Rights, *Window Dressing on the Set: Women and Minorities in Television* (Washington, D.C.: U.S. Commission on Civil Rights, August 1977) p. 75.

25. Ibid., p. 81.

26. Ibid., p. 85.

27. Ibid., pp. 87, 92-93, 108.

28. See *Window Dressing on the Set: An Update* (Washington, D.C.: U.S. Commission on Civil Rights, January 1979) pp. 60-62.

29. See *A Formula For Change,* Report of the Task Force on Minorities in Public Broadcasting, submitted to the Human Resources Development Committee of the Board of Directors, Corporation for Public Broadcasting (Washington, D.C., November 1978), 496 pp.; especially, see pp. XV-XXXII.

30. Ibid., p. 83.

31. Ernest Holsendolph, "F.C.C. Offers A Plan to Add 125 Stations to AM Radio Bands," *New York Times*, December 20, 1978.

32. Ernest Holsendolph, "F.C.C. is Petitioned to Set Aside Frequencies for Indian Stations," *New York Times*, November 17, 1978.

33. See "But Is It Black-Owned?" *Media Decisions*, (November 1978) pp. 72-73, 97-98, 100.

34. Ernest Holsendolph, "Blacks May Soon Direct Big Mississippi TV Station," *New York Times*, November 20, 1978.

35. Federal Communications Commission, *Report on Minority Ownership in Broadcasting*," mimeographed (Washington, D.C.: Federal Communications Commission, May 17, 1978), 46 pp.; see summary, p. 2.

36. See "New Financial Qualifications Standard for Aural Broadcast Applicants," Public Notice (Washington, D.C., August 2, 1978), No. FCC 78-556.

37. See comments of Commissioner Benjamin L. Hooks in *Mid-Florida Case* (TV9), October 6, 1972. 37 F.C.C. 2nd. 559 (1972).

38. See Bernard E. Anderson, "Blacks: Hardly Monolithic," *New York Times*, February 4, 1979, sec. E, p. 19.

39. See "Press Critic Asks Curb on Papers' Ownership by Large Companies," *New York Times*, December 15, 1978.

40. Edwin Emery, Philip H. Ault, and Warren K. Agee, *Introduction to Mass Communications*, 4th ed. (New York: Dodd, Mead, 1975), pp. 71-73.

41. See Kevin Phillips, "Busting the Media Trusts," *Harper's* 255, no. 1526 (July 1977):28-29.

42. Ibid., pp. 33, 34.

43. See Ralph Ellison, "Harlem is Nowhere," in *Shadow and Act* (New York: Random House, 1953), p. 297.

44. See *The Bay State Banner* 13, no. 43 (August 3, 1978).

45. For comments cited here, "But Is It Black-Owned?," op. cit., pp. 72-73, 96, 98, 100.

46. See Resolution 23 of 19th General Conference of UNESCO, Nairobi, 1976. Also, UNESCO, *Medium Term Plan* (1977-82), Document 19 c/4 (Paris: UNESCO, 1977); and, Bernard Rubin, "International Film and Television Propaganda," *The Annals of the American Academy of Political and Social Science* 398, (November 1971):81-92.

47. See Bernard Rubin, "Letter from Cairo," *Nieman Reports*, 22, no. 2 (Summer 1978):33-37.

TWO

COVERING THE DISENFRANCHISED: A WORKING REPORTER'S NOTES

Caryl Rivers

I was asked not long ago to speak on a panel about the discrimination I had personally faced as a woman in my chosen profession of journalism.

"Gee," I said, "I really haven't been hurt by discrimination. There have been incidents, of course, but nothing all that serious." However, I said I would think about the issue. As I left work that day, I was humming as I walked out to my car; my writing had gone well that afternoon; a hint of spring was in the air. Driving home, I started to think about all those little incidents I had mentioned to the man who was putting together the panel. Thirty minutes later, when I pulled up in front of my house, I was fuming. I felt like all those people in the movie "Network" who hollered out their window, "I'm mad as hell and I'm not going to take it anymore."

I had never, until that afternoon, realized how I had simply written off the subtle and not-so-subtle rebuffs I had received to the reality of an unfair world or the stupidity of the person involved. Fortunately for my own psyche, I had never taken discrimination personally. If some idiot didn't want to hire me because I was a woman, I figured it was his loss—the more fool he. I had known in advance that this sort of thing would happen. My mother, a lawyer, had said to me that a woman had to be twice as good as a man in this world to get as far. She knew that from personal experience. She had graduated near the top of her class in law school, with top honors in debate; and for years, the only jobs she could get were secretarial ones. She told me about the day she stepped into an elevator on Capitol Hill and encountered the only black who had graduated with her class in law school. He was running the elevator.

So I was not exactly surprised at the reaction I got when I walked into the editorial offices of the National Observer in the early 1960s, looking for a reporting job, my credentials on display: the Anne O'Hare McCormick award from the Columbia University School of Journalism; three years of experience on a respected small newspaper; a national award, for a special section I had edited, from the School of Journalism at the University of Missouri; and clippings on subjects ranging from education to science to criminal justice to the arts.

The managing editor looked at my clipbook, leaned back in his chair, and said he never hired women as reporters, but he did need a secretary. Would I like the job?

Next, I went to the *Baltimore Sun*, where the managing editor said he didn't hire women, period.

I finally got a job working in a Washington bureau that serviced a group of newspapers around the country. I didn't make much money, but the experience was marvelous. I covered some of the major stories of the day, including the transition from the Kennedy to the Johnson administration, the Dominican crisis, the Bobby Baker scandal. I had always been interested in teaching a course in journalism; so I approached the chairman of the Journalism Department at George Washington University, to see if he would be interested in having a working Washington correspondent teaching a course. He said he wouldn't think of hiring a woman, for they just ran off and got married and had babies.

I pointed out the fact that I was already married, and that I planned to continue my career as a journalist when I had children. There was, after all, no definitive research showing that motherhood rotted the brain and crippled the typing fingers. He merely grunted.

Thinking of my advancement in my career, I cast a hard eye at the city around me. I saw no women who were managing editors, city editors, or national editors of newspapers. I saw none who were bureau chiefs. I saw few who were columnists or top political reporters. I asked a friend of mine who worked at one of the newsmagazines about the prospects there. He told me not to waste my time. They didn't hire women as reporters; the best I could do was to be hired as a researcher, checking facts for a reporter who would probably have less experience than I. I watched as green young men from the good Ivy League colleges waltzed into jobs at the newsmagazines without ever having covered so much as a good sewer-line controversy.

At the time, I was working in the National Press Building, which was convenient, since so many of the newsworthy people who came to town spoke in the auditorium of the National Press Club, located on the thirteenth floor. By virtue of my sex, however, I was not allowed to be a member of the club. There was, in fact, only one club in town I could join, the Women's Press Club. When the Kennedy liberals came to town in 1960, they were appalled by the fact that the prestigious private clubs, where so much of the business of government is done over elegant luncheons and dinners, refused to admit blacks. So they set up the Federal City Club, which possessed all the chic of the New Frontier. Blacks could come and go freely. Women could not join. (My mother had a philosophy about all this. She observed that women usually got into professional organizations a few steps behind the blacks—the rationale being that since everything had gone to hell when black folks got in, the group might as well bite the bullet and take the even more revolting step of admitting women.) I observed, somewhat wryly, that we hadn't much progress from the 1930s, when my mother was getting turned down by the bar association, to the 1960s, when I was being rejected by the press club.

The problem at the press club had an added twist. Not only were women reporters not admitted to membership, but their corporal presence was so offensive to the male hierarchy that women could not even sit on the main floor with males, to cover speeches at the club. Nonmember males were seated at a special table, where they were served luncheon prior to the speech. Often, the members' tables were filled with men who were not reporters—rather, they were lawyers and public-relations men who found the club a handy vehicle for impressing clients. Female working reporters were sent upstairs to a balcony with the TV cameras and engineers. Not only did we have to stumble over the cables and the sound men, but we had few chairs and no tables. I covered many a speech leaning on a marble pillar trying to take notes. One day I had an assignment from the *Washington Star* to write a profile on Carl Rowan, the black journalist who was then head of the U.S. Information Agency. I was supposed to follow Rowan around for a full day for my story, and on this day he was to be the guest speaker at the press club. When I tried to follow him into the dining room, I was grabbed and marched upstairs to the balcony. The full irony of the situation really came home to me as Rowan told the tale of his boyhood in Tennessee—of how he used to go to the movies and watch the white folks take up the good seats on the main floor, while he and the other blacks were sent up to the balcony. As Rowan spoke, the white reporters—many of them involved in covering the civil rights movement—clucked in outrage. I remember wishing I had the nerve to yell, "Here I am, you sons of bitches—segregated in the balcony. And this ain't Mississippi!"

It wasn't long afterward that I was involved in a major national story. Sarah McClendon, a tough, single-minded woman reporter from Texas, was disturbed at the fact that women reporters were cut out of so many good stories because they weren't part of the old-boy network male journalists shared with many of their top sources. We didn't get asked to lunch at the fancy clubs to discuss issues of national import, nor to private dinners in elegant Georgetown townhouses where confidences were shared. So Sarah set up a series of press briefings for women reporters with top federal officials. J. Edgar Hoover was one of these, and in the midst of a briefing with the FBI chief, Hoover said, very deliberately, "Martin Luther King is the most notorious liar in the country." This was, by anyone's assessment, a big story—the head of the FBI calling the nations' most respected civil rights leader a "notorious liar." When Hoover added that his statement was on the record, we all raced back to our offices. Since I filed my story over UPI (United Press International) wires, to one of our bureau's clients, UPI picked up the story with my name on it, and the next day, I wound up on front pages across the country. A reporter from CBS News came to interview me, on camera, for the Cronkite show. He kept asking me the strangest questions: "Was there tea at the gathering, cookies?" I couldn't understand what on earth he was talking about. This was a press briefing. Later, it dawned on me. The man simply couldn't imagine that Hoover would make such a momentous statement to a bunch of women. He had to assume it was a social event where Hoover had let something slip.

As I was thinking about all this on my drive home from work, I realized that not only had I in fact faced major discrimination, but that people had taken cases to the Supreme Court for less. I had been denied jobs, advancement, membership in professional organizations—and none of it on the basis of my own individual talent. Then along came the women's movement, and of course everything changed, right?

Wrong. Here's an example of how much things changed. In 1970 I was living in Boston and working with WGBH-TV, the public-television station in that city, as a commentator on an evening news show. The women's movement was a big story by then, and the women at the station felt that public TV should be among the first to go on the air with a program aimed at examining the new concerns and political action of women. The station management agreed to let women air a show during the summer, but with a minimal budget. The first woman who was asked to moderate the show had no television experience, and didn't work out, so I was asked to take over as moderator. As I was walking onto the set, the night I was to go on, the president of the station was standing by, nervously. I had never even seen the president before.

"Now, you won't be too militant, will you?" he asked. I think he thought he saw Ché Guevara, not the mild-mannered reporter who actually stood in front of him. The show went well, the producers thought. They began to plan the next show. But the program manager said he didn't want me to continue as moderator—I was not "warm and loving" enough; I might threaten suburban housewives. (Let me say here that I am the sort of person who has to grit my teeth before I speak rudely to anyone who has shoved in front of me at the supermarket checkout; I was intrigued by the idea that I might actually threaten anybody.) The producers argued, in vain, that they didn't want a talk-show hostess for this program; in fact, that was precisely what they did *not* want. The upshot of the whole affair was that the show was cancelled—on the fiftieth anniversary of women's suffrage.

If 1970 sounds a bit like ancient history—surely, things have changed in the past decade—here's a more recent example. Last year I was working on a piece on sexual harassment of women on the job, and I interviewed two women who were working as cocktail waitresses to support their young children. A male editor on a prestigious liberal publication questioned the validity of the interviews: "Don't women who take jobs like that ask for it?" The story did not appear in that publication.

THE CONDITIONS AND PREJUDICES BUILT INTO THE NEWS MEDIA

This litany of horrors serves a purpose here other than giving me a chance to engage in a bit of therapeutic catharsis. It touches on conditions, prejudices, and attitudes existing in the news media that affect the treatment of women—and members of minority groups—not only as employees, but also as subject matter. Many of these problems are built into the institutional structure of the media, and many of them do not operate at the conscious level. Today, in fact, many of the more blatant examples of discrimination, the sort I faced early in my career, have disappeared. The newer forms are more subtle, and more difficult to combat. Deliberate and conscious racism and sexism may be the easiest thing to grapple with; it's out front, visible, and a good target. But too often, the worst decisions, the policies that have real discriminatory effect, the story assignments that ignore disenfranchised groups, are made by people who believe they are doing a good job.

Let's take a look at several of the factors that operate at all the managerial and reportorial levels of the media industries: social class, race, and sex. During a televised panel discussion on television news, network news producer Av Westin said that he made his decisions, about what the news was that day, on the basis of his years of experience as a professional newsman. That was, of course, only partly true. A man (or woman) brings to that sort of decision the value judgments and prejudices of an entire lifetime. When the ghetto of Watts erupted in the 1960s, why were the editors of the Los Angeles newspapers caught flat-footed? It was not because of any flaw in their professional judgment, nor for any lack of training. It was due to the simple fact that they didn't regard the things that black people did as news. Black people usually didn't make the paper at all—not when they were born, married, or died. A murder of a white person might make page 1, but if a black person was the victim, newspaper editors shrugged it off. Everybody knew black people were always killing each other off, most likely slicing each other up with razors. Black people never got married, as far as the establishment press was concerned. When my husband was working as a reporter at the *Baltimore Sun* in the mid-1960s, he discovered that the newspapers would not run pictures of black brides. He circulated a petition protesting the practice, which was greeted by total silence from management. The paper, in the meantime, continued running editorials in favor of civil rights in the South. The gag line around the city room was that the *Sun* was for integration in Mississippi, but "moderation" in Baltimore. The same thing could be said of any major metropolitan daily in the North.

It is no wonder that the white media found itself at a loss as to how to cover the ghetto uprisings. It had no sources in the black community, no knowledge of its mores, its geography, its problems. The sad fact is that if the ghettos were to blow up today, the same thing would happen. The black community was covered in the 1960s—often like a foreign battleground—and the problems of the cities became a big story. Urban teams were formed, special reports on poverty were cranked out, and the invisible man—the black—materialized, but only for a time. Today, things are pretty much back to normal. Few newspapers or television stations have any real commitment to coverage of the black community; urban teams have gone the way of the hula hoop, and reporters may wander through the black community when Jesse Jackson comes to town, but not much more often. Otis Chandler, the publisher of the *Los Angeles Times*, has said it's hard to attract minority readers, because a big urban newspaper like the *Times* is simply too diverse and too sophisticated for them. That view reflects the thinking of many publishers, though perhaps few of them would admit it in public.

If it is hard for white male editors to see blacks as being newsworthy, it is even harder for them to see women in the same light. If blacks were regarded as nonpeople on the great map of news, women were another story. Women were a joke. If women made the newspaper at all, it was usually when one of them posed in a bikini as Miss Amalgamated Pickle. The first reaction to the women's movement on the part of editors was raucous laughter and bad jokes about bra burners. No wonder. They had grown up in a society which taught them that men were the serious people, and that women only mattered—only existed, in fact—in relationship to men, as wives, lovers, nice girls, tramps, beauty queens, mothers. The idea of women as a political force was totally alien to them; they could not have been more surprised if an army of ducks marched up to their doors demanding their rights. The suffragettes, after all, were only grey pictures in history books, and most male editors had lived through a postwar era where the serious aspirations of women lay quiescent beneath the return to home, hearth, and children. Anything that had to do with women was automatically devalued. The women's pages on the newspaper were a sort of "marshmallow Siberia." Young women of my generation vowed we weren't going to get stuck there, writing about bouquets of seed pearls and stephanotis. The women's movement certainly raised the consciousness of many an editor in this regard, but it is still an uphill battle. As is the case with the civil rights movement, the women's movement has moved off the streets, and the tendency on the part of the media is to return to the status quo. It is getting harder now for me as a writer to sell editors on stories that are regarded as women's issues. The devaluation of things concerning women is not dead. I know that if I wish to maintain my reputation as a serious journalist, I must be careful not to publish solely in women's magazines. When I applied for tenure at Boston University, I was well aware that my credentials were considered strong because my range of publications and stories went beyond the female ghetto in journalism.

I have a friend, an NBC producer, who won an Emmy nomination for a minidocumentary she had done on battered women. When I mentioned my friend to a male reporter, his comment was, "Oh yeah, she does 'light stuff.'"

The class structure of media management does not only affect minorities and women. It also has a major impact on the treatment of the poor and the working class. Journalism, once considered basically a lower-class trade, has moved up in the world. That fact was impressed on me recently when I attended a party given by a high-ranking newspaper editorial employee in a Boston suburb. Many of the media executives and writers in town were there, sipping good sherry, expensive liquor, or Perrier water and lime on the grounds of a large Victorian house; white-jacketed waiters passed out hor d'oeuvres. I was reminded of a statement made by a legislator from South Boston, a working-class area, that any time you wanted to reach a reporter on the *Boston Globe*, you had to dial 1. What he meant was that today, reporters often live in the suburbs in relative affluence. They are insulated from the problems that many people, who are not so fortunate, have to grapple with every day. If rats crawl in your window and bite your children at night, you will probably regard the problem of rats as a major issue in your life. If that never happens to you, you may not even think of it as a problem—certainly not as news. Affluent media managers tend to be intrigued with stories that they see as intellectually stimulating or exotic. The antics of Idi Amin in Uganda, for example, are thought to be more worthy of news space than the fact that the conditions of local housing projects have deteriorated badly and there are no funds even to maintain existing buildings. I have heard editors refer to news about the poor as "garbage-can journalism." It is not surprising that people in poor and working-class neighborhoods have come to regard the media as "them," and to feel alienated and voiceless as far as their problems, their news, is concerned.

I remember once, in the mid-1970s, watching a television panel show in which network news executives talked about their operations and the problems of getting nightly news on the air. Defensiveness was the prevailing mood. The TV executives seemed to regard criticism as a deadly germ to be stomped on. One of them quoted Jefferson on the free press. Then, a remarkable thing happened. A young black woman in the studio audience stood up. The anger rippled in her voice. She said to the TV executives, "You are arrogant men."

The words tumbled out of her. Why, she asked, when a young white woman was burned to death in a black neighborhood, was the story flashed coast to coast? Where was the national press when a black youth was shot by a white? Why did the cameras and reporters only appear when there was violence and a white woman involved in the story? Where were they the other 364 days of the year?

"We're part of this city. We're part of you," she said, pointing at the newsmen. Why, she asked, did she not see her world reflected, not just on special black shows, but "on the evening news with everybody else?"

A few minutes later, a young white man stood up. He too was angry. He came from a white working-class section of the city. 'Youse guys, [yes, he said "youse"], we never see youse guys unless some white kids are throwing rocks at a bus with black people in it. You make us stereotypes."

Why was it, he asked, that he never saw his world on television, except during the St. Patrick's Day parade or when somebody threw a rock?

The anger, the alienation, the frustration of these two people were echoed by others in the studio audience. It rolled toward the TV executives like a tidal wave. They sat there as if they were protected from it by an invisible wall. There was a station break, and afterward, the executives and the anchormen started talking about another subject. It was as if the angry words had not been heard at all. Exasperated, one of the members of the panel, media critic Edwin Diamond, said, "Wait a minute! These people have raised some real issues here. Aren't we going to answer them?"

The executives dredged up answers, about time constraints, and the fact that one station had once done something on Head Start. They were trying to scoop up the tidal wave with coffee spoons. What the people in the audience were trying to say was this: "I am angry, I am frustrated, because I have no power to determine the images I see of myself and my world. I am not asked. I have no power to shape the images, and the ones I see I do not recognize."

The class bias in the media is subtle and pervasive. My husband, journalist Alan Lupo, has encountered it often, since his major field has been urban affairs. He was the creator of, and editor and anchor on, a program at WGBH-TV in the 1970s called "The Reporters," a nightly news show designed to deal with issues that affected the lives of people in Boston's neighborhoods. It was an innovative concept, and the show received much critical acclaim and a following in the city's neighborhoods. But Alan believes that the station management rather quickly grew bored with the concept, being more comfortable with programs that served its usual upper-class, affluent audience. One executive said in a memo, "We can't shove aside 'Zoom' or 'The French Chef' or opera because of a public-affairs broadcast." A public-relations person put it more succinctly in a memo; people were, she said, "getting tired of the great unwashed."

If the class, race, and sex of media managers provide a formidable obstacle to access for disenfranchised groups, the nature of news itself makes the situation even worse. News is event oriented, and outside the ordinary: dog bites man—no news; man bites dog—that's news. But much of the information that affects disenfranchised groups is negative in nature: people don't get jobs, health care isn't delivered, funds for a shelter for battered women don't materialize. If editors are not perceptive enough to see that it may be more important when things don't happen than when they do, such vital information, which affects so many people, does not get reported.

The event orientation of the news media can make it easy for people with enough savvy—and enough money—to create events that can be billed as news. The press conference is the most obvious of these. A well-managed press conference makes life easy for reporters. Let's say you are mayor X, and you wish to announce your new policy of raising money by taxing disco dancing. First, you have your press officers write up releases which will explain how the city will earn $2 million in new revenue without raising property taxes, a stroke of fiscal genius. You package the releases in a shiny press kit, which also contains a glossy photograph of yourself and a biography listing your achievements. You hold the conference in a special room at City Hall that has enough wattage so the TV crews can plug in their lights and sound equipment. Most likely, you will wind up on the evening news and, the next day, on page 1.

But suppose you are the head of an organization in a working-class neighborhood that has formed to oppose the building of a superhighway through your living room. You have no well-paid public-relations men who are on a first-name basis with newsmen;

you probably don't know the difference between the city editor and the managing editor. You have no one to write press releases for you, no money for a glossy press kit. You have to do all your community work in your spare time, anyhow, because you're working all day and trying to raise a family. There is almost no way you can compete with the special interests and the politicians in creating media events. And because you can't, you don't get page 1, or the lead story on the evening news. You are lucky if you can get an assignment editor to send a reporter out to do any story on you at all.

News has another characteristic that is important to understand. It is cyclical in nature. Problems that affect the lives of disenfranchised groups may be constant and unrelenting, but news about them is not. "We did our story on starvation a year ago," an editor will say. For him, the issue is dead and gone. People may indeed still be starving, but he is concerned with something else—OPEC has raised its prices; the primaries are coming up. News, as it is presently defined, is not only cyclical; but the way it is reported is a process that resembles a merry-go-round. When Lyndon Johnson declared the existence of a war on poverty, one media outlet after another discovered that, in fact, poverty did exist in America. An unemployed coal miner in Appalachia woke up one morning to find reporters from the *New York Times*, AP (Associated Press), UPI, and Reuters on his front step, wanting to interview him about poverty. Today, that same coal miner may be just as poor, just as unemployed, but he is all alone. The reporters have gone. When was the last time you read anything about Appalachia in the national media? There was a time—a brief time—when it seemed that was all you could read about when you opened up your paper. Editors are often so preoccupied with what is new that they forget to follow up on yesterday's stories. Is anything being done to ease minority employment? What is happening to the food stamp program? Are the elderly people who were eating cat food getting real sustenance, or are they still gnawing on Meow Mix? This too is news, important news, but it often gets lost in the shuffle of daily events.

If all this isn't enough bad news, there is still more of it where disenfranchised groups are concerned. The nature of the career ladder inside media organizations is such that it steers talented people away from focusing on news of such groups. The most prestigious beats in the newspaper business are the political ones—Washington, or the state house, or city hall. These are the jobs that lead to columns, managing editorships, city editorships. If you are an ambitious young journalist, you are well aware of the fact that you are not going to climb up the ladder of success by writing about kids who get bitten by rats, or neighborhoods flattened by expressways, or women who get beaten by their husbands. There was a time in the early 1960s and 1970s, when urban reporting was chic and was given attention by editors. For the most part, that is no longer so. Reporters and editors like to be around people of power—presidents, governors, mayors—and they know that coverage of such people can result in journalistic goodies and a step up the ladder. It's not exactly astonishing that reporters are not battling each other for the right to cover poor folks.

If the prestige ladder of the media business is a barrier to coverage of disenfranchised groups, so too is the growing realization, on the part of publishers, of the nature of the market for information in this country. Newspapers in this country used to be vehicles of information primarily for the middle and working classes. Many large urban newspapers aimed specifically at a working-class audience, and this didn't always result in great journalism. Reporters used to say, contemptuously, that they were writing for the 11-year-old mind, and many of the stories dished up were lurid murders or reflected a sob-sister sentimentality. Today, however, publishers realize that the major buyers of information are the upper and middle classes. These are the people that the big advertisers—the department stores, for example—really want to reach. Most of these stores have moved out of the core city to suburban shopping malls; their customers are, by and large, white and affluent. Newspapers today understand that this is the audience they must reach to survive economically. When I did a stint as writer-in-residence at the *Washington Star* in 1976, I heard a great deal of discussion of who the *Star*'s readers were. The Star was, at that time, struggling to survive. It was trying to break the stranglehold the *Washington Post* had on major advertisers. It was trying to survive as an afternoon paper in an era when the TV six-o'clock news had stolen the customers away from afternoon papers. To boost its advertising linage, the *Star* had to reach readers beyond the beltway—that is, in the far suburbs in Maryland and Virginia. I heard more than one heated discussion about the *Star*'s obligation to serve the blacks who made up the majority of the residents of the nation's capital—but even the most passionate debaters realized that economic survival would undoubtedly pull the paper in the other direction.

Today, there is money to be made in providing information to the affluent middle and upper classes, who want to know how to spend their money and want to be entertained. This fact has led to a distressing trend that I have called the "bagel-people" syndrome. Let me explain that jazzy title. The "bagel" part of the syndrome refers to the acres of newsprint that are being devoted to stories about where in town you can purchase the best bagel—or the best wine, or the best stereos, or the best paté de foie gras. Now, there is nothing wrong with this kind of information—it is quite useful to people with change jingling in their jeans, and while it often has more in common with advertising than with journalism, it is of interest to many people. The problem is that this sort of quasi-journalism is spreading like bubonic plague, and respectable journals that were once devoted to serious journalism have turned to touting expensive consumer products. Other serious publications are choking and dying. For example, *New Times* magazine died just one month after publishing an article of mine on the shambles of the mental health system in this country. *New Times* was owned by the giant conglomerate MCA, and its circulation and advertising were not holding steady enough. Its publisher, George Hirsch, said that *New Times* died because the members of the "me generation" weren't interested in the serious political and social issues the magazine covered. *New Times* was far from perfect—it suffered, at times, from a New York wise-guy tone, but it did deal with issues that were relevant to disenfranchised groups. While *New Times* was strangling to death, another magazine owned by the same conglomerate was going great guns: *The Runner*. Why people would pay, month after month, to read about what kind of jogging shoes to wear, and would not pay to read about nuclear power, mental health, or national politics is a mystery to me, but perhaps my reading tastes are slightly arcane.

The "people" part of my syndrome refers, of course, to *People* magazine. It is devoted to information about famous people—most notably, media personalities—and who can resist its mixture of celebrities and gossip? That particular mix has been a part of journalism since cavemen started chipping out news stories on stray pieces of rock. But again, the problem has been in the proliferation of gossip journalism. I had a call not long ago from a friend, a serious and dedicated journalist, who was shaking her head in disgust about the direction her newspaper was taking. "There's no news in the paper anymore," she said. "It's all soft features and gossip." Another journalist I know, whose interest had been in political reporting, quit the magazine she was working for when she was ordered to write a gossip column. My husband was, for a time, the executive editor of *Boston* magazine; and the publisher of *Boston*, G. Herbert Lipson, told him one day that he did not like the kind of stories Alan was running. He said the magazine could not afford to be the cutting edge for blacks and Puerto Ricans, and he didn't want any more stories on unimportant people like 'that guy Salboochi.' (He was referring to a piece Alan had written about Fred Salvucci, the secretary of transportation for the state of Massachusetts, and one of the people who had been most influential in stopping an inner-belt highway that would have ripped through working-class neighborhoods to make it easier for suburbanites to get in and out of the city.) Alan told the publisher he could take his magazine and—to phrase it as delicately as possible—insert it in a tender part of his anatomy. The magazine's senior editor, Nancy Love, quit shortly afterward. Nancy had approached me about doing a cover story on the women's movement in Boston, which Lipson had vetoed with a terse comment: "no broads on the cover."

The significance of the bagel-people syndrome may be hard to calculate in column inches lost for the interests of disenfranchised groups, but I know that it has been considerable. I know that I, as a writer who often tries to probe serious issues, am facing a shrinking market for such stories. I have the terrible feeling that one day soon, I shall have to resort to selling my stories on the street corner, the way men sold apples during the depression: "Brother, can you spare a dime for an exposé on welfare fraud? Two incisive articles on mental health for the price of one. Yes, we have consumer fraud, women's issues, stories about the farm workers, get 'em while they last."

If all this sounds rather bleak, this concentration on the myriad of the problems involved with the media and disenfranchised groups, then it's only fair to say that there are some encouraging trends as well. The most blatant forms of sexism and racism are fading, and there is at least a recognition on the part of many media managers that their past record hasn't been very good, and that they ought to do better. There is a fair amount of goodwill on the part of editors, program directors, and reporters; there are a great many people honestly trying to do a good job, even though they often get so preoccupied with the day-to-day grind that the good intentions stay on hold.

One of the things that must be brought home to media managers is the fact that there are built-in biases in the normal operations of the news media; that it's not a question of overt practices, but of not-so-benign neglect. They will have to recognize that the status quo is not good enough; that to deal fairly and effectively with disenfranchised groups, they will have to make an effort. It's not good enough to sit back and wait for the ghettos to burn or for people to hit the streets. They will have to learn to be as aggressive in their coverage of issues that affect disenfranchised groups as they are in digging up political scandal or racing to five-alarm fires. This means a serious rethinking of some of the axioms they have accepted for years, about what is news and who is newsworthy.

First of all, it is up to the managers to initiate contact with disenfranchised groups—to seek out representatives of blacks, Hispanics, women, and other minorities, and build some kind of continued contact into the system. Media managers should sit down with such groups on a regular basis to get an idea of what their problems and priorities are. Editors and managers have to make an effort to get out of their offices and get a feel for what's going on with the rest of society. People assume that media managers, because of the business they are in, are right at the pulse of new thoughts, news ideas—that they are the first to sense the ripples of change. In fact, many media managers rarely get away from their desks, and they can get so bogged down in the details of getting a paper out every morning, or a show on every night, that they become, in fact, among the last to grasp what's happening in society. They need to get out and get their batteries recharged once in a while. One good example of this is the reaction of Jack Limpert, the editor of *Washingtonian* magazine, to the charge that his slick monthly represented only the affluent whites in a city that is, in fact, a black metropolis. The charge was made by the *Washington Post*'s black columnist, William Raspberry. Limpert recognized the validity of Raspberry's complaint, and decided to take some time off to get to know the black community better. If more managers would follow Limpert's example, the coverage of—and attitudes toward—minorities couldn't help improving. It's not enough, however, to let managers out to get new perspectives, and then have them swallowed up once again in the system. Access for disenfranchised groups has to be a part of the system itself, and it has to be an ongoing process.

Media managers will also have to change their attitudes toward their reporters, who, after all, are their eyes and ears. They can have all the good intentions in the world about covering the disenfranchised, but if they don't build rewards into the system for reporters who cover such groups, nothing will happen. Reporters will not rush eagerly into dead-end streets. Some reporters, out of social conscience or their own concerns, will push hard in these areas, but will eventually get discouraged when they keep seeing their stories stuck under the auto-body ads on page 32.

Both managers and reporters will have to understand that the old definition of news as something that happens is too narrow. They are going to have to unlearn their knee-jerk reaction of saying that when something doesn't happen, it's not news. It takes more imagination, more initiative, more aggressive reporting, to poke around and find out, for example, why the juvenile justice system is not working, than it does to rush out to cover a riot. Editors and reporters are going to have to broaden their sources, so they will know who to call when a story breaks about welfare clients, not just who to call in the bureaucracy. And they are going to have to broaden their idea of reliable sources. For example, a reporter I know was arranging a public-affairs show on the problem of airport noise in urban communities. She had planned to bring on a community leader who had helped organize neighborhoods against the encroachments of a large urban airport; this woman may have been a working-class housewife, but she had become extremely sophisticated in such matters as decibel levels and takeoff patterns. The producer wanted to bring on an MIT professor who, as the expert, had little sympathy with the neighborhood groups. The community leader could not qualify as an expert, the producer said; she didn't have a degree from MIT. In this case, the reporter fought and won, but it is a clear example of the class bias common in the news business.

Media managers are simply going to have to do a better job of covering minority communities, and much of this has to do with assigning reporters to cover specific beats. Too often, the big metro dailies and television stations regard the black and Hispanic communities as alien turf, as remote as the Australian outback. This may mean that editors and reporters are going to have to fight against the pressures to abandon those areas because they are not where the revenue is. It won't be an easy battle, but it is one that has to be fought, if American journalism is to do what it's supposed to do: hold a mirror up to society—all of it, not just white, middle-class America.

It's clear, too, that the big dailies and TV stations are not the only sources of information about, and for, disenfranchised groups. Special-interest publications, by women's groups, black and Hispanic communities, and urban neighborhoods, can be not only an invaluable source of information, but a tool to help organize these groups to lobby effectively in their own behalf. But such publications face almost impossible financial odds. We need talented young people working in these areas of journalism, but we can't expect them to starve. A Boston University graduate, Renee Loth, a talented journalist, spent years as editor of the *East Boston Community News*, an aggressive weekly newspaper in an urban neighborhood that has produced an impressive array of community leaders. Renee worked for a salary a good file clerk would have laughed at, and had to sell ads and try to beg for and borrow money to keep the paper alive. Community journalism can offer real challenges to a journalist, not the least of which is the chance to have a direct and immediate impact on the person's environment. But the whole community-journalism movement needs financial help—it needs funding by foundations, and it needs help from the big media outlets that are so profitable. One way the large media corporations could help disenfranchised groups is by financial aid to community journalism, which does not have access to the lucrative advertising revenue that fills the coffers of the conglomerates.

It goes without saying, of course, that the media in general have to do much better than they have in the past in the area of hiring and promotion. There is still a token mentality as far as members of minority groups are concerned. One problem that black journalists have had to face is the temptation to be pushed along too fast, to be set up to fail. The scenario goes like this: A talented young black person is hired, performs well, and is seized upon by management as the perfect way to show how liberal it is, how a black can do well in the higher echelons. So the talented young person is shoved into a job for which he doesn't have the experience—not for his benefit, but so the company can look good. And if he fails, managers shake their heads, and sigh that, of course, "those people" really don't have what it takes. A good example of this is the failure of the minority program at one of the large networks. It failed, one executive said, because the black journalists in the field couldn't get "producer acceptance" in New York. That's not surprising. The blacks didn't have as much experience as the whites they were competing against, nor did they have the sort of contacts in the organization that would be helpful in getting their stories on the air.

For women, the problem is somewhat different. While women today don't face the sort of discrimination I encountered when I was breaking in, they still have a hard time moving into the jobs where the real power is. Managing editorships, city editorships, the title of public-affairs director—these rarely belong to women, and often talented women are simply not considered for such positions. The major push in the years immediately ahead will be to move talented women into decision-making positions. For blacks and minorities, a major effort must be made to train and recruit journalists and media managers, and to see them move in force into the media professions.

The journalism schools have a role to play in this process, and not an insignificant one. Too often, the schools fall into the assembly-line mentality, simply churning out bodies to fill the slots to do the same old thing in the same old way. For the most part, the journalism schools have not made the questions of coverage of, and access for, the disenfranchised a high-priority issue. The schools should be the spearhead of reform and new ideas in the media industries; they should set the agenda for American journalism in the 1980s and beyond. They are entrusted with the hearts and minds of young journalists, and owe them more than training in how to write a snappy second-day lead. If there are, indeed, any words that should be called the credo of the journalist, I would choose those of H. L. Mencken, who said that the job of the journalist is to "afflict the comfortable and comfort the afflicted." We haven't been doing the job we should in either category. Maybe the problem is that we find it hard to afflict the comfortable—now that we *are* the comfortable.

PART II

LEGAL RIGHTS OF REPRESENTATION AND ACCESS APPRAISED

THREE

THE RHETORIC AND REALITY OF REPRESENTATION: A LEGAL BASIS FOR PRESS FREEDOM AND MINORITY RIGHTS

Everette E. Dennis

When minority voices criticize the press, they usually make a fundamental assumption that news coverage should accurately reflect what their group is doing in the society. Just what dimensions this reflection should take, and how it is to be accomplished, may spark debate, but the notion that public communication should be representative is almost a truism. Since the race riots of the 1960s, various governmental commissions, private study groups, and public conferences have denounced inaccurate and unbalanced treatment of blacks, Hispanic Americans, Native Americans, women, the handicapped, the elderly, youth, and other segments of American society.

Although the spare command of the free-press clause of the First Amendment to the Constitution ("that Congress shall make no law abridging freedom of speech or of the press. . . . ") does not require the press to be fair, objective, or representative, the rhetoric of representation has become an unquestioned, integral part of almost all minority criticism of the press. And this idea is not without some legal basis. In fact, the suggestion that the content of the press should accurately represent the society and its component parts is at the heart of many disputes that have taken the news media into the courts in recent years. The confident rhetoric of minority spokespersons notwithstanding, the issue of whether the press is or should be representative is hardly settled and is not a truism at all, but a controversial, hotly contested legal and ethical question. It is a conflict wherein freedom of expression collides with the concept of representation.

To many media leaders, the idea that they represent anyone or anything is anathema, yet they themselves invoke this concept when it is convenient. "Why do you want the information?" a public official may ask an inquiring reporter. The answer: "Because the public is entitled to know, and I represent the public." And it is not unreasonable to think that this may be the main reason the framers of the Constitution granted some special protection for freedom of the press. Press freedom is a personal, constitutional right that cannot be enjoyed by most people unless there is a full and responsive press to channel information and provide a forum for the exchange of opinions. Thus, in carrying out its constitutional function, the press represents the public because all citizens do not own, or have access to, the communications media. The press stands for and acts for the public. As Justice Lewis Powell put it:

> The people must therefore depend on the press for information concerning public institutions. . . . The underlying right is the right of the public generally. The press is the necessary representative of the public's interest . . . and the instrumentality which effects the public's right.[1]

The extent to which the press has any special responsibilities to the public (as minority advocates say it does) has long been debated by scholars and jurists. Some commentators believe that freedom of the press means freedom to publish without interference, while others say that with rights come duties, and that the press has a particular duty to the society it serves, the same society that grants it special protection. The latter view was accepted and elaborated by the 1947 Commission on Freedom of the Press, which declared that the public deserves a "truthful, comprehensive and intelligent account of the day's events in a context that gives them meaning."[2] To the commission, this meant that the news media should provide

1. a forum for the exchange of comments and criticism;
2. a representative picture of the constituent groups of society;
3. the presentation and clarification of the goals and values of the society; and
4. full access to the day's intelligence.[3]

If these recommendations of the commission were at first dismissed as ivory-tower philosophizing, they would later become accepted dogma for many, if not most, minority critics. Indeed, the next logical step from this representative-picture theory of the press was to ask not only what the press should cover, but also who would prepare the news reports that would make up the representative picture of society. Whether for reasons of equal employment opportunity, or because it was thought minorities could do a better job covering minority news and issues, there has been little disagreement with the goal of greater minority representation on the staffs of news organizations. As other chapters in this book indicate, this has been the concern of many people, from members of the U.S. Civil Rights Commission to critics and educators. Few would argue that the sociological profile of the American Journalist[4]—which is overwhelmingly white, male, and middle class—should be maintained as it exists now. But people part company on the methods to be used in achieving a better balance of minorities in the newsroom. And they also differ on the degree of representation desired—ranging from a rigid quota system to a loose search for qualified minority persons. No matter. The concept of representation is alive and well in all of these proposals.

Therefore, it is possible to speak of at least three aspects of representation that have a bearing on the press—the press as a representative of the public; representative content in the press; and representative personnel in the newsroom—whether they are representative of the racial, national, religious, sexual, and other demographic characteristics of the society.

To ascertain whether all this is mere rhetoric, or the basis for a practical framework to resolve policy conflicts between minority interests and rights on the one hand, and unfettered freedom of expression on the other, requires an understanding of the proper role and function of the news media, and of the nature and dimensions of freedom of the press. These essentially definitional problems are often treated glibly and superficially, but there is a genuine need to thoroughly explicate both.

THE PRESS AND REPRESENTATION

The concept of representation is an intellectual tool evolved and elaborated by philosophers, legal scholars, and political scientists to analyze some of the ways our social and political systems work. Although the concept of representation in democratic theory is most often used for political representation and the institutions of government, it can also be applied in other contexts. The political scientist Hanna Fenichel Pitkin, in her seminal study, *The Concept of Representation,* acknowledges that "representation need not mean representative government; . . . institutions and practices which embody some kind of representation are necessary in any large and articulated society, and need have nothing to do with government."[5] To the extent that the press is a conduit between the organized institutions and interests of society and the public, it is representative. Most commonly in definitions of representation, a surrogate figure (i.e., the representative) stands for or acts for someone else. Representation is not a self-contained end in itself, but part of a larger process. The most common definition of the term is, "making present in some sense something which is nevertheless not present literally or in fact."[6] While the representational problems of the press may not be directly analogous to those of representative government, studies of representation as a political concept can be useful in unraveling what might otherwise be a conceptual thicket.

Early formalistic studies, for example, focused on issues of authority and accountability.[7] These studies ask about the sources of authority to act for others, as well as how and to whom the representative is accountable. Since the press does make representative claims (claims which are echoed by the critics), these questions must be addressed. It is also true that the nature of representation by the press, and the character of the representative's actions will be governed by the way the concept of representation is defined.

The newspaper or broadcast-news organization that is guided by marketing studies and readership reports, to try to give the readers and viewers what they want, is in the category of descriptive representation. An elitist magazine or opinion journal, by contrast, decries such practices as pandering to the lowest common denominator, and provides editorial fare that the editor thinks the reader should have. This is a kind of symbolic representation. The daily newspaper is judged largely on whether it covers the community, that is, whether it accurately represents what is perceived to be happening. A quality magazine like *Harper's* or *The Atlantic Monthly* will be examined against standards of literary quality and new ideas. It has no community to cover and is unabashedly elitist. Newspapers and broadcast stations that are in the business of presenting public-affairs information to a mass audience must be responsive to various minority interests in their communities, for ethical, social, and legal reasons.

The degree to which the press is representative depends entirely on how one views the purposes and functions of the news media, and on what metaphor for representation best describes a particular organ of the press. Four metaphors for representation that demonstrate the complexities of this problem are *picture*, *map*, *mirror*, and *sample*. These metaphors embody concepts that are not as innocuous as they might at first seem. Indeed, the role that the press accepts largely determines its rights. Of even greater concern, though, is the accountability inherent in these terms. A press that is acknowledged to be a picture of society will be expected to deliver a particular news product. This picture of the society can be an exacting photograph or an abstract painting. One kind of picture meticulously represents the scene as most observes might have witnessed it; the other selects an aspect of the event and accentuates it. Imagine, for example, the kind of picture of society delivered by the *New York Times*, with its comprehensive, detailed coverage, and the picture delivered by a feminist journal interested mostly in politics.

In some respects the map theory argues for an important variation in the image of society that the newspaper or broadcast station conveys. A map might cover only the social contours, the highs and lows of the day's news. Inherent in the map is the idea of helping the audience to find its way around, to see details in relationship to a whole, to put things in context. In a sense, a newspaper like the *Christian Science Monitor* is a map. It tries to make sense out of major issues and problems of social importance, with emphasis on long-term trends rather than on the details of here and now. And the *Monitor* is known for putting stories in an international context.

Many critics have suggested that the press should mirror the society. The mirror is, of course, a kind of picture, capturing the passing show and bringing it directly to the public. Television news, in spite of its technological limitations, presents a kind of mirror image. It shows the viewer the event as a television camera caught it. The ideal mirror is the kind of coverage of public meetings that is found on some cabble-television channels in which cameras follow the proceedings from beginning to end, without editing or any intrusion.

A much more recent metaphor for the press is the sample. The sample (as in survey research) is a scientifically selected piece of the whole that accurately represents the whole. A public-opinion survey is based on sampling theory. Precision journalism is an approach to news gathering that uses social science methods to more accurately represent what the public, or a particular segment thereof, is thinking. One of the classic precision-journalism studies conducted after the Detroit riot in the 1960s tried to go beyond the "seat-of-the-pants" approach of on-the-street reporting and scientifically find out what black citizens of Detroit thought caused the riot.[8] Another kind of sample theory in journalism is the so-called supermarketing of the news, wherein market surveys indicating public interests and demands are used to shape news content.[9] This controversial approach, to which we have referred earlier, is the basis for much of the remaking of American newspapers and for the addition of special sections with names like "Lifestyle," "Shelter," and "Weekend." News organizations making heavy use of public-opinion polls for stories about public attitudes toward particular issues, events, or people embrace the sample theory of journalism.

Clearly, the kind of accountability that a particular news medium has depends on the metaphor that best describes its purposes. An advocacy journal that presents a particular interpretation yields one kind of image; a newspaper that uses opinion-poll data, quite another. We set different standards for the avowedly conservative magazine than we do for the more impartial daily newspaper.

Even though students of news definition and critics of objectivity in reporting use the terms picture, map, mirror, and sample somewhat casually, this is not unlike the long-standing debate among representational theorists, which is referred to as the mandate-independence controversy, and which was stimulated by the writings of Edmund Burke.[10] Should the press be a representative with a specific mandate from its audience or community? Should it serve in some democratic majoritarian fashion, or should it take an independent posture, making decisions on the basis of judgments that are not necessarily related to the immediate wishes of the audience? This argument, common in discussions of popular government, has also been mentioned by freedom-of-expression theorists, who ask whether the press should lead or follow. Using the concept in connection with the press requires an understanding of the accepted formulations.

THE AUTHORIZATION FOR PRESS REPRESENTATION

Where does the press get its authorization to act as a representative of the people or the public interest? Justice Hugo Black said that one need look no further than the Constitution, because

> [t]he Constitution specifically selected the press . . . to play an important role in the discussion of public affairs. Thus the press serves and was designed to serve as a powerful antidote to any abuses of power by governmental officials and as a constitutionally chosen means of keeping officials elected by the people responsible to all the people whom they were elected to serve.[11]

Actually, this formulation is a deductive extension of the larger constitutional rationale for free expression. To Thomas I. Emerson, freedom of expression in a democratic society should assure individual self-fulfillment; advance knowledge and discover truth; provide a basis for decision making by society's members; and help to achieve a more adaptable, and thus a more stable community.[12] (Although we are dealing here only with press freedom, it should be noted that freedom of expression embraces speech, press, and assembly.)[13] Emerson's premises, along with Harold D. Lasswell's definition of the functions of communication in society, help clarify the idea of the authorization for freedom of the press and the expected social benefits inherent in letting the press represent the people.[14] Lasswell said the functions of communication were *surveillance of the environment, correlation of the parts of the society responding to the environment, and transmission of the social heritage from one generation to the next.*[15] If the press is to carry out these functions, it must have the freedom and wherewithal to act. Thus, when the press acts on behalf of the public, either in disseminating information, collecting information, or processing that information, it invariably claims that any and all of these activities are authorized by the free-press clause of the First Amendment. The spare language of this fragment of the Constitution, which some critics and jurists have seen as nearly absolute in its admonition against interference with freedom of the press, has nonetheless inspired volumes of debate tied often to preconstitutional authorities.

Philosophical Foundations

The framers were strongly influenced by William Blackstone, who outlined his ideas about freedom of the press in his *Commentaries on the Laws of England*, stating:

> The liberty of the press is essential to the nature of a free state; but this consists of laying no previous restraints upon publications, and not in freedom from censure for criminal matter when published. Every freeman has an undoubted right to lay what

> sentiments he pleases before the public: to forbid this is to destroy freedom of the press. . . .[16]

Blackstone's work provided a useful framework for an integration of intellectual soundings by such seventeenth- and eighteenth-century philosophers as John Milton, John Locke, Jeremy Bentham, Thomas Hobbes, and Jean Jacques Rousseau, whose views of press freedom helped fashion a consenus among the framers that led to the First Amendment. Blackstone believed in the right of the individual to self-expression, which was not inconsistent with Milton's powerful argument for the free flow of information and ideas.[17] Locke's call for freedom of expression arose from a distrust of the state,[18] while Bentham said one of the distinguishing characteristics of a free government was tolerance of communication, including that of malcontents.[19] These views were in a tradition of negative freedom, that is, freedom from governmental controls or restraints. Hobbes, the social-compact theorist who thought that a powerful state could best control the problems of competing individual interests,[20] is also associated with negative freedom, although his ideas influenced Rousseau who said freedom is positive and must be freedom for something.[21] Freedom, Rousseau said, was not simply the lack of coercion; indeed, in some instances, coercion may be required by the general will. The framers, while aware of these conflicting views, opted for negative freedom, which is seen in the negatively phrased First Amendment command.

In America, freedom of the press owes an intellectual legacy to the letters of Cato (a pseudonym for two Whig journalists writing in London newspapers, and whose writings were reprinted in Benjamin Franklin's *Pennsylvania Gazette* in 1721), which linked freedom of speech and press with good government. Later, the trial of John Peter Zenger held great symbolic importance (though it had no binding legal effect) in its defeat of prior restraint of publication.[22] Still, a coherent social and political commitment to freedom of the press did not come about until the adoption of the Bill of Rights in 1791.

In the *Federalist Papers* debate over the Bill of Rights (written under the name of Publius by Madison, Jay, and Hamilton), there was worry expressed that freedom of the press "would leave the utmost latitude for evasion."[23] There was, however, strong-enough sentiment for a free-press provision that one was drafted by Madison and reworked in the First Congress. Although Jefferson and Madison, in particular, wrote eloquently about the meaning of press freedom and the First Amendment, it "is not certain that the

Framers themselves knew what they had in mind. . . ."[24] To some, the free-press clause was a caveat against governmental intervention; indeed, the historian Leonard W. Levy says the framers were clearly reacting to a "legacy of suppression" and wanted to make certain that they imposed limitations on government with regard to speech and press.[25] Madison envisioned specific protection for the information function of the press, in his well-known defense of press freedom, saying:

> A popular Government, without population information or the means of acquiring it, is but a prologue to a farce or a tragedy; or perhaps both. Knowledge will forever govern ignorance. And a people who mean to be their own governors must arm themselves with the power knowledge gives.[26]

The notion of a surveillance or watchdog role for the press was underscored by the Virginia Resolution of 1788, wherein the General Assembly of Virginia, in a debate on the federal Constitution, acknowledged a "right [in the Constitution] of freely examining public characters and measures, and of free communication among the people therein, which has ever been deemed the only effectual guardian of every other right."[27] Once adopted, the simple statement of press freedom in the First Amendment was not tested until the twentieth century. Yet, during the nineteenth century, philosophers were examining and reformulating their understanding of press freedom. Two of the most influential of these commentators were James and John Stuart Mill. Disavowing the suggestion that press freedom was superfluous in a representative democracy, James Mill said, "So far is this from being true, that it is doubtful whether a power in the people of choosing their own rulers, without the liberty of the press would be an advantage."[28] To Mill, the press was absolutely necessary to representative government because it would provide information to the electorate, give the people information about the government, and make the government aware of public opinion, This expanded the surveillance function as it was then understood. John Stuart Mill elaborated on the social value of press freedom in his essay "On Liberty."[29] Even if the government were totally representative—it is "at one with the people and never thinks of exerting any power of coercion unless in agreement with what it conceives to be their voice"—there could still be no right to control free expression.[30] Mill went beyond the value of individual self-fulfillment to describe the benefits accruing to society in the conflict between truth and error. If some commentators would severely limit reckless and irresponsible communication, Mill would not. He saw value in this kind of societal risk taking; to do otherwise was to impose unknowing and perhaps dangerous restraints. As he expressed it:

> [T]o argue sophistically, to suppress facts or arguments, to misstate the elements of the case, or misrepresent the opposite opinion— . . . all this, even to the most aggravated degree, is so continually done in perfect good faith by persons, who are not considered, and in many respects may not deserve to be considered, ignorant or incompetent, that it is rarely possible, on adequate grounds, conscientiously to stamp the misrepresentation as morally culpable; and still less could law presume to interfere with this kind of controversial misconduct.[31]

Mill's analysis effectively integrated individual self-fulfilling aspects of press freedom with social benefits, and did so with less agonized hand wringing over the rationality of man then that which divided the Enlightenment philosophers.

Several of the philosophers mentioned here (especially Hobbes, Rousseau, and Mill) grappled with the concept of political representation, but apparently did not relate this idea specifically to the press. Instead, they perceived the press as being an intermediate part of the process of representation by providing a conduit for information and opinions. However, to the extent that political representation was necessary because of the scale and size of society (given the fact that not all persons could participate efficiently in the democratic process), it might be argued that the press necessarily would play a representative role. The philosophers and the framers did not isolate press freedom from representative government. At least one of the functions of a free press was to facilitate the relationship between the governors and the governed. Just as direct government involving all of the citizens in direct decision making was impossible, it was similarly not feasible for all citizens to enjoy freedom of the press, at least in the direct sense of publishing a newspaper or broadside. Thus, if freedom of the press was to have any real social purpose, the instruments of communication must function in some aggregate sense as trustees for the public at large. Just as no single representative in a legislative body is expected to represent all dimensions of the public interest, neither would a single publication reflect all viewpoints, or be in perfect harmony with views, of the audience or community. The press as an instrument in the democratic process is a channel for public-affairs information that allows the polity to communicate with itself.

Zechariah Chafee, Jr. understood this when he distinguished between individual and social interests inherent in the speech and press clauses of the First Amendment.[32] Chafee said individual interests in press freedom would lead to individual self-fulfillment. If life were really worth living, people must have an opportunity to express their opinions on matters vital to them. To Chafee, social interests would lead to the attainment of truth in a Miltonian sense, and would have the purpose of helping the country adopt the wisest course of action among alternative choices. These individual and social interests are really a statement of desired consequences that will come as the result of cumulative communication, rather than deriving from any single communicative act. However, First Amendment conflicts arise over discrete acts of communication, over fragments that are part of a whole complex pattern of communicative activity. Clearly, the public discussion of public issues is essential to representative government; providing a channel for that discussion is one of the duties the Constitution expects from the press as the price for freedom. Therefore, the press becomes a de facto representative of the people—a role authorized by the Constitution and reinforced in judicial decisions.

PRESS RESPONSIBILITIES AND MINORITY CONSTITUENCIES

Discussing the representative role of the press in society as a guardian of individual and social interests is one thing; applying this concept to specific situations is quite another. Take the case of minority constituencies, for example. Minority critics of the news media want more and better coverage of their communities and interests; they want that coverage to be supportive of them and their interests; they want the press to take a more active investigative posture on their behalf; and they want greater representation of their groups on the staffs of media organizations.

The performance of the press, with regard to minority constituencies in America, is mixed. For the most part, the press has reflected public and governmental sentiment toward particular minorities, though there have been exceptions. The abolitionist editors of the mid-nineteenth century were virulent crusaders for minority rights. Often, though, the press treated minority persons in a derogatory manner until they were able to exert enough influence to demand something better. Racist language and racial designations that were irrelevant (and not applied to the white majority) were once commonplace. And there were instances when minority communities simply were ignored.

Usually, racial, religious, and national minorities in the United States have had to pressure their way to public attention. The civil rights movement put blacks on the front page; Native Americans suddenly became visible after Wounded Knee; people in wheelchairs converging on state capitals brought recognition for the handicapped. Migrant workers, the mentally ill, and a few other groups have fared better in the press. Viewed as powerless to make their own case, they have often won the sympathy of the media and have been the subject of exposés. Other chapters of this book comment on and assess the performance of the press in its dealings with, and treatment of, minorities. Yet, a lingering question about the ethical, legal, and social responsibilities of the press toward these communities remains. The Commission on Freedom of the Press put it bluntly, calling for a "representative picture" of society's constituent groups. The commission wanted the press to deliver this picture voluntarily, without coercion or governmental intervention. This assumed social responsibility, and an informal social accounting to see whether or not the press was living up to its constitutional mandate. Others would regard even this modest proposal as an intrusion on press freedom and the right of the press to publish and boradcast what it wishes—subject, of course, to post hoc legal review.

Although it is the contention of this author that all media—whether print or broadcast—have individual and social duties assigned by the First Amendment, there is little question that broadcast journalists, as holders of government licenses who have promised to serve the public interest (presumably as it is defined by Congress and by the Federal Communications Commission (FCC), can face sanction if they do not do so. In fact, a television station in Jackson, Mississippi, that repeatedly refused to provide coverage of its black citizens lost its license. Broadcast stations also seem to be under stricter mandates to provide equal employment opportunity and affirmative action, though many disagree that this has happened. Print media, on the other hand, present a slightly different case. They are not licensed, but are sometimes subject to governmental regulation in such areas as antitrust action and labor relations.

Sorting out what is meant by the press is a difficult task in any consideration of press-minority relations. This was indicated in the earlier discussion of press functions, and grows even more complex when one considers the different forms and media of mass communication. It is likely, though, that most critics and minority advocates would distinguish between mass media of general dissemination (that reach broad audiences), as opposed to those that exist for specialized purposes. It is doubtful that anyone would contend that a magazine for hog ranchers in Tennessee had any generic responsibility to all of the racial, cultural, national, and other minority groups of its community or nation. But a daily newspaper or network news show does have such responsibility.

Important questions emerge for the press in relating to minorities. First, is a given medium advancing social interests by offering a representative flow of news and information? And does this flow devote some attention to minority persons and interests in the community being served? Secondly, is there a channel for feedback from minority persons? Is the press accountable in some way, by having an open-letters column, or by being willing to meet with spokespersons for minority causes and views? Does the press, in fact, provide some mechanism for an articulation and expression of differing viewpoints? Finally, does a given medium respect the rights of minority persons guaranteed under the Bill of Rights? Does the activity of any given medium do anything to impair or block those rights? If there is such blockage, is it justified?

Again, the differences between print and broadcasting are relevant. Under the FCC's ascertainment procedure, wherein local stations are required to ascertain community needs, there is a mechanism for minority groups to make their views known. With the print media, there are fewer formal channels (some that do exist include bureaus of accuracy or fair play sponsored by papers; ombudsmen or in-house media critics; and readers' representatives and press councils that are voluntary and have only the power of embarrassment) and usually, minority groups and individuals have to make personal contacts to plead their case, or develop strategies to gain attention.

To what degree should the press represent minorities? The formulation will differ with different media and different communities. But it would seem that general-circulation media would have a clear responsibility to provide as full a picture as possible to their community—including the various minority constituencies—with an eye not only to the obvious ethnic blocs, but also to emerging minorities that have not previously been recognized. For example, during the 1970s, the elderly and children have begun to identify themselves as minorities who no longer wish to be invisible. Inasmuch as these and other groups are part of the ferment of community activity and action, they deserve recognition and coverage. Unless such coverage exists, the press is failing to provide a representative picture of the society, and is thus shirking a constitutionally based mandate to serve individual and social interests.

DEFINING PRESS FREEDOM

Philosophical soundings offer a theoretical basis from which courts can derive operational principles as a rationale for dispute resolution. With the exception of its powerful admonition against prior restraint in *Near v. Minnesota* (1931),[33] the Supreme Court only infrequently was asked to explicate press freedom prior to the 1964 defamation case, *New York Times v. Sullivan*.[34] Since the *Sullivan* decision, the Court has experienced a steady flow of First Amendment press cases; the result of these has been a detailing of rights and policies, many of which have implications for the press as a representative of the public and public interest.

The *Sullivan* case underscored a fundamental premise that traces its origins to the framers' conception of the First Amendment, namely, "a profound national commitment to the principle that debate on public issues should be uninhibited, robust, and wide-open and may well include vehement, caustic, and sometimes unpleasantly sharp attacks on government and public officials."[35] This reinforced John Stuart Mill's notion that freedom of expression should accommodate a communicative act that was less than competent or precisely truthful.

In a series of libel cases that followed the *Sullivan* decision, the Supreme Court made it increasingly difficult for public officials and public figures to recover damages in cases against the press as long as the press had fallen short of "knowing falsehood" and "reckless disregard" for the truth.[36] For a time, it seemed that the law of libel had been all but abolished, but by the mid-1970s the *New York Times* standard had been modified somewhat to afford greater protection to private persons. The flow of press cases to the high court, while raising idiosyncratic questions about quite different factual situations, often centered on two fundamental and still largely unresolved questions. First, what are the dimensions of press freedom? What specific rights does this concept embrace? That is, it is freedom to do what? Secondly, to whom does press freedom extend? Is it the right of the individual to freedom of expression, or is it a structural right in the realm of policy that extends to the institution of the press? The two areas are, of course, interdependent.

Freedom To Do What?

Unfortunately, press cases have not arisen in clean philosophical categories. And as Alexander Bickel lamented, the result is: "The First Amendment is no coherent theory that points our way to unambiguous decisions, but [it points] to a series of compromises and accommodations confronting us again and again with hard questions to which there is no certain answer." For most of our history, freedom of the press has meant freedom from censorship, the right to publish without restraint, especially the restraint of government authority. This has been called a right of dissemination. Most of the court decisions in major press-freedom cases since 1964, whether involving public- or private-sector litigants, have elaborated on the degree to which this right extends, and on the possibility of post hoc penalties or recovery of damages for those injured by a communicative act. There could, in some instances, be exceptions, but "any system of prior restraints comes to this [Supreme] Court bearing a heavy presumption against its constitutional validity."[38] The rationale was most often "the paramount public interest in a free flow of information to the people concerning public officials."[39] Even in the Pentagon Papers case,[40] where the government said grave national security was at stake, the high court opted against prior restraint of publication, dramatically affirming the right to disseminate information and opinions. Dissemination means publication and distribution, but this is not a unitary act. Instead, it is the end product of a process, beginning with an unfixed idea, that travels through various steps from assignment to reporting, editing, and printing.

Courts referred to the tripartite aspects of the press's work and identified three distinct aspects of press freedom, namely, acquiring information, processing information, and disseminating information. Journalists have argued vehemently that it is virtually impossible to disseminate effectively unless information is acquired (through various news-gathering methods) and processed (edited and prepared for publication). This view notwithstanding, there is considerable doubt about the degree to which the high court protects information processing and news gathering. While there is powerful constitutional support for dissemination, the other two functions stand on less solid legal ground. Those who believe that news gathering rights are assured frequently cite *Branzburg v. Hayes* (1972),[41] wherein the Supreme Court denied the press any special testimonial privilege. The Court, while recognizing the right of the press to gather information, said that "without some protection for seeking out the news, freedom of the press would be eviscerated."[42] This "right," though, is based on Justice Byron White's less-than-reassuring statement with a double-negative construction, that "newsgathering is not without its First Amendment protections."[43] Where the acquisition issue has arisen in cases involving journalists' privilege, the press has not fared particularly well, even in one instance where there was a near-absolute state-shield law that purported to protect journalists from having to reveal confidential news sources.

A growing number of journalist-privilege cases[44] are testing the dimensions of news-gathering rights that do find some philosophical sustenance in the federal Freedom of Information Act, and in various open meetings and open-records statutes in the states; however, the result to date is hardly a resounding victory for press freedom. And the present Supreme Court is fond of pointing out that less-than-full affirmation for news-gathering can be traced to the late Chief Justice Earl Warren's warning in *Zemel v. Rusk* (1965),[45] a freedom-of-travel case, that "the right to speak and publish does not carry with it the unrestrained right to gather information."[46] The fact that reporters can still serve jail sentences, in some instances where they refuse to reveal their news sources to courts, is ample evidence of that.

The Supreme Court has had even less to say about information processing. However, in the controversial 1979 libel case, *Herbert v. Lando*, the Court was asked to grant special protection to the editorial process, shielding it from attorney's probes in the pretrial discovery process. This, the Court, in an opinion written by Justice White, refused to do. In striking down a federal appellate court ruling that had granted special protection to the editorial process, Justice White wrote:

> . . . It is plain enough that the suggested privilege for the editorial process would constitute a substantial interference with the ability of a defamation plaintiff to establish the ingredients of malice as required by *New York Times v. Sullivan*. . . .[47]

In denying this privilege, Justice White again invoked a double-negative construction, as he had done in *Branzburg*, writing:

> This is not to say that the editorial discussions or exchanges have no constitutional protection from casual inquiry. There is no law that subjects the editorial process to private or official examination merely to satisfy curiosity or to serve some general end such as the public interest; and if there were, it would not survive constitutional scrutiny as the First Amendment is presently constructed.[48]

Still, this did not give much encouragement to the news media, which roundly denounced the court decision as having a chilling effect on press freedom.

In *Miami Herald Publishing Co. v. Tornillo* (1974),[49] the Court struck down a Florida law that would have compelled a newspaper to grant a right of reply. In this instance the Court did favor editorial judgment and control, seeing no reason why a newspaper should be forced to print anything. Earlier, in *Columbia Broadcasting System v. Democratic National Committee* (1973),[50] the Court similarly said that broadcasters were not required to accept paid political advertisements. In that case, Chief Justice Warren Burger wrote that "for better or worse, editing is what editors are for; and editing is selection and choice of material."[51] Inevitably, judicial analyses of the tripartite aspects of press freedom lead to the parties' seeking of special privileges—defining who they are and what their entitlement might be.

Freedom for Whom?

In a modern statement of the traditional philosophical position that distinguished positive and negative freedom,[52] several commentators during the 1960s argued about the implicit meaning of the free-press clause. Was it strictly a negative freedom that prohibited Congress (and the states, through the device of the Fourteenth Amendment) from inhibiting a free press, or was it an affirmative individual right enjoyed by all citizens? The latter view was taken by Jerome Barron, who advocated a right of access to the press, whereby individual citizens would have a positive right to reply and a right to buy advertising.[53] Barron's proposal suffered a serious setback in the *Tornillo* case, but is still alive as an expression of positive press freedom. Again, the issue of representation arises. Does the First Amendment protect the press as a representative of the people, or does it protect all citizens in an affirmative right of expression? This led to arguments about institutional rights of the press versus individual rights of citizens. If a citizen does not have access to the channels of communication, is he deprived of press freedom? Barron thought so, but the Supreme Court did not, in *Tornillo*.

A press that asks for news-gathering and news-processing privileges, as a matter of social policy, must necessarily trace this request to the constitutional interest in the free flow of information that serves the public and the public interest. This has been mentioned repeatedly by journalists and others supporting the freedom-of-information movement and the so-called people's right to know. The individual and social interests mentioned by Chafee are very much at issue today in discussions of who should be extended press freedom. It may be that individual interests and social interests are joined in the modern conception of press freedom. After all, an individual in a mass society can hardly have any free-press rights unless there is a vital and vibrant institutional press to convey his message to the community. In a speech at Yale Law School in 1974, Justice Stewart redognized this in supporting the concept of institutional rights of press freedom:

> The free press guarantee is, in essence, a structural provision of the constitution. Most of the other provisions in the Bill of Rights protect specific liberties or specific rights of individuals: freedom of speech, freedom of worship, the right to counsel, the privilege against compulsory self-incrimination, to name a few. In contrast, the Free Press Clause extends protection to an institution. The publishing business is in short the only organized private business that is given explicit constitutional protection.[54]

This striking advocacy of institutional freedom is at odds with the position of the Court in the *Branzburg* case, which characterized freedom of the press as a "fundamental personal right,"[55] encompassing "the right of the lonely pamphleteer who uses carbon paper or a mimeograph," as well as that "of the large metropolitan publisher who uses the latest photocomposition methods."[56] Freedom of the press as a "fundamental personal right" that is not confined to newspapers and periodicals was first affirmed by the high court in the 1938 Jehovah's Witness case of *Lowell v. Griffin* (1938).[57] A natural extension of the near-absolutist interpretation of the First Amendment, found in the views of Justices Hugo Black and William O. Douglas in their many years in the Court, embraced institutional rights as a part of the doctrine of preferred freedom. Accepting Alexander Meiklejohn's position that freedom of expression was the preferred freedom because of the essential nature of knowledge in informed decisions,[58] Justice Douglas, in a dissenting opinion, said:

> The press has a preferred position in our constitutional scheme, not to enable it to make money, not to set newsmen aside as a favored class, but to bring fulfillment to the public's right to know. The right to know is crucial to the governing powers of the people. . . .[59]

Of course, the distinction between individual and institutional rights need not be dichotomous. In most instances, both can probably coexist, but there are times when rights come into conflict, and when the press claims special privileges that go beyond those of the individual citizen. The matter becomes more urgent because of the steady increase in press cases in the courts. The reasons for this increase may be related to the litigation explosion in society generally, or more specifically to conflicts between press and government, beginning in the late 1960s, as the media became more critical of government.[60] The press often sees itself as the victim, attacked by government and private interests that would, for self-serving reasons, erode press freedom.

In the years since Watergate, there has been considerable muscle flexing by the press as investigative reporting of the public sector has accelerated.[61] In a time of press ascendancy, it is useful to know whether the claimed institutional rights of the press, long a part of media rhetoric, and now championed by Justice Stewart, have any real basis in the law. Unfortunately, our understanding of the current status of the free-press clause must necessarily be fashioned from legal fragments, from similar instances that touch on, but do not always address completely, the issue of greatest interest or importance. Courts must take cases as they come. And because of this, many of the questions that minority critics may have about the content of the news media, especially the coverage of their concerns, have not been raised or answered in a legal context.

CONCLUSION

What does all this mean for minority voices concerned about the press representing them with full and accurate coverage? Inasmuch as the press (and, as we've pointed out, this includes only some organs of the media) claims to represent the public and public interest, any of the constituent groups of society can make persuasive arguments for inclusion in the news columns. There may not be any legal remedy that would force any publication to include or exclude certain material; indeed, this smacks of censorship, but there is certainly a moral and ethical case to be made in the forum of public sentiment.

What evidence about press representation does suggest is that the media franchise for press freedom can and must be evaluated in terms of its individual and social benefits. For minority groups, there is a need to articulate their role and rights within this representative scheme. And the wedding of the concepts of representation and freedom of expression has in it the beginnings of a yardstick for evaluating, both individually and cumulatively, the degree to which the press is representative. As this chapter indicates, there may be different standards set for different kinds of publications and broadcasts, but at the same time, there is a real need for some cumulative social accounting, some evaluation of the press as a whole, both in its coverage of minority communities and in its patterns of personnel selection. This social accounting demands the attention not only of minority critics of the press, but of all critics who care whether we are getting our constitutional money's worth by letting the press, as an institution, manage our individual right to freedom of the press.

NOTES

1. *Saxbe v. Washington Post Co.*, 417 U.S. 843, 864 (1974), Justice Powell dissenting.
2. Commission on Freedom of the Press, *A Free and Responsible Press* (Chicago: University of Chicago Press, 1947).
3. Ibid.
4. This statement is supported by the first national sociological study of the American journalist, John W. C. Johnstone, Edward J. Slawski, and William W. Bowman, *The News People, A Sociological Portrait of American Journalists and Their Work* (Urbana: University of Illinois Press, 1976). For a regional study with similar findings, see A. H. Ismach and Everette E. Dennis, "A Profile of Newspaper and Television Reporters in a Metropolitan Setting," *Journalism Quarterly*" (Winter 1978):739-43, 898.
5. Hanna Fenichel Pitkin, *The Concept of Representation* (Berkeley: University of California Press, 1972, reprint ed.), p. 2.
6. Ibid., pp. 8-9.
7. This refers to theorists who thought of representation in formalistic terms, for example, Thomas Hobbes. See the useful discussion of formalistic theorists, and selections from their work, in Hanna Fenichel Pitkin, ed., *Representation* (New York: Atherton Press, 1969).

8. See, generally, Phillip Meyer, *Precision Journalism* (Bloomington: Indiana University Press, 1973); see also chapter on precision journalism and its import in Everette E. Dennis and William L. Rivers, Other Voices: *The New Journalism in America* (San Francisco: Canfield Press, 1974); a recent update is seen in Arnold H. Ismach, "Precision Journalism: Coming of Age," *News Research Report* (American Newspaper Publishers Assn.), no. 18, March 9, 1979, pp. 7-9.

9. See treatment in "Supermarketing the Newspaper," *Columbia Journalism Review* 15 (September/October 1977); also, Phillip Meyer, "In Defense of the Marketing Approach," *Columbia Journalism Review* 16 (January/February 1978):60-62.

10. Edmund Burke, *Burke's Politics,* eds. Ross J. S. Hoffman and Paul Levack (New York: Alfred A. Knopf, 1949).

11. *Mills v. Alabama*, 384 U.S. 214, 219 (1966).

12. Thomas I. Emerson, *The System of Freedom of Expression* (New York: Random House, 1970), pp. 6-7.

13. This idea was expressed succinctly by Chief Justice Hughes in *De Jonge v. Oregon*, 299 U.S. 353, 365 (1937):

> [I]mperative is the need to preserve inviolate the Constitutional rights of free speech, free press and free assembly in order to maintain the opportunity for free political discussion, to the end that government may be responsive to the will of the people and that changes, if desired, may be obtained by peaceful means. Therein lies the security of the Republic, the very foundation of constitutional government.

14. Harold D. Lasswell, "The Structure and Function of Communication in Society," in *The Communication of Ideas*, ed. Lyman Bryson (New York: Institute for Religious and Social Studies, 1948), pp. 37-52.

15. Ibid.

16. William Blackstone, *Commentaries on the Laws of England, Of Public Wrongs*, vol. 4 (Boston: Beacon Press, 1962), p. 161.

17. John Milton, "Areopagitica, Speech for the Liberty of Unlicensed Printing."

18. John Locke, "A Letter Concerning Toleration" (1689), "Essay Concerning Human Understanding" (1960), *Two Treatises of Government*, ed. Peter Laslett (Cambridge: Cambridge University Press, 1960).

19. Jeremy Bentham, "Fragment on Government."

20. Thomas Hobbes, *The Leviathan* (1651).

21. Jean Jacques Rousseau, *The Social Contract*, ed. Sir Ernest Barker (London: Oxford University Press, 1960).

22. For a useful historical review of the influence of Cato's letters, and a discussion of the Zenger trial, see Edwin and Michael Emery, *The Press and America*, 4th ed. (Englewood Cliffs, N.J.: Prentice-Hall, 1978).

23. Ralph H. Gabriel, ed., *Hamilton, Madison and Jay On the Constitution, Selections from the Federalist Papers* (New York: Liberal Arts Press, 1954), p. 195.

24. Leonard W. Levy, *Legacy of Suppression* (Cambridge: Harvard University Press, 1960), pp. 236-38.

25. Ibid.

26. G. Hurst, ed., *The Writings of James Madison* (1910), p. 103.

27. Jonathan Eliot, ed. *The Debate in the Several State Conventions on the Adoption of the Federal Constitution* (1836), pp. 553-54.

28. James Mill, "Essay on Liberty of the Press" (1825).

29. John Stuart Mill, "On Liberty" (1859).

30. Ibid.

31. Ibid.

32. *Supra* note 5.

33. *Near v. Minnesota*, 283 U.S. 697 (1931).

34. *New York Times v. Sullivan*, 376 U.S. 254 (1964).

35. 376 U.S. 254, 270.

36. The so-called *New York Times* standard is found at 376 U.S. 254, 279-89.

37. *Supra* note 4, at 57.

38. *Bantam Books, Inc. v. Sullivan*, 372 U.S. 58, 70 (1963); also, see *Near v. Minnesota*, 283 U.S. 697 (1931); *Organization for a Better Austin v. Keefe*, 402 U.S. 415, 419 (1971); and *New York Times Co. v. Washington Post*, 403 U.S. 713 (1971).

39. *Garrison v. Louisiana*, 379 U.S. 64, 77 (1964).

40. *New York Times Co. v. Washington Post*, 403 U.S. 714 (1971).

41. *Branzburg v. Hayes*, 406 U.S. 655 (1972).

42. *Id* at 681.

43. *Id* at 707.

44. For example, *Zurcher v. Stanford Daily*, 46 LW 4546 (1978), *Branzburg v. Hayes*, 408 U.S. 665 (1972), *Nebraska Press Assn. v. Stuart*, 427 U.S. 539 (1976); also, see Mark Neubauer, "The Newsman's Privilege After 'Branzburg': The Case for a Federal Shield Law," 24 *U.C.L.A. Law Rev.* 160-193 (1976); David Gordon, "Newsman's Privilege and the Law," *Freedom of Information Foundation Series*, no. 4, August 1974.

45. *Zemel v. Rusk*, 381 U.S. 1 (1965).

46. See Chief Justice Warren's opinion for the Court, 381 U.S. 1, 16-17.

47. *Herbert v. Lando*, 4 media Law Reporter 2575 (1979), 47 LW 4401, 4405 (1979).

48. 47 LW 4401, 4406 (1979).

49. *Miami Herald Co. v. Tornillo*, 418 U.S. 241 (1974).

50. *Columbia Broadcasting System v. Democratic National Committee*, 412 U.S. 94 (1973).

51. *Id.* at 120-21.

52. See "Two Concepts of Liberty," in Isaiah Berlin, *Four Essays on Liberty* (London: Oxford University Press, 1969), pp. 118-72.

53. Jerome Barron, *Freedom of the Press for Whom?* (Bloomington: Indiana University Press, 1971).

54. Potter Stewart, "Or of the Press," 26 *Hastings L. J.* 631 (1975).

55. *Branzburg v. Hayes*, 408 U.S. 665, 704 (1972).

56. *Id.* at 704.

57. *Lowell v. Griffin*, 303 U.S. 444 (1938).

58. Alexander Meiklejohn, *Free Speech and Its Relation to Self Government* (New York: Harpers, 1948).

59. 408 U.S. 665, 713 (1972).

60. See William E. Porter, *Assault on the Media: The Nixon Years* (Ann Arobr: University of Michigan Press), 1976.

61. Documented in dozens of books on contemporary reporting practices since the Watergate period; see, for example, Paul Williams, *Investigative Reporting* (Englewood Cliffs, N.J.: Prentice-Hall, 1977); useful historical review in Emery & Emery, *supra* note 22.

FOUR

OPEN AND CLOSED ACCESS: A LAWYER'S VIEW

John Taylor Williams

INTRODUCTION

Law is merely the codification of acceptable social behavior. We must first understand that behavior to fully comprehend the problems we presently face in communications rule making. Man views himself as the most social, acquisitive, communicative, and intelligent of life forms. Whether this is in fact true matters little, since it is this view of himself that has colored all his approaches to rule making in the "media" (a word as uniquely expressive as "movies" is for continuous exposed film). Man's first reaction to tangible forms of expression, from Assyrian clay tablets to Caxton and Gutenberg pressings, has been his approach to all tangibles. He determines, either peacefully or forcefully, who owns them.

Two general types of ownership have resulted: public—controlled, at first by royal libraries and now by the state television and publishing houses of socialist countries; and private, from the early patrons, printers, and publishers to the multinational communications conglomerates of the non-socialist West. Once ownership has been settled, man's more social instincts come to the fore, since under either form of ownership, tangible forms of communications have been viewed as too valuable a public resource to remain unexploited.

Man's scholarly and inquisitive instincts have historically generated continuous pressure for access to tangible knowledge and information. This pressure, and society's recognition of the basic appropriateness of this pressure have ultimately led to every society's establishment of access rules. In fact, any particular society is probably more distinctly capable of classification by its access rules than by any other identification factor.

Those societies which are basically open in their approach to access now dominate the West, and those which are closed, the East. It is the purview of social anthropologists to trace the paths by which we came to form these basic rule-making systems. They lead us back to the hereditary king/priest castes, and to cults which handed their knowledge down only to the initiate, and forward to the invention of tangible symbolic communications, to which certain religions and cultures, for various reasons, began to permit open access.

Open and closed access will never be capable of permanent definition since both are based on a particular society's perceptions of what is the best and highest use of information and knowledge. Certainly, what Western man seems increasingly to believe is that any restriction on access erodes his ability to make intelligent judgments. Vietnam provides a recent example in the United States of a subject about which more open access might have had considerable influence on society's view of the war. Conversely, the Soviet and Chinese people and governments express grave concern over the potential harm of open-access rules. The very lives of their citizens may depend upon their ability to achieve preestablished socioeconomic goals. Open access to elitest and nonutilitarian information and ideas regarding luxury products and nonproductive behavioral modes, such as rock culture, could inhibit or destroy their ability to meet those goals. The concerns of both East and West may well become academic as the development of systems of computerized storage and retrieval of knowledge, combined with satellite communications systems, make data increasingly accessible for persons in either open or closed systems.

THE HISTORICAL RELATIONSHIP BETWEEN MINORITIES AND THE MEDIA

Since social change is most likely to be produced by restive minorities, they often become the focus of the majority's inherent fear of change. From the Sons of Liberty in the American colonies and prerevolutionary France, to the English Protestant sects under

Charles I, to the Bolshevik and early Chinese Communist cells, minorities dictated the social upheavals that formed our present world.

They often achieved their dominance by understanding the inherent power of mass communication, and its manipulation, more clearly than their royal counterparts, who relied on the classic mode of a censored, closed-access system.

With the rise of the popular democracies came a new and hard-won admiration for the power of the press. Each society, whether closed or open, recognized that without access, a minority, whether ethnic, sexual, or religious, could not easily replace the new majorities.

The new majorities that dominated the world's communications resources were, with the more recent exception of Japan and China, predominantly white, male, and nominally Christian, a group which is strangely a minority, on a global scale, in each category. These dominant groups, to use a Spenglerian or Darwinian term that we shall later find employed by the Federal Communications Commission (FCC), had also come to power with new concepts of the moral obligations such control placed on them. Words such as "racism" and "propaganda" were not part of their predecessors' vocabulary, although certainly known to them by other names (as the public monuments of imperial Rome and of Shakespeare's *Othello* attest). In recognition of the enormous power either closed- or open-access systems confer upon the dominant majority, each system has attempted to establish rules that avoid propaganda in the form of false or slanted information, and racism in the form of racial or ethnic disparagement.

One of the few forums in which the open- and closed-access blocs have been able to discuss common concerns, without totally giving in to their mutual fear of criticism (propaganda?), has been the United Nations. On November 22, 1978, a Media Declaration was adopted at the Twentieth General Conference of UNESCO, after the usual politicking between the open and closed blocs. It set forth, in 11 articles, a call for the world media to take an active role in "countering socialism, apartheid and incitement to war," by disseminating information exposing such conduct; refusing to engage in racially, sexually, or ethnically discriminatory activities; opening media career opportunities to minorities; and, lastly, promoting governments which "guarantee the existence of favorable conditions for the operation of the mass media."[1] This, then, may represent the best universal expression of both systems' highest moral base for access rule making. Each bloc, however, remains fearful that its language may be used adversely to embarrass the other.

AMERICA'S APPROACH TO AN OPEN-ACCESS SYSTEM: PRIVATE OWNERSHIP OF MEDIA AND FREE SPEECH

The United States faced the problem of developing an access system in a position unique to other cultures or societies. Its independence coincided with the dawn of the great technological developments in mass communication. The country had just completed a popular revolution that left it with an extremely homogeneous population, with the exception of its then mainly undiscovered Native American population. It remained a society committed to the prerevolutionary principles of English common law, private property, and religious and political tolerance. Statutory racial tolerance did not arrive until the abolition of slavery and the ratification by the states, from 1865 to 1870, of the Thirteenth, Fourteenth, and Fifteenth Amendments.[2] To a lesser degree, statutory sexual tolerance only began with passage of the Nineteenth Amendment in 1920 enfranchising women,[3] and the more recent extension of the antidiscrimination laws to prohibit both racial and sexual discrimination.[4]

Two dominant themes were present at the time of the making of the Constitution that still control our approach to access rule-making. These are the provisions of Article 1, Section 8, regarding Congress's power to control commerce among the several states—which has become known as the Commerce Clause[5]—and the First Amendment to the Constitution,[6] which prohibited Congress from interfering with freedom of speech or the press. This counterposed the legislative and judicial branches, each attempting to carry out their constitutional duties in communications rule making.

The Legislative Approach to Rule Making

The Commerce Clause has been interpreted by the courts as giving Congress the power to preempt rule making from the states in important interstate-commerce areas, such as navigation, air and rail transportation, and communications.[7] The views of the Supreme Court and Congress in this area often appear to have been in conflict, but this is belied by their joint achievement in communications rule making. Basically, both the courts, beginning with Chief Justice Marshall, and the post-Jacksonian democratic legislatures have viewed it as proper that the federal government should have general rule-making authority over commercial interstate communications. This choice of federal, rather than state, authority has merely insured uniformity of law, not ownership. Neither the courts nor Congress had any wish to interfere, at least through World War II, with the capitalist free-enterprise form of communications ownership as long as the federal rule-making power was respected. In fact, the prerevolutionary recognition of private ownership in the expression of ideas was readily adopted by the founders.

Prior to the revolution, England had adopted a copyright act,[8] which was first incorporated into American law in Article 1, Section 8, of the Constitution.[9] This recognized the creator or proprietor of an original readable work as the holder of a monopoly for its exploitation. The creator-proprietor, however, was required to publish in conformity with the relevant copyright law, regarding notice and registration, to gain copyright protection. The intent was to encourage the widest possible dissemination of ideas by encouraging tangible expressed creativity through grants of limited monopoly.[10] Thus, the press was viewed as a business whose product could be the subject of limited monopolies and, in a much more romantic mode, as the guardian flame of liberty.

A government's initial interest in most communications systems is primarily to determine a system's potential for maintaining order, either military or psychological. The press was not viewed with genuine military interest by the founding fathers, but its psychological potential for the state was of some complexity.*

The psychological potential of the press is exemplified in the Constitution's First Amendment guarantee of a free press and free speech. This special position accorded the private press remains one of the most unique of Anglo-American concepts. Indeed, it represents the key to an understanding of America's open-access approach to communications rule making. Of course, it was first viewed as merely the right to express oneself in written or oral form upon matters of state, politics, or religion, without fear of government suppression. However, the courts and Congress have created a tension which has found Congress or state legislatures passing legislation barring the use of communications media for discrimi-

---

*This conclusion does not ignore governmental fits of paranoia, such as the Alien and Sedition Acts of 1798 and similar government abuses during wars and civil unrest.

natory or racist purposes, and courts, in turn, holding that even racist comment is protected speech under the First Amendment.[11]

Justices Douglas, Black, and Brennan were not the first members of the judiciary to express the absolutist view that all speech, of whatever moral or aesthetic value, is absolutely protected under the First Amendment.[12] It was, in fact, James Madison who, in response to Alexander Hamilton's challenge to define freedom of speech, said simply that it meant freedom from despotic control by the federal government.

The Context of the Recent Case Law

We now have before us all the dynamics of the open-access system of American communications: private ownership of both the tangible expression of ideas and the technology for their dissemination; and the almost mystical belief, held by courts and Congress, that free press and free speech are the constants of our liberty.

These traditions have now to contend with the rising expectations and demands for media access (and eventual control) for minorities and women. America's rather complacent and benign racial and sexual views are also increasingly questioned by nonminorities on moral grounds. Certainly, until the *Bakke* case, both state and federal legislation mirrored this growing sensitivity.

America's racial, ethnic, and linguistic homogeneity is constantly unmelting as blacks, women, Chicanos, Native Americans, Asians, and gays seek access to media still owned and dominated by middle-class, white, English-speaking males.

The cases cited in this discussion have been limited primarily to those which depict the FCC's growing sensitivity to minority access in the context of broadcasters' license renewals. They do not contain the final answer to this clash. They may illustrate how this tension between conflicting goals makes law. It is the opinion of most believers in America's approach to open-access rule making, including the author, that as long as this tension exists, ultimate stability, and progress toward open access will continue.

The New Media and the FCC

Private ownership remains the vehicle for radio and television, as with the print press; however, the broadcasting profile is one of greater concentration (e.g., ABC, NBC, CBS, and PBS). The hands-off regulatory stance that Congress and courts have adopted toward the print press has not been true of the electronic media.

While the print press remains relatively unlicensed or regulated, except for a growing interest in preserving diversity of ownership under the antitrust laws, the new nonprint media have been historically excluded from a niche in the revolutionary pantheon along with the pen. This may also be because much of radio and television is transitory in nature. Or perhaps it is that, prior to the recent advent of public broadcasting, advertising was an inherent or even primary part of all radio and television programming.

Also, radio and, later, television sprang from a technology that was seen as militarily useful. Initially, radio waves were used for Coast Guard and maritime purposes, and civilian use was strictly limited and licensed. The Commerce Department, to whom this licensing process had been assigned, was not equipped for the commercial boom that cheap crystal sets brought to radio technology. Licensees battled for valuable commercial frequencies, disregarding the assignments made to them by Commerce.[13] From this turmoil emerged, in 1934, our present Federal Communications Act, which merged the Federal Radio Commission into the Federal Communications Commission.

The act charged the FCC with regulating "interstate and foreign commerce in communications . . . so as to make available, so far as possible to all of the people of the United States, a . . . communications service with adequate facilities at reasonable charges . . ."[14]

The FCC has authority both to grant original licenses and assign frequencies or make spectrum allocations to broadcasters, as well as consider renewals for existing broadcasting-station licenses every three years. Both procedures require the FCC to make its rulings consistent with the "public convenience, interest or necessity,"[15] which is the key language that both courts and Congress have looked to when reviewing the FCC. This broad language is actually administered within a rather narrow range of pure licensing rulings, with little or no authority to influence ownership per se (which is controlled by the Sherman and Clayton Antitrust Acts), or advertising content, which has been left to the Federal Trade Commission (FTC).[16] Those access remedies that the FCC can bring to bear have therefore centered predominantly in the licensing area.

The licensing process is, by definition, one contrary to the basic schema of the First Amendment. We would be appalled if newspapers, magazines, or books were subject to limited federal mandatory licenses. Limited airwave frequencies allegedly made licensing a necessity.[17] In order to encourage broad participation, Congress chose to use short-term licenses, for which no license fee was charged, conditioned only upon the licensee's ability to show that the public interest would be served by the proposed license.

AN OVERVIEW OF MINORITY-ACCESS LEGISLATION AND CASE LAW

Media Ownership

Media ownership is increasingly a rich-man's club. The days of the flourishing ethnic, foreign-language, and racially oriented newspaper have drawn to a close. Union wages, postal costs, and, in some cases, loss of a literate audience have helped, but are probably not the crucial causes of their extinction.

America has a unique relationship with its minorities. The desire to be absorbed, and be perceived as, first, an American and, only secondarily, by ethnic or racial origin, is still a dominant tradition. This wish of the immigrant or minority person to lose himself in the melting pot has, however, gained a new sophistication. Today's minorities wish to be seen as having retained all the unique qualities of their ethnic or racial life style, but they do not want to share this life style only with members of their own race or ethnic group. They, like all Americans, wish to be represented on prime-time television, because that is where Americans are depicted and watched by other Americans. Recent research appears to suggest that, in many instances, guaranteed access for minorities to any media forum other than prime-time commercial television, including public television or CATV (community antenna television) channels, would not achieve increased minority-audience access, because the minorities simply would not listen, read, or watch.[18] Their rationale is not a disingenuous one; put bluntly, if they are to be given true access, it must be to prime-time media and not to nonmainstream high-culture programming or CATV, which, in many instances, minorities may not be able to afford.[19]

The ownership club is also rich because it is small. As of 1976, there were only 514 VHF television stations and 197 UHF stations. Ownership of many of these stations was grandfathered, and exempted from the new restrictions on multiple ownership adopted by the FCC.[20] It is also unlikely, due to the potential for spectrum overlap, that except in the CATV field, the FCC will create many new station licenses.

Government programs to encourage minority ownership have, in the main, been pathetic. In 1978 the FCC took additional steps to encourage minority ownership by making available a minority-buyers list, for private sales to minorities; and it has begun a program of providing economic incentives to owners who make sales to minority buyers.[21] At the FCC's request, in 1978, the Small Business Administration (SBA) relaxed its regulations in order to make loans more available to minority entrepreneurs seeking broadcasting ownership. Of the 32 SBA-loan recipients to date, under the new rules, only seven were minority. One of these nonminority recipients was a group led by the NBC-TV "Today" show's host, Tom Brokaw, who was provided $345,000 under an SBA loan guarantee for the purchase of a station in a predominantly American Indian region of South Dakota.[22] Brokaw admitted his salary exceeded $250,000 annually. Meanwhile, such groups as the Native American Public Broadcasting Consortium continue, without avail, to seek financing or guaranteed access.

Media-Management Access

Management access for minorities has exhibited vastly greater progress than has outright ownership. However, as with most minority progress, it is a slow move up the employment ladder toward the management apex.[23] At the pinnacle of media management lies the FCC, with its seven commissioners. All are presidential appointees approved by the Senate. No more than four may be members of the same political party, and they serve for staggered seven-year terms.[24] The FCC remains firmly in the hands of the dominant majority, which is white, male, and middle class.

It is doubtful that any of this legislative progress in minority management and employment would have resulted without the soul-wrenching reexamination of American racial relations that followed the Supreme Court's 1954 decision in *Brown v. Board of Education.*[25]

Access to the top tiers of management, for most minorities, only began to open with the passage of the Civil Rights Act of 1964, and the accompanying creation of the Equal Employment Opportunity Commission (EEOC).[26] At first, only the EEOC brought pressure on the media to engage in affirmative action; but in 1969 the FCC also began to require all licensees or applicants to adopt affirmative action programs to insure equal employment opportunity in hiring, training, and advancement.[27]

The FCC began to focus on the fact that minority employment by broadcasters should not be limited to gross employment data, which permitted broadcasters to hire minorities and women only in the lowest job categories. Employers, beginning in 1970, were required to break down their employees, by sex and minorities, into nine job categories on FCC Form 395 (Annual Employment Report). The FCC announced it would not only focus on the total number of women and minority persons employed, but also on the number employed in the higher-paying, most desirable upper-four employment categories (officials and managers, professionals, technicians, and sales personnel).[28]

The FCC began to employ affirmative action compliance and progress as one of its tests for determining the suitability of new applicants or renewal applicants in the licensing process.[29] The problem was, and remains, that unlike the EEOC, the FCC does not concentrate solely on the affirmative action profile of a licensee at the time of license renewal or application. The strong, potentially negative, chilling First Amendment effects that vigorous civil rights enforcement could have on licensing seem to have made the FCC's approach a more vague and general one than that of EEOC. The FCC continues to consider all employment data, including the long-term statistical history of an applicant, extending to all postcomplaint employment data available at the time of a hearing. This synoptic approach to statistical data is combined with the FCC rule that all statistical employment data must be measured against a standard of "the public interest, convenience and necessity," as opposed to the EEOC's standard of "reasonable cause" to believe that the evidence available constitutes *prima facie* discrimination.[30]

The act provides that the FCC need only hold a hearing in a license-renewal challenge if it finds the challenge raises specific allegations of "substantial and material fact" regarding the applicant's performance during the license term, or other reasons why renewal would not be in "the public interest."[31] It further provides that all appeals directly from FCC licensing decisions shall be heard only by the federal Court of Appeals for the District of Columbia Circuit.

THE LICENSING OF BROADCASTERS: SELECTED CASES IN THE PUBLIC INTEREST

The "Zone-of-Reasonableness" Doctrine

The FCC and the courts began to examine the progress and standards for minority employment access in an important series of cases commencing in 1972 with *Stone v. F.C.C.*[32]

Stone involved a Washington, D.C., citizens' group that had filed a challenge to the renewal of the license of station WMAL-TV, on grounds which included allegations that its programming and employment practices were discriminatory to blacks. The FCC determined not to hold a hearing, and this denial served as the basis for appeal. In *Stone*, the court of appeals, in affirming the FCC's decision that the challengers had not made a prima facie showing of discrimination, nevertheless established a base for future progress.

Cognizance was taken, for the first time, of the license applicant's employment statistics, gathered on Form 395. The court compared WMAL's statistical employment profile with the minority population in the standard metropolitan statistical area (SMSA) in which it was located. (In smaller areas, where SMSA information is not available, Census general-population characteristics and general social and economic characteristics are used.)[33] Although the court finally held that in the absence of affidavits setting forth allegations of specific discrimination, mere statistics showing racial employment inequities could not serve as a prima facie case, it suggested that in future cases where comparative statistics alone were so disproportionate as to take the applicant's hiring profile outside "the zone of reasonableness," a prima facie case of discrimination could be proved.

Thus, *Stone* became the originator of the FCC's zone-of-reasonableness test. The court, in *Stone*, relied on the fact that the applicant had an affirmative action program, that no specific allegations of employment discrimination were made, and, finally, that 7 percent of its employees were black. The Washington, D.C., metropolitan area's population then was 24 percent black, which the court viewed as sufficient to sustain the commission's grant of a renewal as being in the public interest, and apparently also within its new zone of reasonableness.

The zone-of-reasonableness test was still anything but clear.[34]

In 1974 the court of appeals heard arguments in *The Bilingual Coalition of Mass Media, Inc. v. FCC.*[35] (commonly referred to as *Bilingual I* to distinguish it from the subsequent case involving many of the same issues and parties).

A citizens' group in San Antonio had challenged the license renewal of San Antonio's station WOAI-TV. As in *Stone*, no affidavits of specific discrimination were filed, but the SMSA statistics, upon which the petition was based, showed that 48 percent of San Antonio was Mexican-American, as opposed to only 12 percent of the station's employees, or a roughly 4-1 ratio. Again, however, the FCC denied the challengers a hearing. The court, on appeal, affirmed the FCC's placement of heavy emphasis upon the vigorous affirmative action recruitment policies of the station. It did, however, for the first time, acknowledge that a challenger is at an enormous disadvantage in "raising substantial and material questions of fact" if it cannot engage in a discovery of the station's employment data before the FCC decision on the request for a hearing.

While an employer's statistical data would be readily discoverable by a plaintiff in a civil-rights action under Title VII, the FCC only grants a right of discovery to a challenger if a "hearing" is designated. This is rendered almost nonsensical, because the FCC will not grant such a hearing without a prior showing of substantial questions of fact. The court, in *Bilingual I*, suggested that the FCC attempt in the future to avoid this conundrum by a more careful study of statistical employment data at the challenge stage, since it intimated that it viewed permissible minority parity percentages under the zone of reasonableness as a "contracting-zone" theory.[36]

Progress in focusing the commission's attention on the problems inherent in its zone-of-reasonableness test was slow. From the first citizens' petition for a license challenge, in 1966, through 1976, only four challenges to renewal applications, on the grounds of discrimination in employment, had even been granted a hearing by the FCC. This, of course, meant that these were the only cases where a challenger could gain discovery of the employment data necessary to prove a prima facie case raising a substantial and material question of fact.

The interim cases between *Bilingual I* and *Bilingual II* are of interest because in them, the FCC began, perhaps unconsciously, to demarcate its zone of reasonableness, sometimes without even referring to it by name. In *Leflore Broadcasting Company, Inc.* (1974),[37] the FCC denied a renewal application of a Greenwood, Mississippi, AM and FM radio station without any specific reference to the zone of reasonableness. The renewal had been opposed by a citizens' group that alleged that three black announcers were unlawfully discharged when the station changed its format from rhythm and blues to country and western. The FCC's administrative-law judge found that this constituted classification of job capacity by race, in violation of the Civil Rights Act of 1964. The applicant's affirmative action program was also found to be mere window dressing.

Cases followed that added specific refinement to the parameters of the zone-of-reasonableness test. Racial statistical employment data were used to place two renewal applicants outside the zone of reasonableness, upon challenge by citizen groups. First, in 1972, Alabama's eight educational-television stations, which had only one full-time black employee in a state that was over 30 percent black, were denied a renewal of their license.[38] Thereafter, in 1975, a Rochester, New York, AM-FM station's license was denied renewal in an FCC hearing where the statistical data showed that the employer-applicant had only one black employee (a janitor) in an SMSA that was 6.5 percent black.[39]

These cases actually illustrate the extremely conservative approach to employment statistics taken by the FCC in applying its zone-of-reasonableness test. This conservatism, when combined with a license challenger's limited right to the discovery of employer statistics and a corresponding lack of success in obtaining hearings, continued to result in few successful challenges by minorities. The FCC's tradition of accepting postchallenge affirmative action data also enables a challenged broadcaster to "stock up" on minority employees between the date of the challenge and the hearing, in order to present an affirmative action posture complying with FCC standards. The FCC and the court of appeals also clearly did not intend that the zone-of-reasonableness test require parity between a particular licensee's minority employment statistics and the relevant SMSA minority population.

Basically, the FCC continued to resist the EEOC and the judiciary's approach to minority employment statistics, which held that a disparity between employment and SMSA data could give rise to a rebuttable presumption that the employer was engaged in discriminatory employment practices, where discrimination charges had been filed by a protected minority.[40]

Bilingual II

In May of 1978, the court of appeals handed down its most comprehensive and important review, to date, of the zone-of-reasonableness test, in *Bilingual Bicultural Coalition in Mass Media, Inc. v. F.C.C., et als.* (popularly known as *Bilingual II*).[41] In *Bilingual II*, the court was not in unanimity. The carefully delineated differences between Circuit Judge Wilkey's majority opinion, the dissent of Judge Robinson, and the concurring opinion of Chief Judge Bazelon must be studied with extreme care by anyone truly interested in the present status of the law of minority access.

The case dealt definitely with prehearing discovery for challengers, the parameters of the zone-of-reasonableness test, and the legitimacy of classifying minorities as dominant or nondominant.[42]

Actually before the court were two separate citizen appeals resulting from FCC renewals of AM radio licenses in San Antonio (station KONO) and San Francisco (station KCBS). In the case of station KONO, the issue was its employment of Mexican-Americans, and for KCBS, Chinese-Americans. Both citizen-group challengers were denied a hearing by the FCC. Their principal contentions on appeal were that they should have been permitted discovery, and that hearings would have shown that the licensees' minority statistical data were outside the zone of reasonableness.

The court affirmed the FCC's denial of a hearing, and affirmed the license renewal for KCBS, but remanded the renewal of KONO, for further investigation by the FCC. It did, however, affirm the FCC's denial of discovery or a hearing for the KONO petitioners.

The court, in affirming KCBS's license renewal, noted that there were no allegations of specific discrimination, and that the petitioners were relying solely on statistical disparity. Also, the FCC, as in past cases, had considered KCBS's postchallenge-date employment data, which, together with amended earlier data, showed that it presently had a 6.1 percent minority of Asian-American employees, in an SMSA area with a 6 percent Asian-American population. However, its percentage during its prerenewal license term was considerably lower.

On the other hand, the statistics which led the court to return KONO's renewal application for further FCC investigation were considerably more dramatic. KONO operated in an SMSA area with a 44 percent Mexican-American population, and yet during its previous license term, Mexican-Americans never exceeded 17 percent of its total employees. The FCC itself had made a finding that these statistics were outside the zone of reasonableness, and had found that its affirmative plan was inadequate and "passive." Nevertheless, it granted the renewal, subject to certain requirements it imposed upon KONO to provide detailed reporting as to its efforts to recruit women and minorities.[43]

The court went out of its way to state what it viewed as the "governing principles" to be used by the FCC in considering renewals of applicants charged with employment discrimination, noting that, unlike EEOC, the FCC's goal was the public interest, and not enforcement of the antidiscrimination laws:

> [T]he F.C.C. is not the Equal Employment Opportunity Commission, and a license renewal is not a Title VII suit. The Supreme Court has consistently held that "the use of the words 'public interest' in a regulatory statute is not a broad license to promote the general public welfare" [citing *NAACP v. FPC*, 425 U.S. 662, 669 (1976)] and that these words "take meaning from the purposes of the regulatory legislation" [citation omitted]. In view of the purposes of its regulatory legislation, the F.C.C. analyzes the employment practices of its licensees only "to the extent those practices affect the obligation of the licensee to provide programming that fairly reflects the tastes and the viewpoints of minority groups, and to the extent those practices raise questions about the character qualifications of the licensee" [citation omitted].[44]

The Differing Goals of Discovery under the EEOC and FCC

Having established these basic "governing principles," the court used them to clarify the difference between the EEOC's affirmative action policies and those of the FCC. It confirmed that the FCC's are inherently "prospective," since its ability to deal with the past lies in the future, in the form of renewals and other prospective sanctions. Unlike the EEOC, it has no statutory power to right past wrongs through awards of reinstatement, promotion, or back pay for aggrieved minority employees.

The FCC was, however, seen as having a continuing duty to investigate any broadcaster's past employment practices and hold a renewal hearing if substantial and specific allegations of fact were raised in the petition to deny. The court thus seemed to reaffirm its vision in *Stone*.[45] Hearings, because of their administrative expense, should be granted only if the specific allegations of discrimination raise substantial or material questions of fact, or, in the alternative, general allegations raise substantial prima facie statistical disparity, such as would place an employer outside the zone of reasonableness. This would be particularly true where statistical disparity is combined with a languishing affirmative action program.

While the court agonized over the burden it continued to place on petitioners, by restricting their ability to obtain statistical data necessary to raise substantial material facts, it reiterated its belief that the FCC was the appropriate body to make such inquiry.

Of course, the FCC's investigation of statistics would be somewhat limited, the court admitted, as "[T]he Commission considers over 3,000 license renewal applications each year [citation omitted]; to require that its 13 Administrative Law Judges assume the burden of passing upon the propriety of an inevitable host of interrogatories would create a regulatory nightmare [citation omitted]."[46]

The court, however, expressed its hope that such increased FCC investigatory power, if exercised vigorously, would provide the petitioners with the data it required, without discovery.

Dominant versus Nondominant Minorities

Judge Robinson's dissent in *Bilingual II* was directed toward the lack of a coherent judicial approach toward the setting of standards for the FCC to follow in attempting to meet its avowed goal of denying license renewals to broadcasters who engaged in "intentional discrimination."

He noted that if the views of the entire minority community, both the dominant and nondominant groups, were not considered, the commission could not fulfill its statutory duty:

> [T]o ensure that its licensee's programming fairly reflects the tastes and viewpoints of minority groups [citation omitted], the Commission in turn has identified two related ways in which discrimination can frustrate that objective. First, the duty to ascertain and meet the programming needs of all segments of the community served is undercut when the licensee himself has indulged conspicuously in employment bias—both because minorities might not bother to present their preferences to him and because he might well be insensitive to them [citation omitted]. Second, minority employees are more likely to originate programming that rectifies deficiencies encountered by their groups [citation omitted].[47]

His dissent raised, as its central concern, the majority's consent to the commission's classification of Asian-Americans in KCBS as a nondominant minority. Judge Robinson felt that the majority had not followed its own guidelines by such classification, since it ignored the very large aggregate minority in KCBS's broadcast SMSA area, including women, and the black "dominant minority."

The majority reaffirmed the FCC's approach of considering the overall percentage of minorities in the SMSA workforce, except that "where one minority group predominates the 'dominant minority' becomes the focus of comparison."[48]

The problems inherent in such a focus were recognized, but the majority felt the FCC could avoid the problem by careful consideration of both groups:

> After checking to see that the percentage figures for *all* minorities and for the *largest* individual minority group are acceptable, therefore, the F.C.C. investigates discrimination against smaller groups by looking to other types of evidence. Evidence of actual discrimination in hiring, evidence of recruiting aimed selectively at one minority, and evidence that a particular group has had little or no representation on a station's payroll are clearly relevant, and should be examined to determine whether an employer is in fact discriminating against a "non-dominant" minority, notwithstanding acceptable overall figures. Like the dissent we "see no reason whatever for countenancing purposeful discrimination merely because it is aimed at only one small group" [dissenting opinion at 26-27], and we firmly believe the F.C.C. shares our conviction.[49]

The above language set forth the very test Judge Robinson castigated the majority for failing to apply to KCBS. He noted that it is historically the smallest groups that have often been the most heavily victimized by racial prejudice or stereotyping. The majority's failure to carefully analyze the employer's statistics, in line with its announced test, confirmed Judge Robinson's view that both the court and the commission did not believe that statistics alone could show intentional discrimination. Without such a careful statistical analysis of all minority employment data, with particular emphasis on the upper-four job categories and increasingly less reliance on an employer's post challenge statistical employment data, Judge Robinson felt discrimination could not be eradicated:

> It makes little difference whether a licensee purposely calculated that an applicant was unable to handle the responsibilities of a position because of his race or whether a licensee's socialization

was so imbued with the stereotype that it simply never occurred to him that the applicant could do the job. Improper purposes and neglect have the very same impact on the policies that the Commission's job bias rules seek to further. As has been said in another context, the arbitrary quality of thoughtlessness can be as disastrous and unfair to private rights and the public interest as the perversity of a willful scheme [citation omitted].[50]

The Application of the Governing Principles of Bilingual II

Shortly after its entry of judgment in *Bilingual II*, the court of appeals decided *Los Angeles Women's Coalition, etc. v. F.C.C.* on September 12, 1978.[51] This case gave the court the opportunity to apply the tests of *Bilingual II* in challenges to the renewals of three Los Angeles television stations.

The court reiterated the *Bilingual II* rule of thumb that total minority employees at the stations should represent at least 50 percent of the SMSA minority workforce, and 25 percent of those in the upper-four job categories. The court, however, now went further:

> Moreover, the zone of reasonableness must contract over time, and substantial disparities, such as those claimed with respect to all three licensees, may necessitate further inquiry and action even if falling slightly short of the rule of thumb definition of reasonableness. This is particularly true where, as is alleged here, recruitment efforts are not in fact aggressive and result-oriented; where similar recruitment efforts have failed to produce significant or lasting improvements in the past, at a minimum, commission monitoring may be necessary to ensure there will indeed be improvements in the future, as the zone of reasonableness contracts.[52]

It also clarified its ruling on *Bilingual II* that the FCC may elect either to grant a hearing and the correspondent discovery to a petitioner-challenger, or make its own investigation. If it elects the latter, "the Commission must ensure that the petitioner has a meaningful opportunity to examine and comment on the information received."[53]

Access Through Media Program Content

The fact that one may even seriously address the issue of program content by government regulation highlights the differences between printed and electronic media. A doctrine such as the fairness doctrine in broadcasting[54] would clearly be held violative of the First Amendment if applied to publications.[55]

In *Red Lion Broadcasting* (1969), the Supreme Court stated:

> [B]ecause of the scarcity of radio frequencies, the Government is permitted to put restraints on licensees in favor of others whose views should be expressed on this unique medium. But the people as a whole retain their interest in free speech by radio and their collective right to have the medium function consistently with the ends and purposes of the First Amendment. It is the right of the viewers and listeners, not the right of the broadcasters, which is paramount [cases omitted]. It is the right of the public to receive suitable access to social, political, esthetic, moral and other ideas and experiences which is crucial here. That right may not constitutionally be abridged either by Congress or by the F.C.C.[56]

Thus, a means of minority access to the program content of broadcasters has been created. It has not been the subject of much litigation to date, as the case law still predominantly revolves around the fairness of coverage of political, religious, and hard news. But like the zone-of-reasonableness test, it can be seen in several guises without any particular name.

Perhaps the most elemental right to control program content begins with the right of minorities to gather news. This was legally insured after *Brown v. Board of Education* in 1954. For, it was as recently as 1947 that black reporters were excluded from the congressional press gallery.[57]

Once the news is gathered, its re-creation as a program is a task for the media licensee's employees, who may or may not be aware of, interested in, or sensitive to, the needs of minorities in program content. Two recent cases illustrate the problem.

In *Cosmopolitan Broadcasting Corp. v. F.C.C.* (1978), the court ruled on the appeal of a foreign-language radio station, resulting from denial of its license renewal by the F.C.C.[58] The station (WHBI in Newark, New Jersey) devoted 68 percent of its schedule to ethnic programs in some 18 foreign languages.

The facts indicated that the station maintained poor records as to program content, and that much of its foreign programming had little if any substance. However, it had a large foreign-language audience, and evidence showed that its programs were "valuable to immigrants and to second and third generation members of ethnic groups."[59] The court differed with the FCC's conclusion that it could not consider foreign-language programming as being *per se* meritorious."[60]

The court remanded the case to the FCC for further consideration, with the following admonishment:

> In determining whether the past programming of WHBI may have mitigated its derelictions of character, the Commission should therefore consider whether denying Cosmopolitan's application for a license renewal will silence a unique outlet serving "a specialized audience that would feel its loss."[61]

The F.C.C. has listed "service to minority groups" as one of the 14 major elements necessary to meet the public interest, needs, and desires of the community in which a station is located.[62] In *National Organization for Women (NOW) v. F.C.C.* (1979), these necessary elements were considered.[63]

NOW challenged the program content of a station seeking renewal, on the grounds that media treatment of women was a controversial issue of public importance, and that the station's program content regarding women violated the fairness doctrine. The station's programming allegedly failed to give equal time to women in the news, and failed to present issues of interest to women except in stereotypical character presentation.

Both the court and the FCC conceded that a controversial issue of public importance, under the fairness doctrine, had been raised. The court, however, upheld the FCC's determination that the overall programming of the station was balanced, since it did not find that "the public was uninformed on the present issue of women's role in society."[64]

It should also be noted that the fairness doctrine, when applied to minorities, has been held by the courts not to require mathematical equality, unlike the zone-of-reasonableness test for employment of minorities.[65]

CONCLUSION

Strangely, it is the First Amendment that represents the greatest obstacle to minority access. On the one hand, without its protection, no minority could freely expound views which are abhorrent to those held by the majority. On the other hand, since the media of expression are primarily owned or dominated by nonminorities, governmentally decreed minority-access rules for ownership, employment, or program content may not be so chilling as to affect the majority's exercise of its First Amendment rights.

The judiciary and the legislature have seen fit to separate the media into two categories—the print press, which has been left almost totally unregulated, and the electronic, which both have felt free to regulate on the theory that it is merely licensed privilege to use the state-owned airwaves. To return to our original thesis, it appears that while the First Amendment basically decrees an open-access system for the United States, the broadcasting industry is one of less open access than the print.

Even in the area of licensed media, both the courts and Congress have tended to approach rule making in an extremely vague and broad manner in order to avert any conflict with the First Amendment, and for perhaps the best of reasons. Democracy and art may, as Isaiah Berlin has noted, be philosophically incompatible. How does the government decide that a community should retain its only classical-music station (desired by only 8 percent of the population), as compared with awarding the license to a licensee representing the second or third black-oriented station in a community with a 45 percent black population?[66]

America's open-access system for minorities continues to be one of balancing the interests of all citizens in free and open debate, against the wishes of many for greater guaranteed access for their particular race or sex.[67]

It has been said that "ownership is the most significant factor influencing the content of media."[68] This probably truer for the broadcasting media than for the print, since only in broadcasting is ownership limited by governmental regulation. Perhaps this explains our present open-access system's determination to divide the media. This division leaves the unregulated printed media free to explore the outermost bounds of the First Amendment, while reserving the broadcast media as a laboratory for learning—if, at the same time, access for minorities can be imposed by regulation without affecting its ability to serve both the public interest and the First Amendment.[69]

NOTES

1. 4 Med. L. Rptr., News note (December 12, 1978).
2. U.S. Const. amends. XIII, XIV, XV
3. U.S. Const. amend. XIX
4. 42 U.S.C. §§ 1971, 1975(a)-(d), 2000(a)-(h)(6) (Civil Rights Act of 1964).
5. U.S. Const. Art. 1, § 8, cl. 3
6. U.S. Const. Amend. I
7. *Gibbons v. Ogden*, 22 U.S. (9 Wheat) 1 (1824).

8. *The Licensing Act of 1662*, 13 & 14 Car. 2, c. 33 (lapsed in 1694); *Statute of Queen Anne 1709*, 8 Anne, c. 19. For a history of the Anglo-American copyright law, See American Bar Association, *Two Hundred Years of English and American Patent, Trademark and Copyright Law*, (symposia), 1976. (Symposium by ABA Patent, Trademark & Copyright Section)

9. "To promote the Progress of Science and Useful Arts, by securing for limited Terms to Authors and Inventors the exclusive Right to their respective Writings and Discoveries." 1 U.S. Const. Art., § 8, cl. 8.

10. The first major revision in American copyright law in almost 70 years is embodied in the Copyright Act of 1976, 17 U.S.C. §3 01 *et seq.*

11. *Collin v. Smith*, 578 F.2d. *1197* (7th Cir. 1978), 3 Med. L. Rptr. 2490, cert. denied sub nom. *Goldstein v. Smith* 436 U.S. 953 (1978) (First Amendment prohibits restraint under city ordinance or by court injunction of American Nazi Party march through predominantly Jewish suburb of Skokie, Illinois) and *Pittsburgh Press v. Commonwealth.* 2 Med. L. Rptr. 2337. (1972 decision in Pennsylvania Commonwealth Court) (First Amendment bars prosecution of paper which carried ads that disclosed job seeker's race, color, sex, etc. in violation of Pennsylvania Human Relations Act).

12. Cf. *Near v. Minnesota*, 283 U.S. 697 (1931). For a scholarly and influential presentation of the "absolutist" view of the First Amendment, see Meiklejohn, *The First Amendment is an Absolute*, 1961 Sup. Ct. Rev. 245.

13. cf. *U.S. v. Zenith Radio Corp.*, 12 F.2d 614 (N.D. Ill. 1926).

14. 47 U.S.C.A. § 151

15. 47 U.S.C.A. § 307

16. cf. *U.S. v. Radio Corp. of America*, 358 U.S. 334 (1959)

17. As of January 1, 1974, there were 7,785 radio stations and 925 television stations and the potential broadcast spectrum has still not been exhausted.

18. Greenberg & Derwin, *Mass Media and the Poor*, 74-415 (1970); Kasserjian, *Blacks as Communicators and Interpreters of Mass Communications*, 50 Journalism Q. 291 (1973)

See *Garrett v. F.C.C.*, 513 F.2d 1056, 1063 (1975) ("[T]he entire thrust of *TV 9* is that black ownership and participation together are themselves likely to bring about programming that is responsive to the needs of black citizens.")

19. Allen Hammond has pointed out, in a provocative article in the *Black Law Journal*, the affect of CATV upon the poor who now receive television free: "An access requirement that allows the poor to communicate with those who can afford to subscribe but not with others like themselves has serious shortcomings and will do little to alleviate the present distortion of the world which the poor receive on broadcast television. Hammond, *Federal Communications Commission's Cable Accent Rule and the Fiction of Public Participation* Black L.J. Vol. V No. 3 at 371 n.25.

20. The F.C.C. has enacted a series of "multiple ownership" rules designed to thwart market dominance through multiple ownership of facilities or multi-media conglomerate ownership, such as ownership by newspapers or television stations in the same community. cf. 47 CFR §§ 73.35, 73.240 and 73.636; 50 F.C.C. 2d 1046 (1975); See also *Chronicle Broadcasting Co.* 40 F.C.C. 2d 775 (1973).

Proceedings of the F.T.C. *Symposum on Media Concentration* December 14-15, 1978. Former F.C.C. Commissioner Nicholas Johnson expressed the view in light of increasing monopoly that minority groups may have to have "guaranteed access". Professor Ben Bagdikian of University of California (Berkley) stated that mass media concentration leads to a "homogeneous" mass media population which includes minorities only in a pre-selected manner. Minorities are increasingly unable to read or see themselves outside this mass media stereotype as small minority or local paper and stations are acquired. Today only one paper exists in 97.5% of American cities, where once there were many.

21. F.C.C. Open Meeting of October 31, 1978.

22. Boston Globe, November 16, 1978 at 43, Col. 1 ("Brokaw Gets SBA Loan Guarantee").

23. The F.C.C.'s publication *Employment in the Broadcasting Industry*, 1975, stated that of the 378 broadcasters and group owners with 10 or more full time employees which were located in areas with more than 5% or greater minority populations, 209 had no minority employees in any capacity.

24. 47 U.S.C.A. § 154(a)

25. 347 U.S. 483 (1954)

26. 42 U.S.C. § 2000(e) *et seq.*

27. 47 CFR § 73.680 (1969), which provided in part: "Equal opportunity in employment shall be afforded by all licenses . . . to all qualified persons, and no person shall be discriminated against in employment because of race, color, religion, national origin or sex". See Nondiscrimination Employment Practices of Broadcast Licensees, 18 F.C.C. 2d 240 (1969).

28. 47 CFR §§ 73-125, 73-301 et seq., 18 F.C.C. 2d 522 (1973). The F.C.C. has recently attempted to increase the breadth and accuracy of the job categories on Form 395 so as to accurately reflect the structure of the broadcast industry. *Petitions for Rulemaking to Amend F.C.C. Form 395* and *Instructions*, 66 F.C.C. 2d 955 (1977) cf. *Bilingual II* 16 EPD ¶8290 at 5496 n. 59 (majority opinion).

29. 40 Fed. Reg. 31625 (1975) (Notice of Inquiry, July 16, 1975, Docket No. 20550).

30. Bowie and Whitehead, *The Federal Communications Commission's Equal Employment Opportunity Regulation; An Agency in Search of a Standard, Black Law Journal* Vol. V No. 3 (1977).

31. 47 U.S.C.A. § 309(d)(e).

32. *Stone v. F.C.C.*, 466 F.2d 316 (D.C. Cir. 1972)

33. Nondiscrimination of Licensee Employment Practices, 54 F.C.C. 2d 354 (1975)

34. As F.C.C. Chairman Burch stated in 1973: "If I were to pose the question, what are the F.C.C.'s renewal policies and what are the controlling guidelines, everyone in this room would be on an equal footing. You couldn't tell me. I couldn't tell you and no one else at the Commission could do any better (least of all the long-suffering renewal staff)." Address to the International Radio and Television Society, (September 14, 1973).

35. 492 F.2d 656 (D.C. Cir. 1974) (*Bilingual I*).

36. *Bilingual I* at 658.

37. *Leflore Broadcasting Company, Inc.*, 46 F.C.C. 2d 980 (1974) (F.C.C. No. 75D-45).

38. *Alabama Educational Television Commission* 50 F.C.C. 2d 495 (1972), but cf. *Puerto Rican Media Action*, 51 F.C.C. 2d 1178 (1975).

39. *Rust Communications Group, Inc.*, 53 F.C.C. 2d 335 (1975).

40. Cf. 42 U.S.C. §§2000(e) *et seq.* The bruden of proof placed on an employer under Title VII of the Civil Rights Act of 1964 is set forth in *Green v. McDonnell Douglas Corp.*, 411 U.S. 792 (1972).

41. *Bilingual Bicultural Coalition in Mass Media, Inc. v. F.C.C.*, 16 EPD ¶8290 (D.C. Cir. No. 75-1855, decided May 4, 1978).

42. *Bilingual II* had originally been heard by a panel of the Court of Appeals a year earlier on April 20, 1977. The panel reversed the F.C.C.'s renewal orders for both stations on the ground that the F.C.C. should have granted petitioner's prehearing discovery. Because of the importance of the case, the Court ordered a rehearing en banc (before the entire bench) of the Circuit Court. *Id.* 16 E.P.D. ¶8290 at 5481.

43. Judge Robinson in his dissent set forth a scholarly recapitulation of the F.C.C.'s development of the "zone of reasonableness" test. He pointed out that while previous opinions from *Stone* forward seemed to suggest that minority employment of 29% of parity with the relevant SMSA statistics was acceptable, this was not to be taken as sufficient except for those particular cases. He questioned any arbitrary approach to parity including the F.C.C.'s expressed intention to question licensees employment of minorities where minorities represented less than 50% of parity with the relevant SMSA figures and 25% in upper-level positions. He suggests that the best approach would be a step-approach beginning at 50% of parity to be increased by 5% each year to a maximum of 90% of parity. *Bilingual II supra* at 5489 and dissenting opinion fns 71-78.

44. *Bilingual II, supra.*, 16 EPD ¶8290 at 5481.

45. *Stone supra*, 466 F.2d 316 (1972)

46. *Bilingual II, supra.*, at 5484

47. *Bilingual II, supra* at 5485. Judge Robinson relied in part on the earlier cases of *Black Broadcasting Coalition v. F.C.C.*, 556 F.2d 59 (1977) and 2TV 9, Inc. v. F.C.C., 495 F.2d 929 (1973), cert. denied 419 U.S. 986 (1974).

48. *Bilingual II, supra* at 5492 (The majority opinion n. 7. cited with approval the F.C.C.'s use of the "dominant minority" focus in *Mission Central Co.*, 56 F.C.C.2d 782, 784 (1975) (finding Mexican-Americans dominant minority group where they comprised 44% of SMSA and 84% of composite minority population in SMSA and 84% of composite minority population in SMSA) and *KRMD, Inc.* 53 F.C.C.2d 1179, 1186-87 (1975) (finding blacks' dominant minority group where they comprised 33% of SMSA and 99% of composite minority population in SMSA).

49. *Bilingual II, supra* at 5492 n. 7 (majority opinion).

50. *Bilingual II supra* at 5497 n. 14 (dissenting opinion).

51. *Los Angeles Women's Coalition, Etc. v. F.C.C.*, 584 F.2d 1089 (D.C. Cir. 1978).

52. *Id.* at 1092 n. 3. In *Los Angeles Womens Coalition* women in the upper four categories for two of the licensees were less than 15% of women in the SMSA.

53. *Id.* at 1092.

54. The Fairness Doctrine began with a series of F.C.C. rulings which were later incorporated in the 1959 Amendments to Section 315(a) of the Communications Act.

55. The Supreme Court in a precedent setting case held that broadcasters must cover matters of "great public concern" or risk the loss of their license as not in the public interest. *Red Lion Broadcasting Co. v. F.C.C.*, 395 U.S. 367, 394 (1969).

56. *Red Lion, supra* at 389, 390.

57. See Marbut, "The Standing Committee of Correspondents," *Congress and the News Media*, 40, 45-46 (R. Blanchard ed. 1974).

58. *Cosmopolitan Broadcasting Corp. v. F.C.C.*, 581 F.2d 917 (D.C. Cir. 1978).

59. *Id.* at p. 928

60. 61 F.C.C. 2d at 260.

61. *Cosmopolitan, supra* at 931

62. F.C.C. Form 301, Rad. Reg. 2d (P & F) 98:301-18 (Forms 1977) citing *En Banc Programming Inquiry*, 20 Rad. Reg. (P & F) 1902 (1960).

63. *National Organization for Women v. F.C.C.*, 555 F.2d 1002 (D.C. Cir. 1977).

64. *NOW, supra* at 1015. N.B., the Court in *NOW* did not include any women judges.

65. *Brandywine—Main Line Radio, Inc. v. F.C.C.*, 473 F.2d 16 (D.C. Cir. 1972) cf. *In Re Storer Broadcasting Co.*, 60 F.C.C. 2d 1097 (1976) (black's allegations that news programs excluded them from coverage except in conjunction with criminal violence held not ground for challenge because of broad discretion of licensee in covering newsworthy events and in racial fairness programming.)

66. See Geller, "*First Amendment and Electronic Media: Raising the Issues*," The Black L. J., Vol. V, No. 3 at 355 (1977).

67. See *National Black Media Coalition v. F.C.C.*, (D.C. Cir. 1978); 4 Med.L.Rptr. 1685 (1978)

68. Case Note *43 U.Cin.L.Rev.* 669, 677 (1974)

69. Bolinger Book Review, 76 Colum.L.Rev. 1354 (1976) (B. Schmidt, Jr., *Freedom of the Press v. Public Access*).

PART III

SOCIAL STEREOTYPING AGAINST THE PUBLIC INTEREST

FIVE

BLACKFACE IN PRIME TIME

Melvin M. Moore, Jr.

BACKGROUNDS IN AMERICAN MINSTRELSY

The portrayal of Afro-Americans in television drama has been an issue of concern and debate since the early 1950s. Throughout the past 29 years of television's development and growing influence, this issue has been addressed by numerous scientific and impressionistic studies, resulting in little significant change. Today, it is argued that Afro-Americans are depicted in a more positive manner than ever before, and that there has been a notable increase in the number of Afro-American characters in dramatic television. This argument finds considerable support when portrayals of the 1950s are contrasted with those of 1970s television; however, stereotypic portrayals of Afro-American characters and culture, although less blatant since the "Beulah" and "Amos 'n' Andy" programs, still persist.

Unfortunately, when these same portrayals are contrasted with the images from which they were derived, time appears to stand still. Any discussion of television's portrayal of Afro-Americans must curiously, but necessarily, begin, not with "Beulah" or "Amos 'n' Andy," but with the birth of mass entertainment in America. Afro-American portrayals existed throughout the development of mass entertainment, through nineteenth-century minstrelsy, motion pictures, and television. Tragically, while mass entertainment developed and matured, the growth of the Afro-

American image was stunted, forced to remain within rigidly imposed standards, with slight modifications coming only with changing technology and social climate. Significantly, what did not change, even while the images themselves changed, was the concept that structured the portrayals of Afro-Americans. From the minstrels in blackface to the black characters in prime time, the identity of Afro-Americans was, and continues to be, defined in the mind of white America.

Long before *Beulah* and *Amos 'n' Andy* were introduced to American television in the 1950s, nonwhite characters were used for comic relief. As early as 1769, a West Indian slave, a "profane clown of little authenticity," was introduced to the American theater in a comedy titled *The Padlock*. And, in 1795, the "shuffling cackling, allegedly comic Negro servant" appeared in *Triumph of Love*.[1] Such comic portrayals of Afro-Americans were common in theater throughout the late eighteenth and nineteenth centuries.[2] However, it was the minstrel show of nineteenth-century America that had the greatest initial impact on the American mind in its perpetuation of negative stereotypes of the Afro-American. Robert Toll, author of *Blacking Up*, wrote that "minstrelsy was the first example of the way American popular culture would exploit and manipulate Afro-Americans and their culture to please and benefit white Americans."[3] Its importance in the present discussion lies in its legacy to modern mass entertainment. Minstrelsy's image, whether reflecting the fantasies of its performers or the beliefs, attitudes, and values of its audience, have influenced the portrayals of Afro-Americans in mass entertainment since that time—in drama, motion pictures, and television.

The seeds of minstrelsy were planted shortly after the War of 1812. During this period, popular entertainment in America was fragmented into two forms. One form, referred to as highbrow or elitist entertainment, reflected and refined European forms and concepts. The other was lowbrow or popular culture—"a common man's culture that emphasized and glorified American democracy and the average white man."[4] This "common man's culture" offered to rural immigrants, in the rapidly expanding and seemingly incomprehensible urban environment of the early 1800s, a substitute for the folk culture that they had left behind. Orientation and adjustment to the cities necessitated the adoption of new values, the incorporation of different norms of behavior, and the discovery of new amusements to replace the entertaining and instructive verbal arts of folk society. This culture form helped the new urbanites develop a sense of group identity and community.

The early elements of this new entertainment form closely resembled the verbal arts that its audience enjoyed in simpler times: full-length plays, singing, dancing, animal acts, and juggling and acrobatic acts. However, central to its development were its stage characters, characters designed to make heroes of common white Americans, and representing what "common" white Americans wanted to believe about themselves. The most important hero of the period was the Yankee character, Brother Jonathan, "a symbol of American democratic society—proud, independent, morally strong, brave and nationalistic." Brother Jonathan, was joined by the Frontiersmen and Mose the B'howery B'hoy, a New York City-bred Irish firefighter. Such folk characters were extremely antiaristocratic. They glorified the American common man and denounced the "corrupt, immoral city slickers."[5] The attitudes they expressed on stage emphasized the fundamental conflict offstage between the common man and the European-oriented elite groups, a conflict that eventually resulted in a complete separation between high- and low-brow culture. From this separation, and the evolution of low or popular culture, emerged minstrelsy and the blackfaced character that was to become its notorious trademark.[6]

White American performers in blackface first appeared on stage during the late 1820s, about the same period that white performers were creating positive stage images of themselves. This, however, was to be the only similarity between the stage portrayals of Afro-Americans and the white heroes of the white common man. In every way, the portrait of black Americans was the antithesis of what white Americans wanted to believe about themselves. Not only were black stage characters, whose faces were smeared with burnt cork, actually black, but many were portrayed with exaggerated physical deformities. In contrast to the strength, fearlessness, vitality, and aggressiveness of white stage heroes, the standard portrayal of the plantation slave emphasized traits suggested by such adjectives as lazy, shiftless, improvident, stupid, ignorant, and slow, and those reflected in a fondness for watermelons, chickens, gin, crap games, razors, and by big words.[7] Toll, in *Blacking Up*, remarked:

> From the onset, minstrelsy unequivocally branded Negroes as inferior.... Even sympathetic black characters were cast as inferiors. Minstrels used heavy dialect to portray Negroes as foolish, stupid, and compulsively musical.... Minstrel blacks did not have hair, they had "wool".... They had bulging eyeballs,

> flat, wide noses, gaping mouths with long, dangling lower lips, and gigantic feet with elongated, even flapping heels.[8]

In addition to the general traits and descriptions attributed to all black Americans, minstrelsy also created symbolic images of black Americans in the characterizations of the "old uncles," "old aunties," and the "yaller gal." Minstrelsy's "old darky" or "old uncle" was a submissive and ideally forgiving character with tender and sentimental qualities and with an undying love for his master.[9] Complementing the "old uncle" was the plantation "mammy" or "old auntie", a strong, tough, yet tender and devoted matriarch. Together they offered white America "openness, warmth, devotion, and love."[10] The "tragic mulatto," often referred to in modern criticisms of Afro-American portrayals in film and television, is a descendant of minstrelsy's "alluring 'yaller gal'"; she had the light skin and facial features of white women, combined with the exoticism and "availability" of Negroes. In minstrelsy, yaller gals "provided coquettish flirtations, happy romances, and sad, untimely deaths."[11]

From the late 1820s to the early 1890s, white men in blackface portrayed black characters throughout the nation. Innumerable minstrel troupes performed from New York City to California, played at the White House for Presidents Tyler, Polk, Fillmore, and Pierce, and before countless common folk in small saloons and great theaters. These blackfaced performers were professional entertainers, yet billed themselves as delineators of black life. In fact, minstrels took great pains to prove themselves more authentic than all others. Many blackfaced acts were based on Anglo-American folklore, but because of the competitive advantage of being authentic, minstrels increasingly made use of Afro-American folklore.[12] They consciously borrowed songs and dances, adapted folktales, and mimicked speech patterns and behavior. Minstrels often made claims that they had lived with slaves, knew their ways, understood them, and could present an authentic representation of their lives. However, regardless of how minstrels came by their material, it fell short of the reality. Although the stage portraits of Afro-Americans did contain factual elements of black culture, they were twisted into caricatures and stereotypes. This was the inevitable result of portrayals based on white fantasies, expectations, and interpretations of black culture; minstrelsy was "composed by whites, acted and sung by whites in burnt cork for white audiences."[13] Minstrels were entertainers. Their purpose was to entertain audiences whose sole purpose as patrons was to be entertained—to get what they paid for. Minstrelsy's method was characterized by J. H. Haverly, the greatest minstrel promoter, who remarked, "Find out what the people want and then give them that thing."[14]

In addition to providing captivating entertainment, minstrelsy served important social and psychological functions. One of its chief functions was to provide a nonthreatening way for white Americans to work out their ambivalence about the proper place for Afro-Americans, during a period when the issue of slavery was paramount. Minstrelsy, by portraying Afro-Americans as inferiors, provided its audience with a way to rationalize their behavior without contradicting their ideals of nationalism and euqalitarianism.[15] As minstrelsy evoked, it increasingly attempted to reflect changing social trends and the anxieties and concerns of its audience. It also provided information about the problems of modern life. After the Civil War, minstrels began to concentrate on national developments. They condemned and lampooned the early women's-rights movement, attacked the social and moral decay of the cities, the inequities of wealth and the evils of industrialization. Minstrels, seemingly in an attempt to help their audience understand the increasing ethnic diversity of America, also devised stage portrayals of racial-ethnic groups other than Afro-Americans. Native Americans, and Chinese, Japanese, German, and Irish immigrants were all, at some time during minstrelsy's popularity, of passing or of considerable interest. But no group aroused as much curiosity as did the Afro-Americans.[16] Regardless of topic and purpose of presentation, the message to the audience, always delivered in blackface, was always at the expense of the black image.

In the late 1850s, Afro-Americans entered minstrelsy. This entrance marked the beginning of black participation in American show business, yet it was not without a price.[17] Locked into white created images, black minstrels were unable to make significant modifications in minstrelsy's black caricatures. They became "caricatures of caricatures".[18] In order to survive, black minstrels fulfilled the expectations of minstrelsy's patrons. And, being "acknowledged minstrel experts at portraying plantation material," they, through their performances, unwittingly lent credibility to minstrelsy's black caricatures.[19]

By the early 1890s, minstrelsy's popularity began to decline.

> But like the Cheshire Cat in the topsy-turvy world through the looking glass where appearances offered few clues to reality, the

minstrel show, long after it disappeared, left its central image—the grinning, black-mask—lingering on, deeply embedded in the American consciousness.[20]

MOTION PICTURES AND STEREOTYPECASTING

After minstrelsy's decline, white America's apparent obsession with a perverted image of Afro-American character and culture was to find expression in the theater, on the vaudeville stage, and eventually in motion pictures. However, the early portrayals of Afro-Americans in films, although still stereotypic in keeping with the dominant southern literary and theater tradition, were more favorable than they had been during minstrelsy. Unfortunately, this had nothing to do with changing racial attitudes, but with the primitive nature of motion-picture technology. In the late 1890s, during the infancy of motion pictures, filmmakers had little technical sophistication, and consequently little technical control over their material. Editorial cutting, film editing, and the film narrative did not exist, making it difficult for this new medium to convey stereotyped portrayals and conceptions.[21] The filmmaker had use of a single camera on a tripod and could only record "the objective reality before it without artifice, staging, or editing."[22] This did not, however, prevent the production of films demeaning to Afro-Americans. Films such as Thomas Edison's *Watermelon Contest* (1899), depicting four grinning blacks who "wolfed melons and spat seeds with a will," were frequently produced, yet films generally deviated from racial stereotyping and often portrayed blacks outside their prescribed place and in positive sexual roles. These films included *Colored Troops Disembarking* (1898); *The Ninth Negro Cavalry Watering Horses* (1898); and *Sambo and Aunt Jemima: Comedians* (c. 1899-1900), in which "two handsome Negroes coyly kiss without gross racial overtones."[23] But this was to change. The period of relatively positive portrayals lasted only as long as the technology permitted. By 1905, the film narrative had developed into a minor art, and the old stereotypes resurfaced. Film catalogues of the period advertised such films as *The Nigger in the Woodpile*; *Interrupted Crap Game*, featuring "darkies who neglect their game to pursue a chicken"; *Prize Fight in Coon Town*, depicting "two bad coons"; and *A Night in Blackville*, "'hot stuff' with 'two coons' out with their 'best babies.'"[24] By 1907, the further development of motion-picture technology was to lead to further definition of the Afro-American film image. Film directors became skilled in editorial cutting and film editing, and the film, in its portrayal of Afro-Americans, turned more and more to "heavy-handed old-style race humor."[25]

The film historian Donald Bogle asserts that all of the early black film characters, from approximately 1903 to 1915, were "filmed reproductions of black stereotypes" carried over from slavery and popularized in American life and art. These characters, which entertained and stressed Afro-American inferiority, Bogle describes as "character types." These types bore the names Tom, Coon, Tragic Mulatto, Mammy, and Brutal Black Buck; they represent the stereotypic roles that black actors have performed since the beginning of motion pictures.[26]

As early as 1895, Afro-Americans appeared in films, but it was not until Edwin Porter's *Uncle Tom's Cabin* (1903) that a black figure appeared in a central film role. That figure was Tom (actually a white man in blackface), who Bogle described as "the American movies' first black character . . . the first in a long line of socially acceptable Good Negro characters."[27] The Tom of motion pictures, as the old uncle of minstrelsy, never turned against his master; was submissive, stoic, generous, selfless; and always represented, for white Americans, positive race relations and equality.[28] The long line of Toms began in 1903 and appeared in the remakes of *Uncle Tom's Cabin* (1909, 1913, 1927), and in the shorts *Confederate Spy* (c. 1910) and *For Massa's Sake* (1911). This theme was also followed in the Shirley Temple films *The Little Colonel* (1935) and *The Littlest Rebel* (1936). It is also recognized in aspects of Sidney Poitier's characters in *Lilies of the Field* (1963) and *In the Heat of the Night* (1968).[29]

The Coon represents the Afro-American as a buffoon and an object of ridicule. Bogle identified three types of Coon: the Pure Coon, the Pickaninny, and the Uncle Remus. Coons are generally regarded as "no-account niggers . . . unreliable, crazy, lazy, subhuman creatures, good for nothing more than eating watermelons, stealing chickens, shooting crap or butchering the English language."[30]

The Pure Coon was introduced in *Wooing and Wedding of a Coon* (1905), and, still early in motion pictures, during 1910 and 1911, appeared in a series of slapstick comedies as the character Rastus, portrayed as a buffoon "possessing only the minutest intelligence."[31] One of white America's most celebrated Coon character types to emerge in the late 1920s was Stepin Fetchit. (Bogle states that in the early 1930s, Fetchit was the best-known and most successful black actor working in Hollywood. He was the first Afro-American to receive featured billing, and special scenes were often written into pictures for him.) As his popularity declined, he was replaced by two other able Coon types, Willie Best and Mantan Moreland, whose antics spanned from 1931 to 1948.[32]

Today, this trio can be seen in reruns of old Charlie Chan movies on late-night television: Stepin Fetchit in *Charlie Chan in Egypt* (1935); Willie Best in *The Red Dragon* (1942); and Mantan Moreland in *The Chinese Cat* (1944), *The Jade Mask* (1945), and *The Chinese Ring* (1947).[33] Unfortunately, like all other types, the Pure Coon survived to provide comic relief for the audiences of the 1960s. This type formed elements of Sammy Davis, Jr.'s characters in *Sergeants 3* (1962), *Robin and the 7 Hoods* (1964), and *Salt and Pepper* (1968).[34]

The Pickaninny is a child actor, described by Bogle as "a harmless, little screwball creation whose eyes popped, whose hair stood on end with the least excitement and whose antics were pleasant and diverting."[35] Bogle credits Thomas Edison with exploiting this type in his film *Ten Pickanninnies* (1904), the forerunner of the *Our Gang* series, which was the 1920s and 1930s vehicle for the pickaninnies Sunshine Sammy, Farina, Stymie, and Buckwheat (and which still airs on major-market television).

The third, and minor, member of the Coon family is the Uncle Remus character type. A relative newcomer, Uncle Remus is known for his quaint and naive manner and his comic philosophizing. Most moviegoers remember his appearance in the heavily criticized films *The Great Pastures* (1936) and *Song of the South* (1938).[36]

In addition to the Coon character type, there is the "victim of divided racial inheritance"—the Tragic Mulatto. This type is usually depicted living a sad and unfulfilled life. The Mulatto suffers while passing for white and fearing discovery, or wanting to be white while hating being black. However depicted, the inference is often made that the Mulatto's life is ruined because of black blood. Initially presented in *The Debt* (1912) and *The Octocoon* (c. 1913), the Tragic Mulatto appeared and reappeared throughout movie history, most recently in *Pinky* (1949), *Kings Go Forth* (1958), *Night of the Quarter Moon* (1959), the 1959 remake of the *Imitation of Life* (1934), and *I Passed for White* (1960).[37]

Not to be forgotten is the prominent Mammy character type usually depicted as "big, fat and cantankerous." This American earth mother made her debut in a 1914 comedy titled *Coon Town Suffragettes* and made significant appearances in *The Birth of a Nation* (1915), *Saratoga* (1937), *The Mad Miss Manton* (1938), and *Gone With the Wind* (1939). While Hattie McDaniel popularized the

Mammy type during the 1930s, Louise Beavers is most identified with the Mammy's offshoot, the Aunt Jemima. The characters of this type are either "blessed with religion," like Toms, or they "wedge themselves into the dominant white culture," like Mammies; but they are always "sweet, jolly and good tempered." Almost all of Mae West's and Shirley Temple's maids fall into this category.[38]

D. W. Griffith's *Birth of a Nation* (1915) introduced the last of the character types, the Black Brute and the Black Buck, both variants of the Brutal Black Buck.* The Black Brute is a barbaric figure, out to cause trouble, raise havoc. Bogle describes his portrayal in *Birth* as "subhuman and feral." The Black Brute's film descendants include the rebellious slaves in *So Red the Rose* (1935), Crown in *Porgy and Bess* (1959), the hood in *The Pawnbroker* (1965), and the militants of *Putney Swope* (1970). Bogle describes Black Bucks as "big, baaddd niggers, oversexed and savage, violent and frenzied as they lust for white flesh."[39] In modern cinema, elements of the Black Buck character type have appeared in the heroes of *100 Rifles* (1968), *El Condor* (1970), *Shaft* (1971), and *Superfly* (1972).[40]

Bogle's "mythic types" became household words in America's black communities long before they were recognized as such by scholars, being better publicized than black historical figures. Today, while Hollywood and the rest of white America boasts of improved film portrayals, black Americans continue to be offended. Bogle argues that the character types have not "improved," but have only been camouflaged. The illusion of change, he asserts, has been accomplished throughout the history of motion pictures by the repackaging of the character types into various "guises"—butlers, maids, villains, heroes, entertainers. Stereotypic treatment continues to plague the portrayals of black characters; what continues today are the least objectionable of the old stereotypes.[41] At best, they appear as superficially positive portrayals lacking three-dimensional characterization.

In Neil Simon's comedy, *California Suite* (1979), two Coon types masquerade as a dentist and a physician and appear in the film's only slapstick scenes. These Coons, along with the film's other major characters, are guests at an exclusive California hotel. The situations in which the white characters are depicted include: a divorced couple debating the custody of their young daughter; an

*Bogle credits D. W. Griffith with portraying all of the character types, except the Pure Coon and the Uncle Remus, in his epic *Birth of a Nation*.

unfaithful, middle-aged Jewish husband caught by his wife; and the relationship between an aging actress and her homosexual husband. The film's white characters were all presented in plausible situations, and the situations were done with humor (interestingly enough, the only other portrayal that approached slapstick proportions was that involving the Jewish couple). There is a striking contrast between these situations and those in which the film's black characters find themselves. The antics of the black doctors, played by comedians Richard Pryor and Bill Cosby, include auto accidents, name calling, threats of violence, an overflowing toilet, a sprained ankle, falls, broken furniture, and a fight between the two doctors. At the film's conclusion, both doctors and their wives leave the hotel bandaged from head to toe—it was ridiculous.

What emerges from even a cursory examination of the history of Afro-American portrayals in American mass entertainment is a pattern of white domination and control and black exploitation. From minstrelsy to the motion pictures of the 1970s, white America has seemed unable (or unwilling) to significantly alter its representations of Afro-American identity, unable to extricate itself from the self-serving complex of myths it has woven around the Afro-American. By maintaining control of mass entertainment, white America has also maintained control over its black images. In doing so, it seems to be asserting its right to define the black images it projects because it controls the means to project them. Supporting this right seems to be a presumption of accuracy in defining the images projected—the delineator concept of minstrelsy.

In motion pictures, black actors playing white roles were little more than black minstrels playing out predetermined patterns of behavior. As television developed and became the most popular mass-entertainment form of the twentieth century, the rigid patterns and traditions of the past remained, and trapped within them, the image of the Afro-American.

TELEVISION

The 1950s

An Afro-American image did not appear on American television until approximately 23 years after television's first drama was experimentally broadcast in 1928.[42] Unlike the world of minstrelsy and the motion pictures, the world of television that Afro-

Americans entered was, according to the broadcasting historian Erik Barnouw, "explicitly and glaringly white."[43] The absence of black faces on the television screen seemed a constant reminder to America, black and white, that Afro-Americans did not exist except when and how white America permitted it.* Unfortunately, in the 1950s this was rare, and on those rare occasions, only in the old familiar roles—entertainers, servants, and buffoons. As entertainers, Afro-American performers appeared on the weekly variety shows of Milton Berle, Ed Sullivan, Sid Caesar, and Arthur Godfrey; as servants, black actors were seen as maids on the sitcom "Beulah," and on "The Great Gildersleeve"; as the valet Rochester, continuing from radio to the television version of "The Jack Benny Show"; and as Willie, the handyman of "The Stu Irwin Show"; and, as buffoons, black actors starred in the all-black, the unforgettable, and the unforgivable "Amos 'n' Andy."

The Afro-American presence on television during the 1950s might have gone relatively unnoticed if the Columbia Broadcasting System had not broadcast this electronic minstrel show. Originally broadcast as a radio series in 1929, "Amos 'n' Andy" was created by two white delineators, Freeman Gosden and Charles Correll. Intended to depict black life in Harlem during the Depression, the series "allegedly drew from the life of the urban black—as the white writers knew of it."[44] The comic and supposedly reality-based situations in which the series characters found themselves revolved around "various schemes pursued . . . to achieve status and dignity." The shows were structured to be understandable to the millions of unemployed and the struggling wage earners in the radio audience. However, despite any lofty intentions,

> . . . the show was in reality an updated minstrel show adapted to the mass media audience. Correll and Gosden retained the accepted Negro idiom and the familiar characteristics of the minstrel stage. Thick dialect, intellectual presumptuousness, simple-mindedness, laziness, and buffoonery were integral aspects of the situations.[45]

But "Amos 'n' Andy" was popular, so popular that a television version was created. In a special demonstration held at the 1939 World's Fair, Gosden and Correll re-reated their radio characters—

---

*The pervasive whiteness of the television industry during its early years was responsible for the demise of "The Nat King Cole Show." Because advertisers feared linking their product to a black face, Nat King Cole was never able to acquire full sponsorship for his show. It folded after a year on the air.

in blackface.[46] In 1951 CBS paid Gosden and Correll $2.5 million for 20-year rights to the show. Black actors were to be cast in the familiar roles of Amos 'n' Andy, the prospect of which, according to Barnouw, caused considerable concern among the series' white following. In what appeared to be an effort to mitigate any discomfort the screen presence of black actors might have had on a white audience, Gosden and Correll trained the series' black actors to portray the characters "in the nuance of the stereotype."[47] (This has to be the classic example of how television gives the people what they want.) An example of such training was cited by E. T. Clayton in *Ebony*. In true minstrel tradition, Gosden, in trying to give Spencer Williams (Andy) some pointers on black dialect, claimed that because he created the series, he "ought to know how Amos 'n' Andy should talk." Williams retorted that he "ought to know how Negroes talk, having been one all my life."[48]

The training of the black actors may have helped alleviate the discomfort of the white audience, but the show's implausible plots and demeaning stereotypes and characterizations only incensed the black community. In 1951, the National Association for the Advancement of Colored People (NAACP) campaigned to have "Amos 'n' Andy" taken off the air. It charged:

> It tends to strengthen the conclusion among uninformed and prejudiced people that Negroes are inferior, lazy, dumb and dishonest.
>
> Every character in this one and only TV show with an all-Negro cast is either a clown or a crook.
>
> Negro doctors are shown as quacks and thieves.
>
> Negro lawyers are shown as slippery cowards, ignorant of their profession and without ethics.
>
> Negro women are shown as cackling, screaming shrews, in big mouth close-ups, using street slang, just short of vulgarity.
>
> All Negroes are shown as dodging work of any kind.
>
> Millions of white Americans see this Amos 'n' Andy picture and think the entire race is the same . . .[49]

One must conclude that the $2.5 million and its potential returns spoke louder than words. Amos 'n' Andy aired on network television until June 1953, and was then released for syndication. Not until 1966 did CBS bar further syndication or overseas sales.[50] (In the February 20, 1966 edition of the *New York Times*, it was reported that in 1963, Kenya and West Africa banned "Amos 'n' Andy" after CBS announced that it had been sold in those two countries. In 1966 CBS withdrew the series from its catalogue, announcing that it was outdated.)

The 1960s

On February 1, 1960, four students at North Carolina Agricultural and Technical College started the sit-in movement at a Greensboro, North Carolina, five-and-dime store.[51] What followed was a chain of demonstrations, freedom rides, boycotts, voter-registration drives, and tragic race riots that focused national media attention on black America. These incidents and confrontations were to change the consciousness of black Americans and the racial climate of the United States. This, in turn, helped bring about limited but significant changes that occurred in the frequency and portrayals of Afro-Americans on television during the 1960s. But change was slow. During most of the 1960s, no matter how visible in the streets, Afro-Americans on television were rarely seen outside the context of national and local news.

In 1962 the Committee on Integration, of the New York Society for Ethical Culture, sampled two weeks of prime-time television to determine the nature of the roles in which black Americans appeared. Black people were found to appear in only 89 units of the 398 half-hour units sampled. Of these, 27 units featured black entertainers in transient, nonweekly appearances. In the remaining 62 units, the majority of black people appeared in hard news and documentary programs, while a small fraction appeared in dramatic programs as walk-ons—maids, doormen, faces in a crowd—or in minor roles. The minor roles included such efforts as those of Ossie Davis in "The Defenders," and "Car 54, Where Are You?"; and Cicely Tyson in "East Side/West Side." In 1964 the Society for Ethical Culture conducted a second study, a study of frequency of appearance. That study of New York City's three network stations documented the invisibility of black Americans at that time:

> If one viewed television in April 1964 for five hours, on any channel at any time, he would have seen about three Negroes, two of them for less than a minute and one for a longer period. In only one-fifth of the appearances of the Negro does he receive exposure for more than three minutes.[53]

These studies indicate the manner in which black Americans were represented on television up to that time—in limited, minor roles (corresponding to the status allowed in American society) or in none at all.

In 1965 Bill Cosby costarred with Robert Culp in the NBC espionage-adventure series, "I Spy." Cosby's "cover" was as trainer for a professional tennis player, Culp. In reality, of course, Cosby was a brilliant spy, a Rhodes scholar, and a superb athlete, fluent in several languages. "I Spy" not only launched Cosby's television career, but initiated, in the portrayal of the Cosby character, two trends that were to influence the portrayal of black Americans through the late 1970s. The formula that developed offered visibility and superficially positive images to television's black audience and to the white audience, black images that did not offend. The first of these trends was that of presenting black actors in the role of "black second banana," the pal of, or assistant to, the white hero.[54] Although Cosby costarred, it appeared that Culp was the hero. He was given top billing, appeared in the program's opening montage, and was portrayed as the tennis pro, not the tennis pro's trainer. Even the costars' roles communicated the status of blacks and whites in white America. It might be argued that a white rather than a black actor was more believable in the role of tennis pro (there is Arthur Ashe). However, during the same television season, we were asked to believe that a horse could talk (Mister Ed), that the U.S. Marine Corps tolerated anyone as infuriating as Gomer Pyle, and that the Beverly Hillbillies were plausible. The concept of "black second banana" essentially stated that black actors were usually cast in the roles of auxiliaries to white people. Their only reason for existence on the screen, their raison d'être, is for the benefit of white people in the story.[55]

The Cosby character fulfilled this function less then did others that followed. However, as a black character, he was the prototype of television's white man's black man. The Cosby character was portrayed in a "social void where being black only meant having slightly darker skin"—not having to deal with one's blackness or another character's whiteness, only having a romantic interest in black women characters, and talking about collards and mom's home cooking.[56] These and similar elements constituted the second trend: depicting black actors in white roles, in situations where black-white relations were one-dimensional, and in situations where black identity was avoided altogether. This may have been an attempt to portray blacks as just human beings, rather than as black human beings. Unfortunately, the portrayals presented only positive black faces and sanctified whitewashed images.

Almost two years after the debut of "I Spy," during the summer of 1967, racial disorders erupted in 23 cities across America. On July 28, 1967, the National Advisory Commission on Civil Disorders was established to investigate the causes of these disturbances. The mass media were singled out for special attention. In its report, the commission concluded that the mass media had failed to communicate:

> They have not communicated to whites a feeling for the difficulties and frustrations of being a Negro in the United States. They have not shown understanding or appreciation of—and thus have not communicated—a sense of Negro culture, thought or history.
>
> Equally important, most newspapers articles and most television programming ignore the fact that an appreciable part of their audience is black. The world that television and newspapers offer to their black audience is almost totally white, in both appearance and attitude.[57]

The commission recommended that, in addition to news-related programming, television should increase the visibility of black Americans in dramatic and comedy series and create programming aimed at the ghetto and its problems.

The commission erred in its conclusion that television had failed to communicate. It had, since its inception, communicated, to both white and black Americans, the schizophrenia of acceptance-rejection and inclusion-exclusion, and the ubiquity of white self-righteousness. What the commission failed to do was communicate to the networks that they had a responsibility to develop programming that communicates a sense of black culture, thought, and history—programming that is not white, neither in appearance nor attitude. Instead, what the commission communicated was that black Americans should get greater visibility on the tube. And that is what we got, all within the parameters of the black-second-banana roles and those of white-washed images—quantity instead of quality.

By the 1968-69 television season, black actors starred or costarred in 14 prime-time network series; at least one black actor appeared as a regular on 21 of the 56 nighttime dramatic programs.[58]

In a content analysis that included the 1968-69 season, it was found that black actors appeared in 34 percent of all dramatic programs in 1967. That percentage increased to 52 percent in 1968 and 1969. A most interesting finding was that of the 63 percent of black actors appearing in major roles in 1967, only 20 percent were in major roles in 1969. This indicated that the increase from 1967 to 1968 and 1969 represented an increase of black actors in minor and background roles (i.e., the black second bananas). During the same period, it was also discovered that although the number of roles for black actors had increased, these roles reflected white rather than black American values and lifestyles.[59]

The following conclusion by the authors of *Racism and the Mass Media*, Paul Hartmann and Charles Husband, sums up black exposure on American television during the 1960s:

> The greater number of black faces on the screen did not therefore carry with it an increased exposure of black American culture. It would seem that blacks in American television drama are not functioned as representatives of any distinctive black culture; rather they are merely black skins in white roles.[60]

The 1970s

In August, 1977, the U.S. Commission on Civil Rights (CCR) published *Window Dressing On The Set: Women and Minorities in Television.* This report focused on the portrayal of women and minorities on network television and their employment within the television industry. The commission's findings regarding employment were based on data pertaining to 40 major-market commercial and public-television stations, and on an analysis of Federal Communications Commission (FCC) employment reports. *Window Dressing* presented a historical review of television portrayals of women and minorities since the 1950s, and an analysis of a sample of television drama broadcast by the three commercial networks from 1969 through 1974. The commission's findings were hardly surprising to the many critics of the television industry.

It found that improvements had been made in the portrayal of minorities and women since the 1950s. However, in its analysis of contemporary data, the commission also found that white males continued to be overrepresented; that women were generally underrepresented, especially minority women; that minority men were typically cast in "ghetto roles" or in programs set in ethnic locales; and that minority characters generally appeared as tokens in otherwise all-white shows. Further, the CCR found that both women and minorities continued to be underrepresented in the industry's work force and "almost totally excluded from decision-making and important professional positions in the stations studied."[61]

In January 1979, the Civil Rights Commission issued its second report, *Window Dressing On the Set: An Update.* Investigated was the extent to which the portrayals and employment status of women and minorities had improved since the period covered in *Window Dressing.* This updated report based its findings concerning portrayals on an analysis of television drama broadcast from 1975 to 1977. Generally, the commission's findings indicated that underrepresentation and stereotypic portrayals of women and minorities continued during this period. More specifically, the commission found two curious trends:

> Minority males are disproportionally seen in comic roles. Moreover the percentage of minority male characters in comic roles has increased during the past three years despite the fact that the proportion of all characters playing comic roles has decreased significantly.
>
> Minorities, regardless of sex, are disproportionately cast in teenage roles; in sharp contrast, white male characters are disproportionately cast in adult roles.[62]

With respect to employment, the commission found little improvement in the overall percentages of women and minorities holding decision-making positions.

For Afro-Americans, the primary minority group referred to in the commission's reports, negative portrayals not only continued, but their severity increased. In the 1970s the whitewashing of the 1960s and the stereotypic portrayals of the 1950s continued to characterize the black image. Added to them, however, were vestiges of the black character types from minstrelsy and early motion pictures, and video presentations of the weak, absent-father image and of the myth of black matriarchy.

A few examples illustrate the situation. The television version of the movie *Shaft* (1973) is a specific example of the network's natural propensity to reflect a white perspective of the black experience. The television character John Shaft is best described as emasculated and whitewashed. Bogle commented that it was as if they had "poured a bottle of Listerine over him; . . . his sensuality had been taken from him."[63] While the image of a Black Buck might have been a minor element in the emasculated character of

John Shaft, the Coon antics of "Sanford and Son" (1973) are unmistakable—it was an updated "Amos 'n' Andy." Buffoonery and ridiculous plots were the mainstay of the show, much of the comedy being based on the assumption that the characters were not very intelligent.[64]

Further insults to Afro-Americans, under the guise of comedy, were to come in such programs as "That's My Mama" (1974), and "Good Times" (1974). Among other things, both projected minstrelsy's and the early motion pictures' mammy image and each reinforced the black-matriarchy myth. "That's My Mama" depicted a 30-year-old man tied to his mother's apron strings and earning a living in a barber shop attached to her house, in which he lives—hardly a portrayal of a strong, independent male, a portrayal, incidentally, without a white counterpart on television. "Good Times" depicts the life of a black family living in a Chicago housing project. Both father and mother are unemployed, the father chronically. Perhaps the setting and employment status of the adult characters were attempts at realism, but neither are laughing matters in real life. In fact, one might wonder if this was an attempt to make a laughing matter of real life—to make certain realities palatable. In any event, the adult leads were strong characters, and we learned to admire them for their struggle. However positive certain elements of this show might have been, they were overshadowed by three of its more negative ones: first, the creation of a black matriarch, when the father (actor John Amos) left or was eliminated from the show; second, the projection of the notion that the mother (actress Esther Rolle) abandoned her children to live with her new man (Ms. Rolle reportedly left the show because of differences with producers over the portrayal of characters); and third, elevating the oldest son to family head while continuing to develop his Coon characteristics.

In "The Jeffersons" (1976), we are treated to a black professional man, George Jefferson, a shrewd, successful entrepreneur. But he is also bigoted, pretentious, obnoxious, overbearing, and rarely talks below a shout. He is a character in the mold of the freed black legislators of *Birth of a Nation* who were depicted as "arrogant and idiotic."[65] The audience is asked to laugh at Jefferson's antics and his basic insecurity without unconsciously making associations with his blackness.

During the 1970s, situation comedies were not the only programs in which the Afro-American experience was portrayed, nor in which it was misrepresented. Meaningful portrayals of Afro-Americans are found in such critical and commercial successes as

ABS's "The Autobiography of Miss Jane Pittman"; NBC's "A Woman Called Moses," the story of Harriet Tubman and the underground railroad; and "Roots" and "Roots: The Next Generation," ABC's television versions of Alex Haley's book of the same name. Generally, each of these dramas focuses on suffering, struggle, and the triumphs of individual characters. Their triumphs are depicted as triumphs of the will, the will to survive, not the will to change the system, the source of most of their suffering. In fact, the system is never challenged, or even questioned. Evil becomes the act of individual white folks, to be overcome through the belief that solutions are found within the American system and in the American way. Such historical portrayals misrepresent the active struggle, since the early 1700s, of American blacks against racial injustice. Furthermore, these portrayals, focused as they are on the past, tend to shield the television audience from the realities of Afro-American/Anglo-American relationships in the present. Additionally, because of their emphasis on the Afro-American as a problem or victim, they do not address other aspects of the Afro-American experience and the significant contributions of Afro-Americans to American society—in the arts, politics, education, the military, and the sciences. Instead, what is projected is a distorted, whitewashed version of Afro-American history that, in no way, conflicts with the carefully constructed history of white America.[66]

The American television industry, from "Amos 'n' Andy" to "Roots," has demonstrated, in its portrayals and employment policies, its failure to serve the needs of Afro-Americans. Two major factors have been cited by television scholars as contributing to this failure. The first is the fundamental problem involving control:

> It is [that] to allow full freedom of expression to an exploited minority group would be to endanger the existing social structure and people's faith in it. Such freedom would give a platform, not only for black culture, but also for a black critique of white society . . . a questioning of the consensus and a challenge to white hegemony.[67]

From this perspective, the portrayal of Afro-Americans becomes an issue of significant implications. Superficially, the solution to the problem would be to allow Afro-Americans creative and technical control. However, if the above analysis is correct, such control would be a potential threat to the status quo. Programs produced by black Americans, about black Americans, would not be expected to be supportive of the prevailing attitudes, beliefs, and values of white American society. In fact, it would be expected that fundamental assumptions of American society would be challenged. George Gerbner and Larry Gross, of the Annenberg School of Communications, assert that "television is the central cultural arm of American society" and serves to "maintain rather than to alter, threaten, or weaken conventional conceptions, beleifs, and behaviors."[68] The presence of critical voices born of alienation and resentment within such a design could not be tolerated.

The above analysis necessarily leads to the conclusion that control of programming content will always be held by white Americans. Such control assures that the problem of stereotypic portrayals and misrepresentation of the Afro-American experience will continue, as white production lacks both the historical perspective and cultural sensitivity necessary to do otherwise. This leads to the second major factor cited for the failure of American television to serve Afro-Americans, the white media professional:

> As an individual he is identified by his employment with a dominant white elite and its subculture, and his problem lies in trying to comprehend the values and needs of a minority group whose very existence is influenced by its subjugation at the hands of the white group. His income will be such as to remove him physically from contact with the majority of black Americans, and his life-style will be totally different from theirs.[69]

The white professional, in addition to being limited in his ability to understand and therefore accurately depict the black experience, is also socialized to the industry's goals. His compliance shapes his perspective further and numbs his "capacity for critical appraisal of social realities."[70]

Gaye Tuchman, author of *The TV Establishment*, suggests that these white professionals are caught in the competition among the networks to attract larger and larger audiences. This competition creates pressures on production personnel to develop and produce programming that delivers audiences to advertisers. Realistic and diverse images are rare. Stereotypic portrayals of characters and situations become the rule, and there is greater and greater reliance on the tried and true. Tuchman argues that the industry's workforce of upper-middle- and upper-class Americans, by just blindly doing their jobs in "the most expeditious manner," help in "the perpetuation of hegemony, television programming that reflects and reinforces the economic and socio-political structures of the United States."[71]

The above analysis is admittedly self-serving. Yet, it fits the history of the Afro-American portrayal on television and is preferable to a simple accusation that the television industry is racist. That would be unfair—it is that, and more.

Based on this analysis, it is not unreasonable to conclude that the television industry will have to undergo fundamental changes before it will accept a definition of the Afro-American that is not of its own creation. Such changes can only be expected under certain conditions. Among them are the following:

1. Television ownership and production personnel must begin to make a conscious and substantial effort toward changing their attitudes and approaches concerning the portrayal of Afro-Americans and other historically oppressed groups. It must be understood that negative minority portrayals, heretofore stated in such terms as "stereotyping," "unsympathetic depictions," and "lacking diversity," may soon be perceived, if continually countered with indifference, as conscious acts of hostility—acts aimed at the distortion and destruction of identity and culture.
2. The television industry must begin to accept responsibility for the images that it projects, and must begin to concern itself with their destructive potential. The industry must begin to understand that the greater evil is not in its intention, nor in the fact of its portrayals, but in its refusal of responsibility for their effects.
3. Afro-Americans and other historically oppressed groups must acquire the creative and technical control necessary to reflect their own realities, both historical and contemporary.
4. Afro-Americans and other oppressed groups must refuse to accept a distorted image of their experience and insist on their right of self-definition.
5. Afro-Americans and other oppressed groups must intensify their protest against television portrayals that offend and against employment practices that discriminate unjustly. Continual pressure must be applied to those in positions of influence—station managers, network executives, advertisers, congressmen, the Civil Rights Commission, the Federal Communications Commission, and the president of the United States.
6. An alliance of third-world people and all other groups concerned with sexism, racism, and violence in television must be formed. Its primary purpose would be the organization of a national boycott of network-advertised products to dramatize the right and the power of the audience to truly get what it wants. The boycott would be aimed at the products advertised over the network whose programming is deemed most offensive to the interest represented by the alliance.
7. Global television must become a reality, with the increasing development of third-world countries and their resources causing the inevitable shift in the bases and sources of world power.

Until several or all of these conditions occur, Afro-Americans and other groups can only hope for improvements in their television portrayals—modifications on traditional themes. Concurrently, we will also be asked by the industry to continue our deadly game with them—consulting, recommending, and otherwise giving of our experience. This game is simultaneously one of appeasement and cultural borrowing. Token positions of little influence and control are exchanged for aspects of culture to be distorted and exploited for profit.

Afro-Americans can look forward to change, but only that which comes through struggle. Struggle must be seen as necessary, for the alternative is to be accomplices in a system that treats our history, our culture, and our lives as mere material for the longest-running show in the history of mass entertainment.

NOTES

1. Loften Mitchell, *Black Drama* (New York: Hawthorn Books, 1967), pp. 16-18.
2. Sterling Brown, *Negro Poetry and Drama* (Washington, D.C.: The Associates in Negro Folk Education, 1937), pp. 105-7.
3. Robert C. Toll, *Blacking Up: The Minstrel Show in Nineteenth-Century America* (New York: Oxford University Press, 1974), p. 51.
4. Ibid., pp. 3-4.
5. Ibid., pp. 13-14. See also Francis Hodge, *Yankee Theatre* (Austin: University of Texas Press, 1964), pp. 41-59.
6. Ibid., p. 13.
7. Harold E. Adams, "Minority Caricatures on the American Stage," in *Studies in the Science of Society*, ed. C. P. Murdock (New Haven: Yale University Press, 1937), pp. 1-26 as cited by George E. Simpson and J. M. Yinger, *Radical and Cultural Minorities: An Analysis of Prejudice and Discrimination* (New York: Harper and Row, 1972), p. 639.
8. Toll, op. cit., p. 67.
9. Ibid., pp. 78, 79. See also Mitchell, op. cit., p. 33.
10. Ibid., p. 79.
11. Ibid., p. 76.
12. Ibid., pp. 31, 42-45.
13. See Mitchell, op. cit., p. 21. See also Toll, op. cit., pp. 48-51.
14. See Toll, op. cit., p. 25.
15. Ibid., p. 272.
16. Ibid., pp. 160-94.
17. Allan Morrison, "One Hundred Years of Negro Entertainment," in *Anthology of the American Negro in the Theatre*, ed. Lindsay Patterson (New York: Publishers Co., 1967), p. 4.
19. Ibid.
20. Ibid., p. 274.
21. Thomas Cripps, *Slow Fade to Black: The Negro in American Film, 1900-1942* (New York: Oxford University Press, 1977), p. 8.

22. Ibid., p. 11.
23. Ibid., p. 12.
24. Ibid., p. 13.
25. Ibid., p. 22.
26. Donald Bogle, *Toms, Coons, Mulattoes, Mammies, and Bucks* (New York: Bantam Books, 1974), pp. 1-22.
27. Ibid., p. 3.
28. Ibid.
29. Ibid., pp. 3-6, 62-71, 306.
30. Ibid., p. 8.
31. Peter Noble, *The Negro in Films*, (London: Skelton, Robinson, 1948), p. 28.
32. See Bogle, op. cit., pp. 99-104.
33. Ibid., p. 103.
34. Ibid., pp. 304-5.
35. Ibid., p. 7.
36. Ibid., pp. 93, 191.
37. Ibid., pp. 9, 212, 271-73.
38. Ibid., pp. 10, 115-24.
39. Ibid., pp. 10-17, 294.
40. Ibid., pp. 311-14, 333-37.
41. Ibid., p. 21. See also Thomas Cripps, "The Death of Rastus: Negroes in American Films Since 1945," *Phylon*, Fall 1967, pp. 268-69.
42. Federal Communications Commission, Bulletin, (Washington, D.C., June 1978), p. 24.
43. Erik Barnouw, *The Golden Web: A History of Broadcasting in the United States, 1933-1953*, vol. 2 (New York: Oxford University Press, 1970), p. 297.
44. Joseph Boskin, "Sambo, The National Jester in the Popular Culture," in *The Great Fear: Race in the Mind of America*, ed. Gary B. Nash and Richard Weiss (New York: Holt, Rinehart and Winston, 1970), p. 181.
45. Ibid., p. 181.
46. See Barnouw, op. cit., p. 126.
47. Ibid., p. 297.
48. E. T. Clayton, "The Tragedy of Amos and Andy," *Ebony*, October 1961, p. 70., as cited in Marilyn Diane Fife, "Black Images in American TV: the First Two Decades," *The Black Scholar*, November 1974, p. 9.
49. "News from NAACP," July 19, 1951, quoted in George E. Simpson and J. Milton Yinger, *Racial and Cultural Minorities*, rev. ed. (New York: Harper and Brothers, 1958), p. 716, as cited in U.S. Commission on Civil Rights, *Window Dressing on the Set: Women and Minorities in Television, An Update* (Washington, D.C.: Government Printing Office, January 1979) p. 5.
50. Daniel Blum, *A Pictorial History of Television* (New York: Chilton, 1959), p. 102, as cited in Fife, op. cit., pp. 9-10.
51. Lerone Bennett, Jr., *Before the Mayflower: A History of the Negro in America*, 1619-1964 (Baltimore: Penguin Books, 1966), p. 404.
52. See Fife, op. cit., pp. 11-12.
53. Regina Loewenstein, Lawrence Plotkin, and Douglas Pugh, "The Frequency of Appearances of Negroes on Television," (New York: Society for Ethical Culture, Committee on Integration, November 1964), p. 4., as cited in U.S. Commission on Civil Rights, *Window Dressing on the Set: Women and Minorities in Television* (Washington, D.C.: Government Printing Office, August 1977), p. 10.
54. Martin Maloney, "Black is the Color of Our New TV," in *Television: A*

Selection of Readings from TV Guide Magazine ed. Barry G. Cole (New York: The Free Press, 1970), p. 257.

55. Art Peters, "What the Negro Wants From TV," in *Television: A Selection of Readings from TV Guide Magazine* ed. Cole, p. 260.

56. See Fife, op. cit., p. 13.

57. *Report of the National Advisory Commission on Civil Disorders* (Washington, D.C.: Government Printing Office, 1968), p. 383.

58. Cole, op. cit., p. 252.

59. Paul Hartmann and Charles Husband, *Racism and the Mass Media* (London: Davis-Poynter, 1974), p. 196.

60. Ibid.

61. U.S., *Window Dressing on the Set: Women and Minorities in Television*, op. cit., p. 148.

62. U.S. Commission on Civil Rights, *Window Dressing on the Set: An Update*, op. cit., p. 61.

63. Joel Dreyfuss, "Blacks and Television, Part I: Television Controversy: Covering the Black Experience," *Washington Post*, September 1, 1974, p. K5.

64. Eugenia Collier, "'Black' Shows for White Viewers," *Freedomways*, 14 (1974):212.

65. See Bogle, op. cit., p. 14.

66. See Roscoe Brown, Jr., "Let's Uproot TV's Image of Blacks," *New York Times* (February 18, 1979), p. 35D; Pamela Douglas, "The Bleached World of Black TV," *Human Behavior*, December 1978, pp. 63-66; op. cit., pp. 209-17; Philip Wander, "On the Meaning of 'Roots,'" *Journal of Communication*, Autumn 1977, pp. 64-69; Jean Carey Bond, "Roots Recycled—Part I," *Chamber Notes*, Winter 1979, p. 8.

67. See Hartmann and Husband, op. cit., p. 197.

68. George Gerbher and Larry Ross, "Living With Television: The Violence Profile," *Journal of Communications* 26 (Spring 1976):175.

69. See Hartmann and Husband, op. cit., p. 198.

70. Ibid.

71. Gaye Tuchman, ed., *The TV Establishment: Programming for Power and Profit* (Englewood Cliffs: Prentice-Hall, 1974), pp. 5, 6, 28-31. See also Muriel G. Cantor, *The Hollywood TV Producer* (New York: Basic Books, 1971); George Gerbner, "The Structure and Process of Television Program Content Regulation in the United States," in *Television and Social Behavior*, vol. 1, ed. George A. Comstock and Eli A. Rubinstein (Washington, D.C.: Government Printing Office, 1972), pp. 386-414.

SIX

DENIALS: THE MEDIA VIEW OF DARK SKINS AND THE CITY

Joseph Boskin

"The subtlest and most pervasive of all influences," wrote Walter Lippmann, in *Public Opinion* (1922)—the earliest analysis of the nature and ramifications of stereotypes—"are those which create and maintain the repertory of stereotypes. We are told about the world before we see it. We imagine most things before we experience them. And those perceptions, unless education has made us acutely aware, govern deeply the whole process of perception."[1]

Lippmann's optimism regarding education's potential for offsetting the pernicious effects of stereotyping—insofar as minority and ethnic groups are concerned—has not been borne out. Once implanted in popular lore, an image attached to a group, an issue, or an event tends to pervade the deepest senses, and profoundly affects behavioral action. A stereotype is basically a standardized mental picture, or series of pictures, representing an oversimplified opinion or an uncritical judgment that is staggeringly tenacious in its hold over rational thinking. It gains its force by repetitive play, often presented in different guises, so that the image it projects becomes firmly imbedded in reactive levels of thought and action. As an integral aspect of a culture code, an image often operates within and at most levels of society, frequently without question and/or criticism.

Such an image affects the thoughts and movements of even those who may be aware of its existence. Equally important, it influences those who are not. It is not an exaggeration to claim that stereotypes are so pertinacious that they are dislodged only after a series of powerful assaults on them. This is primarily due to their collective quality, but more specifically to their oral and visual passage from one generation to another. The collective energy of the image also generates a self-fulfilling or centripetal force that gives it a strong semblance of reality, a "kernel of truth" as the historian H.R. Trevor-Roper observed in his study of the witch anxieties of the sixteenth and seventeenth centuries. What happens, he noted, is that the stereotype, "once established, creates, as it were, its own folklore, which becomes in itself a centralizing force."[2]

Furthermore, the image may actually have little relationship to reality. Gordon Allport, in his voluminous study, *The Nature of Prejudice*, concluded that "it is possible for a stereotype to grow in defiance of *all* evidence."[3] And since stereotyping can proceed virtually unhindered or unchallenged, the image can stand apart from all circumstance, a separate entity, an inviolate concept.

Stereotyping need not be pejorative, but in the history of race relations in the United States, the process has been used in a particularly vicious manner toward Afro-Americans, Hispanics, and other nonwhite groups. Since the institutionalization of slavery in the seventeenth century, the black person has been envisioned either as a Sambo or a savage, and these constructs developed by the majority culture have been extremely effective and long lasting. In fact, of the various stereotypes assigned to minority groups—lazy and dumb, for the Mexican-Americans; inebriated and thickheaded, for the Irish; venal and shrewd, for the Jews; fecund and untrustworthy, for the Asiatics; muscular and stupid, for the Poles; and so on—only the dual image of the Afro-American can be cited for its longevity, tenacity, and barbarity. Without exaggeration, its staying power has been evidenced by the rationalization and maintenance of the institution of slavery; the peonage system; a segregated educational and social system; the bureaucratization of welfare; an urban program of limited funding and dubious policies; race riots, lynchings, and other acts of cruelty. By labeling and perpetuating Sambo—meaning lazy, indolent, carefree, optimistic, and intellectually limited—and the savage—a synonym for sexual prowess, dangerousness, and impulsiveness—white society created and sustained a social and psychological distance. Moreover, it attempted to inculcate the notion of inferiority in black persons themselves.

If images are false, wrote Robert Bone, "if there is no real correspondence between portrayal and event, then the emotional life of the nation is distorted, and its behavior becomes pathological."[4] There can be little doubt that although the system of stereotypes functioned in ways beneficial to the majority, the consequences have been disastrous. Over the past 40 years, the nation has witnessed over a 100 major and minor uprisings in the cities alone, each one more intense than the last; the resultant violence has taken a heavy toll in lives, property, maimed psyches, and damaged institutions. While not all race conflict and violence can be attributed to ill-conceived stereotypes, the institutionalization of these stereotypes in the popular culture has contributed immeasurably. Moreover, welfare and affirmative action programs, urban policies, social service programs, and others have been continually underfinanced and undercut as a direct consequence of the attitudes and images that the populace shares regarding minority and lower-class groups.

Furthermore, in spite of official deference to the goal of equality, the media, from print to visual, continue to depict nonwhites in a deleterious manner. A 1979 report by the U.S. Commission on Civil Rights charges that television is extremely derelict in its treatment of minorities and women. In the preface, the commission stated its concern: "Because of the medium's capacity for fixing an image in the public mind, its responsibility for avoiding stereotypic and demeaning depictions becomes central to its role."[5] What the commission found was evidence to match its anxieties: "Television drama continues in its failure to reflect the gender and racial-ethnic composition of the American population." White males, who comprise 39.9 percent of the population, for example, made up 62.7 percent of the characters in a 1975-77 programming sample. Women, both white and minority, were underrepresented, and minority males, though slightly overrepresented (9.6 percent of the characters, compared to 8.9 percent of the population), disproportionately appeared as teenagers and in comedic roles. Excepting blacks, minority persons rarely appeared in dramas, and of the minority persons who did get roles, over half appeared in the same small number of shows.

Most distressing is that about half of the minority persons who act in prime-time shows are consigned to situational comedies such as "Good Times," "Chico and the Man," "What's Happening," "Sanford and Son," "That's My Momma," "Baby, I'm Back," and "The Jeffersons." The commission accurately concluded that its investigation "lends support to the claim that minorities are often portrayed in ridiculous roles and are not depicted as seriously as whites."[6]

This situation has been compounded by the treatment accorded the cities. In a nation in which the forces of urbanization have been unrelenting, there has been, simultaneously, an unrelenting conviction, as Lippmann observed, that the city must not be acknowledged as the American ideal. Consequently, attitudes about the city are, at best, ambivalent; at worst, condemnatory. The media have consistently reflected and perpetuated these antiurban biases, to the detriment of the minority groups who now constitute the bulk of inner-city residents. The popular arts in general delineate the urban community as violent, alienating, unaesthetic, corrupt, and polluted. Implicit within this message is the idea that the city is an especially harsh environment in which to raise and develop children. In contrast, life in the countryside, suburb, and exurb is frequently portrayed in nostalgic, rapturous, and upbeat terms.

The ramifications of anticity bias are heavy. Both majority and minority cultures view the suburbs as the proper place in which to reside, with the result that many, when they can afford to do so, leave the city. And so American cities continue to decay and deteriorate. When the poor and disadvantaged and the young, who have been abandoned in the inner sections, protest and riot, their activities are spotlighted by the media as representative of urban living and the violent impulses of nonwhites. Thus the initial stereotypes are reinforced. There is, then, a vicious, interrelated cycle of images that affects minority groups and city dwellers alike.

In emphasizing the violent and bizarre aspects of American culture, the media falsify life. There is no statistical way of demonstrating that there is more violence proportionately in the city than a 100 years ago, or even, for that matter, a decade ago. There is little doubt that the patterns of conflict and violence have changed, but that is a far cry from insisting, on a daily basis, that life in the city "is a war of all against all." Indeed, the urbanologist Sam Bass Warner has noted that the modern metropolis is now "a place of specialized public and private spaces," and with the exception of the poor in the ghettos, "this specialization of space has reduced public conflict, increased the safety of persons and property, and has promoted the efficiency of the defined goals of each place."[7]

Nevertheless, antiurban themes comprise a major formula for fiction and news stories in print, visual, and aural media. The contemporary mass media mirror the situation: in film, television, and popular music the city is portrayed as a violent, polluted, bankrupt, corrupt, alienating, fragmented, lonely, and unseemingly harsh environment. It is, moreover, the home of the lower classes, of poverty groups, of nonwhites, and of deviants. Conversely, suburban and countryside settings are pictured quaintly and serenely, as places where the sole problem is crab grass, or an eccentric eight-year-old named Dennis, or a twitchy-nosed housewife imbued with witchlike powers.

Scores of contemporary films, like *The Godfather*, *Taxi Driver*, *The Brink's Robbery*, *Death Wish*, and *Mean Streets*, as well as television shows, have as their theme the harshness of city existence, and denigrate the city as a Darwinian struggle for daily existence. It is for this reason that the newest form of vigilantism in American culture is represented by the urban law-involved figures seen on TV: Kojak, Mannix, Barnaby Jones, Baretta, Ironside, Cannon, Harry O, Columbo, Barney Miller, Starsky and Hutch, and their backups, the Rookies, S.W.A.T., Adam-12, and similar groups. The fusion between the traditional law-and-order figure of the West and the law-and-stability figure of the East was represented by McCloud, Sam McCloud being an earthy, humorous, intuitive sheriff from Colorado who worked with the New York Police Department and frequently had to overcome the bureaucratic procedures of the department in order to solve baffling crimes.

In the same manner, antiurban messages flow continually, almost subliminally, from popular songs. Contrasts between the city and the West, or the idyllic, natural setting of the countryside, are powerful. New York City is, more often than not, the symbol of the rejected place—as, for example, in the Carole King song "Where You Lead." Further, Cashman and West, in their "American City Suite," rued the changes which have occurred.

Country-western songs celebrate life on the farm, with its attenuating virtues of simple but hard work, and family orientation; one of the more popular songs of the 1970s was "Thank God I'm a Country Boy." In the other culture, however, in the urban settings filled with welfare recipients, a country-western song excoriated the lazy, the chiselers, the fecund: "Welfare Cadilac" (sic) was an unknown song until Johnny Cash, at President Richard Nixon's request, rendered it at a White House performance in the early 1970s. In "Take Me Home, Country Roads," the exhortation is to return not necessarily to the state of West Virginia, but to the state of "almost heaven," the place of the Blue Ridge Mountains, the Shenandoah country roads.

This is not to suggest that all songs have an antiurban bias.

There is, indeed, music which portrays the city in dynamic, vibrant, and creative terms. Yet it is all too evident that the majority culture is constantly inundated by lyrics which condemn the metropolis as the harbinger, if not of antilife values and ideals, then of negative impulses. Moreover, the music entwines with the other media in an identical manner.

The image of the city has been captured in the folk catchphrase initially attached to New York, but which now applies to other urban areas: "It's a nice place to visit—but I wouldn't want to live there." This is a far note from the opening vibrancy of the lyrics of the 1944 musical, "On the Town." Living now should be done in the landscaped regions, in the country, away from the source of enervation. Whites, despite some movement back into the refurbished areas of cities, by young, upwardly mobile persons, or by those who have already achieved status and security—both groups typically without children—continue to view the city not as the promised land, but rather its opposite.

Aided by affluence, but motivated by history, millions of whites have fled from the cities, thereby leaving the cores to blacks, Hispanics, Mexican-Americans, and other minority groups, as well as to the white lower classes. Indeed, as the cities became filled with a darker-skinned population, mainly in the lower classes, a demographic and attitudinal cycle set in. Nonwhite migrations contributed to white movement and flight, which reinforced anticity sentiment, producing, in turn, urban policies often of dubious design and limited funding. One gets the feeling—difficult to substantiate, but implicit in the overall situation—that the protest actions of blacks and browns in the cities in the 1960s and 1970s, while shocking to the majority, to city and other governmental officials, were subliminally welcomed. In this way, the stereotypical images of nonwhites and of city living were fulfilled.

A more recent example of this was the nature of the reporting of the looting and firebombings by blacks and Hispanics that occurred during the blackout in New York City in the summer of 1977. The ahistorical nature of American culture generally, a situation severely compounded by the failure of the media to recognize the power of historical forces, made it appear that the collective violence that distinguished the street scene in New York in 1977 was idiosyncratic. Descriptive language of the actions revolved around pejorative words and phrases: "animals," "mad dogs," "cockroaches," "scum," "vultures," "scavengers," "predators," "bulls," "rats," "buffaloes," "night of terror," and others. The noun most frequently used was "animals." Headlines and news stories in newspapers and magazines quoted heavily from policemen and storekeepers, to this effect. On the front page of the *Boston Globe*, on the morning after the events of July 13, 1977, one read, "like mad dogs and animals going wild." Above the headline was a multicolumned photograph of looters reaching into a store whose metal door had been ripped upward. *Time* and *Newsweek* repeated the phrase. "It's the night of animals," was a typical quote.

It is little wonder that one-third of the nation's urban residents would move away from their cities if given the opportunity, according to a survey conducted for the National League of Cities in 1978. "Those people most likely to express the desire to leave their cities are from the same upper socio-economic groups which have been moving away for the last three decades—residents the cities can least afford to lose"; indeed, "33% want to flee crime-ridden cities."[8] These attitudes attest to the inability of the majority to accept, if not embrace, the city as the representative entity of American civilization.

In the final analysis, the print and visual media can contribute to positive racial interaction by eliminating minority and lower-class stereotyping; altering their views of the cities, as unlivable entities; highlighting the folk diversity of society; and presenting a view of life that focuses on the creative as well as the stultifying, the joys as well as the pains.

NOTES

1. Walter Lippmann, *Public Opinion* (New York: Macmillan, 1922).
2. H.R. Trevor-Roper, *The Crisis of the Seventeenth Century* (New York: Harper & Row, 1956), p. 190.
3. Gordon Allport, *The Nature of Prejudice* (Garden City, N.Y.: Doubleday, 1954), p. 185.
4. Robert Bone, "Teaching Negro History: An Interdisciplinary Approach," *Integrated Education* 5 (February-March 1967):8.
5. U.S. Commission on Civil Rights, *Window Dressing on the Set: An Update* (Washington, D.C.: Government Printing Office, 1979).
6. Ibid.
7. Sam Bass Warner, Jr., "The Transformation of Private and Public Space in the American Metropolis" (Paper delivered at Stockholm University, Stockholm, October 12, 1978), p. 2.
8. *Boston Globe*, November 29, 1978, p. 10.

PART IV

SPEAKING OUT FOR MINORITIES: FROM THE VITAL CAUSES

SEVEN

NO VOICE BUT "AUNT BLABBY": THE ELDERLY AND THE MEDIA

William Alfred Henry III

Many minorities are ill-served by the mass media. Only one is overtly and shamelessly made unwelcome by them. It is the largest minority, the elderly, defined by the mass media, at least for advertisers, as everyone over age 50. These people are about a third of the audience for most newspapers and for television. They tend to be the most loyal and consistent members of the audience, and they may be the most keenly interested: they write the bulk of the letters sent by adults to TV and radio stations and their parent networks. Many older audience members have listened to the same radio station and read the same newspaper all their lives. On average, they read, hear, and see more news reports than younger people do. They vote more often. If media services were allotted to those who need and use them most, the elderly would all but dominate decisions about entertainment programming and news coverage. But media services are allotted, instead, to suit the advertisers who pay the bills. That is the core of the problem for all minorities. It is even more intensely a problem for the elderly.*

---

*For readers who do not share the author's experience in covering the broadcast media, there are few books dealing specifically with the media as they relate to the elderly, but several that explain the general business operations of boradcasting. Les Brown's *The Business Behind The Box*, and his more recent *New York Times Encyclopedia of Television*; Erik Barnouw's *History of Broadcasting in the United States*, and his slimmer, more concise *The Sponsor*; and Bob Shanks's *The Cool Fire* are probably the best places to begin. For a sense of the Federal Communications

If you talk to an executive of a television or radio station, as this writer does daily in his work as a broadcast critic for a major metropolitan newspaper, he will tell you he is not in the news business or the entertainment business. A newspaper publisher, or a candid editor, will tell you the same. They are all in the advertising business. That means, these days, that they are in the demographics business.

Social activists are accustomed to complaining about polls, referenda, gross sales charts, and other measures of popular will, most notably the ratings of audience size from the A.C. Nielsen company.[1] The numbers in all these reports convey only the majority tastes, not values, not individual needs, certainly not any tradition of diversity. But about these numbers there used to be at least a crude democracy. One newspaper reader or book buyer or radio listener was considered just like another. No matter what his age, income, education, or profession, and no matter what his relative power in the community, his tastes were just as important as the tastes of anyone else in determining the income of the medium's owner. Advertising rates were based on total readership or listenership, on how many people were brought into the tent.

Demographic research has changed that. Now the audience can be of equal size but unequal economic value—and therefore of unequal impact on the content of newspapers or broadcasts. Advertisers can learn, from Nielsen and other market research companies, whether an audience is rich and urban and young; old and rural and poor; likely or unlikely to buy the advertiser's product. Different advertisers seek different audiences. The network news draws an older-than-average audience, and its advertisers include health and denture companies. Saturday-morning cartoons attract children, and the advertising featured is mostly for toys, candy, and sugared cereals. Car makers and beer brewers seek sports, feature films, and other programs attractive to men. Soap and toiletry manufacturers seek daytime dramas—Procter and Gamble owns several outright—and other programs popular with women.

Most advertisers do not want the elderly, not even the expansive group of everyone over 50, or at least will not pay as dearly for reaching them. Similarly, most advertisers do not want the poor. They are less likely to have the money or inclination to buy advertised products. Thus, ethnic minorities are often given lesser

---

Commission, the best guide is *Reluctant Regulators*, by Barry Cole and Mal Oettinger. The trade publication *Broadcasting* is a shrill but informed advocate for station owners, networks, and advertising agencies.

weight. The Nielsen company acknowledges that for years, it underrepresented blacks in its ratings report, although the company denies published reports that the distortion was deliberate. Rural people, also generally less affluent, are still underrepresented by the Nielsen agency, and became even more so in the fall of 1978, when Nielsen added home monitors in the San Francisco area to supply an overnight-ratings service. The company conceded it was giving San Francisco added influence on a supposedly national profile. But local stations and advertisers had requested overnight ratings and agreed to pay for them.

There are as many definitions of mass media, and of media service, as there are of the elderly. To focus the discussion, we will limit the meaning of the mass media to the major daily organs of communication—the newspaper, the radio station, and the television station. The definition of the elderly will be the one most often used in advertising-agency data, that is, people aged 50 or more. Media services will mean primarily four things:

1. programs or print columns specifically for the elderly as a target audience;
2. emphasis on news concerning the elderly, or on the results, in regard to the elderly, of general news developments;
3. affirmative treatment of the elderly, with minimal stereotyping, in the course of general news or entertainment;
4. proportionate treatment, in competition with other audiences, in all decisions about what programs should contain or what newspapers should cover.

Even by these minimal standards—that the mass media should be attentive and fair—the elderly have been ill-served.

Some of the discussion below will be general, based on the author's experience in writing for a variety of regional newspapers and national magazines, and in covering and appearing on radio and television. The closest analysis will be of Boston, chiefly because the writer knows it best, but also because it is at once a representative and reputedly enlightened city. It is an academic center and a wellspring of progressive thought and social activism. Its two major newspapers have won eight Pulitzer Prizes since 1965. Its four VHF television stations include the nation's number-one and number-two commercial producers of public-affairs coverage, according to 1977 national rankings published in the *Columbia Journalism Review*; and the nation's number-two producer of noncommercial public affairs, WGBH, which typically accounts for a quarter of the national public-television schedule. The fourth major station was sold in 1978 to local investors, but through the spring of 1979, was still being operated, pending federal approval of the transfer, by one of the country's oldest and biggest media companies, RKO General. Boston is the number-five or -six television market, depending upon the year of survey (it moves above and below San Francisco.) Its dominant newspaper, the *Boston Globe*, is the country's ten largest Sunday paper and fifteenth largest daily, and in 1978 accounted for most of the $160-million gross of the parent Affiliated Publications. The second newspaper, the *Boston Herald-American*, is owned by the large and wealthy Hearst Corporation, although it reportedly operates at a deficit.

As with any study of minority needs, this one faces at least two major problems: a minimum of pertinent, detailed statistical information; and a grouping under one umbrella, not of one group, but of several. Middle-class blacks often have more in common with other members of the middle class than with poverty-class blacks. Stable, professional homosexuals often have more in common with other stable professionals than with the homosexuals whom early researchers interviewed at psychiatric clinics, in the army, and in prison. Fully employed, affluent singles, couples, and empty-nest parents in their fifties have little in common with retired pensioners living alone and consuming television and radio seven or eight hours a day.

The Columbia University scholars who in 1978 published a massive survey of all available television research, *Television and Human Behavior*,[2] nonetheless found themselves forced to rely on Nielsen ratings lumping together all people over 50. No other research on the general audience, or its major components, seemed complete, continuous, and reliable. Most research is funded by people interested in sorting the audience into groups; the people most interested in assessing the differential response to television are networks, stations, and advertisers. For most purposes they prefer women, who are thought to make most choices in small household purchases, and more particularly, women of child-rearing age. Thus, in ascending order, the optimal audience members are all people aged 18 to 49, women aged 18 to 49, and women aged 18 to 34.

The industry rationale was expressed briefly by a vice president of Doyle Dane Bernbach, the advertising agency, in the April 23, 1979, issue of *Broadcasting*, a major trade magazine for station owners and their suppliers. "The conventional wisdom in this business," he wrote, "is to go after only the women 18-to-49 market. They have the larger households. They are believed to be more willing to try new products. And certainly cultivating the younger market is the lifeblood and the future of almost every business." He might have added, but didn't need to, for his audience, that the industries which market themselves through television amount to a small percentage of the gross national product, 6 or 7 percent in the estimate of the longtime television writer Gene Thompson.[3]

Many TV advertisers make disposable household goods, either of debatable necessity (room deodorants, antistick coatings for frying pans) or of all-but-indistinguishable brand identity (soap, toothpaste); most of the rest sell frozen, premixed, fully prepared, or volume-restaurant food. Their products are for the amusement, convenience, or necessity of families, of working mothers pressed for time, of women stuck at home with young children and therefore preoccupied with household maintenance. Car makers, airlines, local department stores, and other prestige or high-price ("big-ticket") advertisers aim less for maternal audiences, because major family expenditures are generally considered by advertisers to be controlled by men. But of the 25 major national advertisers on television last year, 22 were selling food, nonprescription drugs, disposable soaps, and similar household products, or telephone calls (as reported in *Broadcasting* magazine, April 16, 1979).

Newspapers depend much more on local, and particularly classified, advertisements. Their demographic reports to advertisers typically stress education, household income, home ownership, and purchases of automobiles, power boats, foreign vacations, or other signs of affluence. Such statistics tilt less toward the young. But they do not reflect the concern of the typical editorial page for the elderly or the poor.

Station owners and publishers do not, of course, directly solicit advertisers' opinions in determining program or publication content. With the exception of Procter and Gamble, Hallmark cards, and a handful of other companies and products, sponsorship of particular programs has given way to buying a mix of media based on overall demographics and cost-per-thousand-people-reached. Few newspapers accumulate more than 1 or 2 percent of total revenue from any single advertiser. Thus, responsibility for content lies, as it should, with the owners of the media. The owners, however, consciously, and more or less openly, run their businesses in an attempt to attract the most desirable audience demographically, and occasionally try to shed the least desirable.

When CBS News interviewed officials of Boston's two major newspapers for a documentary on trends in the newspaper business, the publisher of the Hearst-owned *Herald-American* lamented the fact that his loyal (if slowly dwindling) audience was old.[4] The general manager of a Boston television station—ironically, the only one with a weekly program specifically for the elderly—complained that the audience for his local news was "old, old, old," and juggled two hours of early-evening programs to change the news demographics.[5] Lawrence Welk, although a survivor through syndication, was dumped in 1970 by ABC as a prime-time performer, purely for demographic reasons. During an era when ABC was the desperate "half network" in "a two-and-a-half network industry," it discarded Welk, one of its steadiest successes, because his appeal was "among the mommas and papas," as Welk himself put it. Welk then organized his own station-by-station (syndication) sale and became, for nearly a decade, the most popular syndicated performer in America.

No publisher or station owner in any but the most benighted community would consider speaking of blacks, Hispanics, Asians, or any other ethnic minority with such baldly commercial distaste. The Federal Communications Commission (FCC) would likely entertain a petition for censure, or even for denial of license renewal, based on disregard for an ethnic minority. But because the elderly are unorganized, diverse, numerous—and because they are avid consumers of all television and radio—they are rarely discussed as an underserved minority. Several Boston TV and radio officials said they feel no pressure to give the elderly major consideration in the community ascertainment of needs mandated by the FCC.

Thus the elderly receive mistreatment, or nontreatment, from Boston media and from national media heard or seen in Boston. We will consider one by one the standards for media services set forth above.

PROGRAMS AND PRINT COLUMNS TARGETED TO THE ELDERLY

Only two regular half-hour television programs for the elderly air in Boston. A national one plays weekdays on the public-television station, WGBH. A local one plays Sunday mornings on the CBS-affiliated TV station. National public TV provides "Over Easy," a talk show starring Hugh Downs that blends chatter with aging film stars, inspirational talk about the vigor and capacity of the aging, and practical information about medical, Social Security, and other service agencies. It airs at 3:30 p.m. on Channel 2, the stronger, in signal, of the stations owned by the WGBH educational foundation. That time, normally less desirable than evening, is considered optimal for "Over Easy" because the percentage of the audience aged 50-plus is at its peak then, and the competition from the networks less keen than at 7 or 8 p.m.

The second program aired in Boston, as of May 1979, with the sale of the producing station pending, is "Elder American." The host of the program was dismissed for indiscretions earlier in 1979, but the owners of record, RKO General, and the prospective local owners said they would continue service to the elderly. "Elder American" is a very low budget talk show, aired at 8 a.m. Sunday, a time of such minimal total viewership that some local stations do not attract audiences large enough to be measured in the Nielsen ratings.

The program's creator and host, Stephen Guptill, was appointed state secretary for elder affairs, but then was forced to resign when it was revealed he had awarded himself fictitious degrees from Oxford and Heidelberg Universities. The station took him back for the duration of his contract. After his dismissal, he was accused, by a competing Boston television station, of having used a guest appearance on a radio program to promote an elderly housing project in which he had a concealed financial interest. The cause of his dismissal, however, appeared to be his testimony in affidavits to the Massachusetts Commission Against Discrimination, charging the station with age discrimination. He testified on behalf of two colleagues, both alleging they had lost their jobs because of their age (both 49) and consequent appearance.[6]

Whatever the integrity of Guptill and his reporting or advocacy, the scheduling of his program reflected a considerably smaller commitment to the elderly than to, for example, blacks and Hispanics, who constitute considerably smaller percentages of the Boston metropolitan community. RKO General airs "Black News" for a half hour every Saturday at 6:30 p.m., a time of high viewership, and assigns the show a staff of several full-time reporters plus producers, cameramen, technicians, and other support staff. "Las Noticias De Hoy" is broadcast for ten minutes, weekdays at 6:50 a.m., just before the CBS morning news, for more total minutes, per week, than "Elder American." Blacks and Hispanics have many valid complaints about Channel 7 and RKO, but they fare better than the elderly because they are organized to make themselves heard. When the station proposed to replace "Black News" with a minority talk show, several hundred demonstrators marched on the station. By contrast, when the station reduced Guptill's elderly reports to a half hour a month, after his state appointment, the elderly made no organized objection.

The general managers of Boston's other major television stations—WCVB-TV, a locally owned ABC affiliate, and WBZ-TV, a Westinghouse-Group W station affiliated with NBC—say they recognize the absence of regularly scheduled programs for the elderly as a shortcoming which they hope to remedy. Until then, they say, the elderly will be served through occasional news reports and documentaries. Between them, the stations produce more than 100 hours of local programming per week. Less than 1 percent of it each year, they say, is targeted to the elderly.

WBZ and WCVB concede it is harder to guide the elderly to documentaries than to regularly scheduled programs. The major way of informing the elderly of a show of interest to them, the stations admit, is by mention on another elderly show.

Both stations have regularly scheduled black and Hispanic shows, and both assign reporters, part time or full time, to cover the black and Hispanic communities. In addition, both emphasize the plights of blacks and Hispanics more often than the plights of the elderly, in coverage of urban affairs.[7]

Within corporate Boston, where the stations say they are based, people old enough to receive Social Security cast a third of the votes. Blacks cast about a sixth; Hispanics, an estimated 3 percent. In metropolitan Boston, blacks and Hispanics together are about 6 to 8 percent of the population. The elderly, even if limited to the over-60 group, are more than 15 percent.[8]

The city's two major newspapers, the *Globe* and the *Herald-American*, publish columns for the elderly. The *Globe*'s "Senior Set" and the *Herald-American*'s "Age Wise" both appear in the home-and-feature sections—"Living," in the *Globe*, and "AM," in the *Herald*—generally in unobtrusive display, often on the lower half of an inside-of-section page. Neither paper lists the column among the principal features in its daily index. Both columns are collections of short items, mostly rewritten press releases, announcements of speeches, and occasionally informative summaries of new Medicaid and Social Security rules. The *Herald* assigns a semiretired reporter. The *Globe* assigns an older staff reporter who has never had major reporting or editing responsibilities.

By contrast, both newspapers run black columnists on the prestigious op-ed pages, and both are seeking Hispanic reporter-columnists. The *Globe* has had Hispanic reportage for nearly a decade, and for several years ran a weekly section in Spanish.

The four smaller commercial television stations (all UHF) in metropolitan Boston and the 45 radio stations lack the staff and budgets to make major program commitments to the elderly. Most buy a national news service and tape some local public affairs, giving admittedly sporadic coverage. The national radio networks provide their stations with scarcely more coverage than the television networks do. Even CBS's wholly owned WEEI-AM and -FM, the former an all-news station, have no substantial continuing program for the elderly.

EMPHASIS ON NEWS CONCERNING THE ELDERLY

News coverage may reasonably be divided among reports which are routine; reports of routine news that may be enhanced by interpretation or original reporting; and reports which require substantial initiative. The editors and news directors of Boston's major media outlets say, in interviews, that they perform adequately on routine matters affecting the elderly, variably on matters requiring interpretation, and often inadequately on matters requiring enterprise.

Every major Boston news outlet, for example, reported the warning of the Social Security trustees, on April 16, 1979, that a recession in 1979 might keep the system from paying benefits in 1983. The warning, part of the system's annual financial report, was blown out of proportion in an Associated Press (AP) report that was carried the next day on page 3 of the *Globe* and on page 30 of the *Herald*. The *Herald*, a conservative Republican newspaper, which has criticized Social Security editorially, further distorted the AP report by eliminating the sixth paragraph, which explained that the potential shortfall was more a bookkeeping problem, of cash flow, than a fiscal instability. The Social Security system, its trustees said, is fundamentally sound for the next 50 years, assuming payroll taxes rise as provided by law.

Most radio stations carried a brief and similarly alarmist excerpt of the AP report. The four major television stations were less alarmist, but, like AP and the *Globe*, they emphasized the marginally likely tight squeeze a few years away, rather than the essential soundness of the system. The latter was really more news, given the recurrence of reports that the system is on the verge of collapse. Most news editors did not amend the story to note that Congress is on record as ensuring that benefits will flow, no matter what fiscal changes may be needed.

Had the story been entirely routine, the coverage would have been adequate. Because the story required interpretation, which the wire-service coverage failed to provide, the public had to depend on local initiative. Little was shown.

Even more venturesome coverage is needed in reporting on conditions in elderly housing projects, in private but state-reimbursed nursing homes, and in hospitals for the chronically diseased. Senior editors at the *Globe* and the *Herald* acknowledged that they could not recall a single instance of investigative or exposé reporting of conditions at an institution, except in the wake of a state or federal investigation.[9]

Both papers assign black, white, and Hispanic reporters to cover conditions in predominantly black and Hispanic housing projects. Both have sent reporters to hospitals and schools for the mentally retarded and emotionally disturbed. Both have sent reporters to high-security prisons (the *Globe*, generally, to cover the prisoners' plight; the *Herald*, to cover the guards). The difficulties of the elderly have been relegated, however, to the fictional or fictionalized accounts of local columnists. Most of the pieces are highly sentimental recitals of how healthy but poverty-stricken elders live in fear of the community at large. Few have discussed institutions.

Just as none of the television stations, except the one run by RKO, has had a target show for the elderly of Boston, so none has assigned a reporter to specialize solely in elderly affairs, since Guptill's departure. None, moreover, has an elderly, or even particularly weathered, on-air reporter. The public-television station, WGBH, has aired frequent reports on runaways, teenage prostitutes of both sexes, juvenile delinquents, and the hungry of all ages. Reporters and news executives there describe the station's coverage of the elderly as "sparse," especially in the context of the station's progressive leanings and the high percentage of elderly people among its viewers and contributors.

Part of the insensitivity to elderly issues is that none of the major media outlets in Boston has old personnel in key roles. The *Globe*'s chairman and two principal editors are in their sixties but are also vigorous and affluent. Among the staff, a mandatory retirement age of 65 has been replaced, following a change in federal law, by an almost equally mandatory set of pension incentives to retire at 65. The *Herald* has younger management, although generally older reporters and no explicit retirement age. A threat of potential layoffs persuaded a number of over-60 *Herald* writers to retire late in 1978.

Among the television stations, according to an attorney for one of the principal craft unions, there is no explicit requirement that dismissal of on-air talent be for cause. The contract, the attorney says, tacitly acknowledges that age, appearance, and similar factors may be grounds for removing an otherwise competent employee. RKO, several years ago, demoted a weatherman in his late forties to weekend appearances and replaced him with a man 20 years younger, on the more lucrative weeknight job. The older weatherman claimed he was the victim of age discrimination and won a case before the Massachusetts Commission Against Discrimination, a quasi-judicial body. After being restored to the job, with back pay, he lasted little more than two years before being demoted to weekends again, to give way to another man 20 years younger.

RKO also pressured one reporter—who had been Boston's first anchorman—into quitting while in his early fifties. It assigned a 49-year-old state-house reporter to train his replacement. During the transition, the older political reporter arranged, wrote, and produced the younger man's on-air appearances, for which the younger man was receiving an on-camera pay premium. The state-house case, like the case of the weatherman, has been referred to the state Commission Against Discrimination, accompanied by affidavits from several members of the staff.[10]

WBZ, the Westinghouse-Group W station, recenlty demoted a newsman, who was nearing 60, to announcing, unseen, from the booth. WCVB moved its senior anchorman from the high-income 6 p.m. and 11 p.m. shows to the low-budget noon news, in part because his looks and energy were in decline, station management officials conceded.[11]

AFFIRMATIVE TREATMENT, WITH MINIMAL STEREOTYPING, IN GENERAL NEWS OR ENTERTAINMENT

Although lobbyists for the Massachusetts Association of Older Americans and similar groups complain gently about the prevalence of feeble-old-lady human-interest stories, particularly in the newspapers, they concede there is no working definition of stereotyping in the news. The press, and to a lesser extent the television stations, have reported on the sexual capacity of those over 60, sometimes of those well over 60. They have reported on elderly people, primarily celebrities, who remain active and employed into their seventies, eighties, even later. The major stereotype in news coverage, the elderly's lobbyists say, is the limitation of the "Senior

Set" and "Age Wise" columns to parochial news items and mundane "housekeeping" reports on elderly organizations, as a sort of bulletin board.

The fundamental problem the elderly face in stereotyping—many say it is their fundamental problem with the media—comes from entertainments. Johnny Carson's Aunt Blabby and Gilda Radner's Emily Littella, on "Saturday Night Live," are funny because they are old, or, perhaps we should say, old and loquacious, even senile, although loquacity and senility are treated as natural consequences of age. Almost as troubling to many elders are the sugar-coated grandparents on such shows as "The Waltons." Although these portrayals are more flattering, they are scarcely more rounded and human. They mark the elderly was different and approach them hypersensitively. The pattern has been the same as in television's dealings with blacks, Hispanics, and homosexuals: absence followed by parody, followed by idealization, followed by problem drama, in which the problem is the minority character's status as a minority person—all to be followed someday, one must hope, by sufficient neutrality so that a character's blackness, sexual preference, or age will not define him, but will instead be merely an incidental attribute.

Like most other minorities the elderly are significantly underrepresented on the television screen. The reasons they appear on the screen less frequently then in the general population are simple, and emphasize television's literary nature, as a medium for narrative, rather than its gradually assumed social function of bestowing legitimacy on whomever it portrays. Elderly people, particularly the retired, tend not to be involved plausibly in dramas about money, power, sex, suspense, and death, which are virtually the only subjects the networks consider universal enough to attract a satisfactorily large audience. Few people seem to find the idea of sexual romance erotic among people of golden age, and many tell researchers they find it distasteful. Thus the few elderly characters in title roles—for example, Barnaby Jones—are discreetly left uninvolved, and uninterested, in sex.

Beyond the dramatic difficulties, there are two strong business reasons for minimizing the appearances of the elderly. First, elderly characters will likely attract an older audience, less appealing to advertisers. Second, most older actors are established enough that they cost more for guest roles and continuing parts than weekly TV series budgets can provide.

Stereotyping of the elderly has been widely publicized through protests by the Gray Panthers and others, but the protests have worked little evident change. Writers of teleplays, and the networks who pay them, are willing to contravene convention, but never without commenting on what they are doing. Thus an older man or woman can leave the house or nursing home where he or she ought to stay put (for his or her own safety, of course). But the script then must explain, even justify, why the character has emerged in public. From that duty, it is a short and obvious step to making the character's age and vigor the focal issue of the episode. The net result is that the audience hears that enterprise and independence among the elderly are eccentric, abnormal. The elderly have a worse image problem, not a betterment.

In fairness to the networks and the creative community, it should be noted that most characters considered offensive by the Gray Panthers and other protestors appear in one-time or occasional skits on talk and variety shows; characters on comic and dramatic series, especially members of the recurring "family," must maintain a higher level of plausibility. They, too, however, are often portrayed as garrulous, extravagant, and combative—for example, the tart grandmother portrayed by the late Judith Lowry on "Phyllis"; the termagant mother-in-law portrayed by the late Zara Cully on "The Jeffersons"; the out-catting-all-night housemother in the short-lived "Coed Fever"; and the cantankerous garage mechanic and the equally cantankerous professor-turned-senator, played by Jack Albertson in "Chico and the Man" and "Grandpa Goes to Washington." Nearly all elderly characters in comedies are given insult dialogue and are expected to provoke laughs. With the exception of Barnaby Jones, whom Buddy Ebsen makes the most intelligent, sane, and courtly over-60 character on television, the elderly have a small role in action dramas. Their role in problem dramas, as we have seen, is most often to be the problem.

PROPORTIONATE TREATMENT, IN COMPETITION WITH OTHER AUDIENCES, IN ALL DECISIONS ABOUT WHAT NEWSPAPERS SHOULD COVER

The inadequate service to the elderly as a target audience, the insufficiency of news for them, the stereotyped treatment in broadcast entertainment—these are all parallel to the past or present treatment of other minorities. And they could all be explained away, as being carelessness or incompetence more than malice or overt mistreatment.

But the deliberate attempt to appeal to the young, and above all, to children and the parents of children, by nearly all broadcasters is undeniable discrimination. In defense of their marketing decisions, broadcasters typically retreat to the dual sanctuaries of the First Amendment and the free enterprise system. But broadcasters do not own their licenses. They receive them, at present for limited three-year terms, from the federal government, in exchange for compliance with specific regulations and a general commitment to the "public interest, convenience and necessity." Like the Bill of Rights, the standard of public interest is intentionally broad, and is meant to be reinterpreted to suit social conditions. In general the FCC has said it cannot intervene in matters of content, and has thus absolved itself from ordering specific mixes of programs. As of this writing, in spring of 1979, the FCC and both houses of Congress were considering administrative or legislative proposals to diminish further the role of government in overseeing the broadcast media; to extend further, perhpas to virtual perpetuity, the duration of station licenses; and to modify or abolish the standard of public interest. Other lobbies, notably Action for Children's Television (ACT), have persuaded both the FCC and the Federal Trade Commission to hold extensive national hearings on the needs of children, and on broadcasting's adequacy in meeting them. ACT has also had a major role in deliberations on deregulation. The unorganized elderly have not.

Yet the elderly are, if anything, more clearly victimized by television's indifference than children are by television's hucksterism. According to the Nielsen agency, the networks' and advertisers' own service, people over 50 constitute 30 percent of the audience in every part of the day, including 11:30 p.m. to 1 a.m. The longest-running programs, for example the "Today" and "Tonight" shows, daytime dramas (soap operas), game shows, and the nightly network news, are also those that appeal most heavily to people over 50. The correlation is imprecise and subject to multiple interpretations. It tends, however, to bear out the seat-of-the-pants belief, of network executives, that older viewers are more loyal to programs, and thereby enhance network profits, by holding down the amount spent on fruitless development of unsuccessful pilot shows.

Research in radio suggests similar loyalty. Women over 50 represent the highest percentage of the audience for news, talk shows, and soft music. In radio, as in television, they tend to listen to particular programs or particular stations, year after year.

The reward for this loyalty and for the highest per-person rate of television consumption—about four hours per day—is utter disregard in program decisions. The CBS vice president for programs, B. Donald Grant, said in a January 1979 press conference, in Los Angeles, that the network had adopted new, more raucous programs "because our audiences aren't as young as we would like." A few days later, the ABC vice president for comedy, Marcia Carsey, said, in a similar Los Angeles press conference, that "evenings are built" on comedies at 8, 8:30, and 9 p.m., all designed to appeal to children. The ABC reasoning is that children will dictate program decisions (research tends to confirm the ABC view), and thus will draw in parents 21-34 or, at least, those 18-49. The NBC vice president for programs, Brandon Tartikoff, says every successful show on television began by appealing to teenagers—who, ironically, watch the least television of any age group, but who are emulated by younger children and are catered to by parents eager to keep teens at home at night. All three of these executives, and dozens of writers, producers, performers, and network managers, routinely speak, on the record, this way to the press. During three years as a broadcast critic, this writer has heard references to demographics, either boasts about a young audience or complaints about an old one, on an average of three or four times a week. This writer has interviewed virtually every major figure in television, and has never heard a word of protest about the discrimination against the elderly, beyond a formula admission that ratings matter too much. The idea that older audiences are undesirable, because they are displeasing to advertisers, is taken as a given, never debated.

The Nielsen ratings system, which has become the economic guide for the networks, is itself of dubious statistical value. Polls taken among 1,200 households, statistical theory runs, will tend to self-correct over time, because different households are involved with each sampling. Political polls can be measured against election results. The Nielsen sample, which uses the same 1,200 households, week after week—many for as long as five years, and in the past, for a full decade or more—proves only that what pleased people in particular households last week still pleases them this week. There is no secure way to test whether the Nielsen households are in fact representative. Their names and whereabouts are not released. For comparison, the Nielsen agency, several times a year, issues written diaries to larger groups of households. But the completion of the diaries is unsupervised, often haphazard or late, and is commonly admitted to be based on recollection rather than hour-by-hour logging. Network executives concede that the diaries and, for that matter, actual viewing habits, are likely to be influenced by the widespread newspaper publicity about which shows are most watched. The self-perpetuating effect of the ratings is reinforced by the gossip and celebrity magazines sold at supermarket checkout counters, which feature cover subjects based on ratings and TVQ (recognition and favorability) indices.

Flawed as the Nielsen ratings may be, in measuring national taste, they are decisive, sometimes sole, influences on programming. As the former ABC radio president, Robert Pauley, suggested in a June 1978 interview, the ratings are attractive to executives less for their reliability in predicting success than for their value in displacing blame for failure. "If the show doesn't work, if the show isn't any good artistically, if it doesn't say anything, the boss can always say, 'I copied what is popular in the Nielsens,'" Pauley said. (He is now a vice president of E. F. Hutton, negotiating acquisitions, and is seeking to buy broadcast properties.)

For the 1978-79 season, the highest-rated series programs were "Lavern and Shirley," "Happy Days," "Three's Company," "Mork and Mindy," and "Angie," all about young adults. With the exception of Angie, who married in an early episode, all the lead characters were single and living away from home; there were subsidiary roles, if any, for middle-aged parents, and no major elderly characters.

The next five programs in ratings were "M.A.S.H," "All in the Family," "60 Minutes," "The Ropers," and "Taxi." Of these, two were domestic comedies about people apparently in their fifties and economically secure; two were workplace comedies; and one was a news magazine. None featured a character of retirement age (although one "60 Minutes" reporter, Mike Wallace, is 60 and within five years of mandatory CBS retirement. Network television, unlike local television, believes viewers want the appearance of age, experience, and stability in the most important newscasters.)

The absence of older characters does not doom these series, even with older audiences, since the elderly are accustomed to seeing themselves only infrequently on the screen. Instead, the presence of older characters, with the potential attraction for older audiences, might doom the shows with advertisers.

In the cases of marginal shows requiring tinkering—"The Tony Randall Show" and "Who's Watching the Kids" are recent examples—the solution invariably has been to add a child or young adult, never an older person. "All in the Family," the most successful show of the past decade, was given a new character in the ninth season after the young-married generation had departed. The addition was an attempt, CBS executives said, to strengthen demographics. The character was an elementary-school girl introduced into the household by contrivance. She qualified as "family" because she was a distant cousin.

Lobbying Difficulties

The difficulties for the elderly, in lobbying the mass media, are more akin to the difficulties for the homosexual and the physically handicapped than to the troubles of ethnic minorities. The elderly, the homosexual, and the handicapped are often implicity assumed to be defective, or on their way to becoming defective. Their equal standing, in claiming civil rights, is still under debate in Congress and the state legislatures. Their conditions are viewed as, in some way, natural or divinely ordained or self-induced, not socially imposed. The elderly, moreover, like homosexuals and, until recently, the handicapped, have not been organized into a cohesive community. They are not preceived as having—and indeed do not perceive themselves as having—broad common interests. The elderly have few organs of communication. The best publicized, the American Association of Retired Persons, is intimately connected with, and in some eyes discredited by, a profit-making insurance company. The climate in Washington, moreover, though receptive to individual rights, as in the raising of the mandatory retirement age, is hostile to government regulation. It is probably not the time to push for more government mandates to the media.

Perhaps the ultimate irony is that the elderly depend on the mass media as their link to information and each other, even information about discrimination, stereotyping, and inadequate attention in the mass media. No movement is likely to come without organization from the outside, and the mass media would likely have to lead it. The elderly have legitimate grievances. But they have no way to voice them. For all minorities, when the grievance is invisibility and silence, the grievance precludes any remedy.

NOTES

1. The Nielsen company and its principal competitor, Arbitron, report to subscribers—primarily networks, stations, and advertising agencies—the rating and share of every program with a measurable audience. A rating point equals 1 percent of the potential audience, that is, every household with a set; a share point equals 1 percent of the audience actually watching at the time of measurement.

Nationally, a rating point equaled about 730,000 households at the time of writing, in May, 1979. The ratio between rating and share differs sharply. At the beginning and the end of the day, far fewer people are watching, and a program with a giant share may have a tiny rating, or total audience. In addition, the number of households wathing varies from night to night, normally peaking on Sundays. Although the Nielsen reports do not reflect it, the company also keeps statistics on the average number of people, within a household, likely to be watching at a particular hour, and thereby estimates the total number of people who saw a show. The ratings tend to overstate the total number of people watching, because they report anyone who saw eight or so minutes as having seen the show; dial turners and those who lose interest are counted as still in the audience, for calculating advertisers' rates.

2. Nathan Katzman et al., *Television and Human Behavior*, New York: Columbia University Press, 1978.

3. Thompson was interviewed in Boston in September 1977. His estimate of 6 to 7 percent appears to undervalue the presence of oil and automobile companies. Most of TV's revenue, however, indisputably comes from relatively trivial products; conversely, most of the marketing of cars, oil, and telephone systems is done outside TV. Television's primary sales link is to products whose market is literally created by television. The classic case is Hazel Bishop cosmetics, which grew from a $50,000 business to a $4.5 million business from 1950 through 1952, solely by television advertising.

4. Robert Bergenheim, who has since been dismissed, was on the air with his remarks during the documentary, "The Business of Newspapers," on CBS nationwide, July 14, 1978, 10-11 p.m.

5. Steven Mathis, who has since resigned, made this and other, similar remarks in interviews throughout the summer of 1978.

6. Guptill's career and allegations were reported repeatedly by the writer in the *Boston Globe*; representative and relatively complete accounts appear in "Guptill Fired By Channel 7," April 13, 1979, and "Ch. 5 Makes Payola Charge," April 14, 1979, both on the television-listings page.

7. Robert Bennett, general manager of WCVB, and Bill Aber, then news director of WBZ, provided most of the information about their stations, confirming the author's published and private observations as a critic, in interviews in January through April 1979.

8. The statistics vary slightly from year to year. They are available from the Department of Labor and other sources. The electoral impact of the elderly was a frequent topic of conversation during the author's years as an editorial writer and political reporter, notably in interviews with State Representative Barney Frank, State Senator (and, later, a mayoral candidate) Joseph Timilty, and State Representative Melvin King, the latter a black community leader.

9. Editors most helpful in preparing the paper, among the many the author has worked with, were Robert L. Healy, then executive editor, Timothy Leland, then Sunday managing editor, and Anne Cabot Wyman, editorial page editor, all at the *Globe*, and Michael Ryan, former assistant managing editor of the *Herald-American*. Maureen Taylor, former women's and features editor at the *Herald-American*, now a copyeditor at the *Globe*, was also a principal source.

10. The cases of the weatherman, Fred Ward, and the state-house reporter, Ken Wayne, were reported extensively by the author in the *Globe*, in, for example, "Guptill Fired By Channel 7," April 13, 1979.

11. The cases of the WBZ newsman, Jack Borden, and the WCVB anchorman, Jack Hynes, were discussed in interviews with Bennett and Aber, cited in note 7.

EIGHT

THE 52-PERCENT MINORITY

Jean Cheyne Reinhard

NEEDED: A NEW IMAGE

Eventually, the 52-percent minority may rise to economic and political parity! We have not fully absorbed the changes in women's roles that have already taken place, and there are more to come. Consider a brief summary of what is taking place. Many women are delaying marriage. Now that they are better able to plan the births of children, they tend to have smaller families later in marriage. As the divorce rate rises, the marriage rate declines and the life span increases. More women are free to work, want to work, and need to work out of economic necessity. Women now comprise about 42 percent of the nation's workforce, and they are demanding equal pay for equal work, or for work of comparable value. Many of them fill dual roles as working mothers.

A few women have overcome the handicap of minority status, and are achieving positions of power and prestige. They are entering management and the professions in growing numbers. They are becoming a bit more visible and significant in politics and public life, particularly at the lower echelons.

The changing circumstances of women's lives offer great challenge and opportunity. They are also the source of much confusion and ambivalence. What qualities are truly womanly? Can a woman be aggressive and still be tender and sensitive? Can she be assertive and dominant and still express her need for a man's affection? How far can she adjust her behavior to the biased expectations of others without compromising herself? Is androgyny dull?

Women need reference points in this process; they need touchstones, and imagery: "Unless those others who share the work with us can point to an image which represents the selves we are, they cannot see us at all. And without this label of image, the self becomes a jibbering ghost . . . unable to reach the world."[1] The old stereotypes no longer represent the diversity of roles women play in the world. They are misleading impediments in human relations. However, until we invent and popularize a new imagery, we are bound by the old. Men are nostalgic about familiar feminine stereotypes and cling to them:

> My brave little Ilsebill,
> on whom I can utterly rely,
> of whom, to tell the truth, I would like to be proud,
> who with a few deft strokes fixes everything shipshape,
> whom I worship worship
> while she, through inner recycling,
> becomes entirely different, differently strange and self-aware.
>
> May I still give you a light?[2]

There is some substance of truth in the ancient images. Women did not live with them for centuries without investing them with qualities of value, with some beauty and dignity. They also contain chimerical elements, idealizations of a distorted reality, conventional limitations of role and character which inhibit women's lives. Woman as enchantress is the subject of ancient myth and a whole tradition of idealized female sexuality and romanticism. The role is flattering and enthralling. But the power of the enchantress is transitory and illusory; when it passes, nothing remains. The media continually subject the image of enchantress to fashionable and glamorous metamorphoses and reintroduce her as a new discovery. Francine du Plessix Gray says, "We are all victims of romanticism. . . . An enormous modern organism that I call the sexual-industrial complex . . . brings billions of dollars to thousands of men by brainwashing us into the roles of temptress and seductress. . . . I saw Madame Bovary at Bloomingdale's clutching a copy of *Cosmopolitan.*"[3]

The most powerful of the stereotypes is that of the good woman. In this guise she is pious and chaste; she is obedient and submissive to her husband, a diligent homemaker and a loving, self-sacrificing mother. These idealized qualities placed her on a pedestal; they entitled her to respect and even reverence. The refined moral and emotional sensibility that was imputed to woman was considered an adequate compensation for her presumed weakness of body and intellect.

This view of women was highly exaggerated in the American South during the nineteenth century. The romantic medieval fancy of the chivalrous knight and the virtuous woman were projected into real life. A married lady of comfortable means might live up to such a role, but it was irrelevant to a poor, black, or unattached woman. With the increasing affluence of the industrial North, the notion spread to the rest of the country. The good woman was the dominant ideal of the Victorian middle-class lady.[4]

The emergent popular press took up the concept and exploited it. Ladies of leisure avidly read ladies' magazines, such as *Godey's Lady's Book, Graham's*, and *The Lady's Companion.* During the 1850s the yearly sales of Thoreau, Melville, and Whitman combined did not equal the sales of a popular domestic novel by the now-forgotten Sara Payson Willis (Fanny Fern). It is sad that women created most of this literature and used the press to popularize a distorted view of their own sex. Instead of challenging the stereotype, they idealized and sentimentalized the qualities the good woman was permitted, her piety, sensibilities, intuitions, and affections. This literature did not seriously or honestly explore the realities of women's lives. They are works of sentiment and self-delusion, an attempt by a politically powerless group to justify and dignify their position and exert moral suasion.[5]

In the nineteenth century, women had no political power and very little legal protection. They were not subjected to the stress of serious education that might turn weak brains. Ladies did not work for pay. The propriety of every move was an important consideration. They were denied even the right to know their own minds and make personal decisions for themselves.

In short, individuals of the female gender were honored members of a suppressed group. In an appendix to *An American Dilemma*, Gunnar Myrdal's 1944 study of the situation of blacks in the United States, he wrote that the problems of women in society "reveal striking similarities to those of the Negroes."[6]

In a sense, it is an abomination to compare the situation of the lady, whose heaviest responsibility was to be the "spiritual exemplar" and the "shining ornament" of her family,[7] with the lot of a black field hand with no rights whatsoever. Yet, in a way, the ladies did suffer. Their very idleness and purposelessness appeared to make them ill. In the second half of the nineteenth century, an astonishing proportion of middle-class ladies claimed to be chronically ailing.[8] Male doctors secured their dominance of the medical profession during this period.[9] Some built their practice on the care of affluent, delicate ladies. Accepted medical theories that guided the practicing physician "from the late 19th century to the early 20th century held that woman's *normal* state was to be sick."[10]

Historically, women have constituted a minority group in that they have been singled out for differential and unequal treatment. But there is another part to the definition of the term: Members of the minority group must recognize that they are being discriminated against. Even today, many women do not admit an awareness of any significant discrimination. Sometimes they perceive that they are treated differently, but they accept this as appropriate.[11] This is not just true of affluent ladies of the upper and middle class, but lower-class women as well.[12] All too often women tend to hold themselves and their contributions in low regard.[13]

In a 1972 study of the sex-role stereotypes, researchers asked college students to list attributes and behaviors in which men and women differed. The results yielded 41 items comprising a stereotypic profile of men and women on which male and female respondents substantially agreed. Twenty-nine of the 41 characteristics were favorable to the male, showing him to be an ideal leader and achiever—aggressive, logical, independent, dominant. The qualities ascribed to women suggested greater warmth and expressiveness. These included such little-valued characteristics as neatness, tact, gentleness. The self-concepts of male and female subjects appeared to be closely modeled on the stereotypes.[14]

Although most women would not go so far as to identify themselves as members of an oppressed group, they have adopted a number of behavioral characteristics that are typical responses of oppressed minority groups. In a 1951 study, Helen Mayer Hacker pointed out that women have acquired "accommodation" behaviors similar to the Uncle Tom role that some blacks assumed. She cites the feminine wiles and flattery, the smiles and tentative, modest manners, the assumed helplessness. Because our image of ourselves is based in part on the "defining gestures" of others, "it is unlikely," she argues, "that members of a minority group can wholly escape personality distortion."[15]

In his 1954 work, *Psychology of Prejudice*, Gordon Allport discussed a number of "traits of victimization" in reference to minority groups. The two categories of these traits that apply most significantly to women are those of self-punishment and withdrawal. The intropunitive reactions to discrimination include self-hatred, aggression against other members of the group, denial of membership in one's own group, and identification with the dominant group. Examples of these attitudes are very common. Women who have succeeded in male-dominated fields are sometimes proud to believe they think like a man. They are contemptuous of crybaby women's libbers and women with traditional lifestyles who are devalued by men. Housewives often see feminists and career women as affronts to their values. Some feminists in turn look down on housewives and see them as gullible and inferior. Women who become passive and withdrawn fear the challenge of stepping outside their place. They tend to fail in roles which demand aggressive action or unfeminine skills, such as math or science. They fear success and are prone to mental depression.[16]

Superficially, the media now depict modern, liberated women. Essentially, nothing has changed very much. As *Cosmopolitan* puts it, "We've just redefined the terms a bit. . . ."[17] The conventional stereotype may have been "obscured with an equalitarian veneer," but it is still there, still powerful, "because alternative beliefs and attitudes about women go unimagined."[18]

Scientists may prove that women are intellectually equal to men, that their personalities vary only because of social conditioning, but real change will come about when women act in nonstereotypic roles. When women assume leadership in politics and in business; when more of them become doctors and judges; when they join the army, or work as policemen, telephone linemen, or engineers—this is when they challenge prejudice. Their success in these professions forces the adoption of new attitudes. The more radically the behavior of women in atypical roles conflicts with the traditional limitations of the stereotype, the greater the likelihood that biased social attitudes will change.[19]

One additional thing is necessary if women are to permanently escape the limitations of their place. The images of these liberated women must drive derogatory portrayals and pernicious stereotypes from the mass media.

THE LIMITS OF PROPRIETY

When Betty Friedan attacked "the feminine mystique" in the mid-1960s, a number of women journalists expressed their distaste.[20] Writing in *Harper's* magazine in 1965, Marian K. Sanders, a distinguished editor and journalist, described Friedan's book as "a shrill, humorless polemic," based on interviews with bored and gabby neurotics who had nothing better to do with their time. Sanders was mystified that the book was a best-seller.[21]

Feminists in the late 1960s had learned, from the experiences of the civil-rights movement, that a sure way of attracting the media attention they needed was to be loud and outrageous. This provided new opportunities for criticizing them. When Friedan led a sit-in at New York's Plaza Hotel's Oak Room (an exclusive male enclave) in February 1969, the columnist Harriet Van Horne called her "Kate the Shrew." "Militancy on the part of the gentle sex is always stupid," she continued. "Any clever woman who wants something from a man . . . knows she must campaign in a soft whisper, not a scream."[22]

These remarks expressed the viewpoint of a majority of women who were committed to the traditional ideology regarding women's proper role. They had no wish to see their lifestyle challenged and devalued. Today, many women still resent the feminist movement. They have expressed this attitude by espousing Marabel Morgan's "total-woman" movement,[23] or by voting against the Equal Rights Amendment (ERA).

Phyllis Schlafly has led the campaign against ratification of the amendment. Schlafly describes ERA supporters as "the militant women who are determined to erase all differences of treatment between the sexes in order to force us to conform to a 'gender-free' society . . ."[24] She calls on all "positive women" to take, as their goal, "the right of a woman to be a full-time mother and to have this right recognized by laws that obligate her husband to provide the primary financial support and a home for her and their children."[25] The ERA, Schlafly contends, "does not give women any rights, benefits, or opportunities that they do not now have."[26]

A midwestern organization called Housewives for ERA argues that the constitutional basis for equality that the amendment would provide is necessary because "the subordinate status of women has been firmly entrenched in our legal system."[27] The organization's leadership feels that the press has given ERA's opponents extensive coverage, while many of its supporters are not "taken seriously," or are unfairly "categorized as radicals"—a designation which seems strange indeed to housewives who feel they represent the majority of average Americans.[28]

In a 1974 poll conducted by the Roper organization, 57 percent of the women questioned endorsed efforts to secure more equality. Only 25 percent were opposed. More than half said they were aware of discrimination in employment. Burns W. Roper said the poll results indicated to him that "the general drive toward sexual equality is now a mainstream movement."[29] Particularly in the younger generation, there is evidence of changed perceptions of relationships with men, and of new expectations of opportunity and fair treatment.[30] "We begin to act upon new assumptions without even being aware of the singular changes. . . . Women's liberation suits society much more than society itself is prepared to admit. The wife economy is as obsolete as the slave economy."[31]

Still, the traditional stereotype of virtuous womanhood claims deep-seated responses of respect and admiration. Too bold an attack, or excessively unconventional behavior, on the part of feminist leaders still leads to reprisals in some quarters. Insensitive journalists continue to employ ad hominem attacks and ridicule, with righteous good conscience, when the behavior of a prominent woman seems overly aggressive or eccentric. A dose of such treatment frequently restores the miscreant to docility, and the incident serves as a warning to the group.

Bella Abzug is the most prominent recent victim of media scapegoating. As a congresswoman from New York, she was combative, flamboyant, salty of tongue—and she wore big hats. The congresswoman was also competent and serious, but inevitably, a focal point for media flippancy. The season was always open on Bella. There are lots of vulnerable congressmen, but it was Bella the cameramen shot from a rear view. When it snowed, the paparazzi hung about all day, hoping she would take an ungainly fall down the Capitol steps.[32]

Abzug was ridiculed in press-club skits. Congressmen played pranks on her. She has now been defeated in three political campaigns, twice by little more than 1 percent of the vote. Finally, Abzug was fired from her position as nonsalaried cochair of the National Advisory Committee on Women, after the committee's first meeting, on January 12, 1979, with President Carter. The president, his top political aide, Hamilton Jordan, and his White House counsel, Robert J. Lipshutz, were angered by Abzug on three counts: the committee's cancellation of a 15-minute meeting scheduled with the president eight weeks earlier; the issuance of a press release, prior to the January meeting, that accused the administration of negligence in failing to develop a public policy on women's role in the changing economy; and finally, her lecturing tone toward Carter. Abzug says she informed the president's aides that she had opposed the cancellation of the earlier meeting, but the other members of the committee "were unanimously insistent" that the time allotted was too short. She stated that she was absent from the committee meetings at which the positions taken in the press release were adopted.)[33] In an interview on American Broadcasting Company's (ABC) "Issues and Answers" program (January 14, 1979), Abzug said she thought the real reason for White House irritation was that the committee had dared to speak out on the economy.

Black leaders had already confronted the president with similar criticisms on behalf of the black minority. In the spring of 1978, some members of the congressional black caucus actually walked out of a meeting with the president, as an expression of their dissatisfaction with his response to the problems they had raised. A strong, abrasive tone is a customary technique employed by leaders seeking to call attention to urgent inequities on behalf of their constituents. Are all female political leaders to be denied this approach, or was Abzug just unusually vulnerable? Jody Powell, the president's press secretary, felt he could remark, with confidence, "I don't think most women in the country identify with Bella Abzug."[34] Abzug's behavior conflicted so strongly with conventional norms that the public's reaction was a kind of intense culture shock.[35]

Norman Lear's Tandem/TAT Productions ended the situation comedy series "Maude" with her election to the U.S. Congress. The idea was recast with a black congressman called Mister Dugan, played by Cleavon Little. The program was withdrawn at the last minute after some congressmen and black leaders had viewed it and concluded it lacked dignity. Tandem/TAT should have stayed with "Maude." Most women didn't identify with her either.[37]

Some 24 members of the Advisory Committee for Women resigned in support of Abzug. President Carter selected Marjorie Bell Chambers, a Republican and a former president of Colorado Women's College, as temporary chairman. Chamber's well-modulated demeanor conveys the message that she is intelligent, reasonable, and a lady. The president informed the new chairman at their first meeting, according to a White House press aide, "that he expected her panel to be 'independent,' but to stick to women's issues."[38]

On another occasion, Chambers, when asked about political behavior for females in public office, said: "I'm afraid the stereotypes still remain.... Women are supposed to be genteel, soft spoken, passive, dainty.... You'd better follow the traditional pattern if you want to be acceptable." The very drive and combativeness that is a requirement for success in politics must be controlled and masked by women. "There has to be suppression,"

Carol Bellamy (president of the New York City Council), says. "There is just a churning inside all the time. . ." Says Frances (Sissy) Farenthold (president of Wells College, Aurora, New York, and the first woman nominated for vice president of the United States, at the Democratic Convention of 1972): "You do it by keeping a lid on your feelings, by really watching them—by sensing, assessing, constantly evaluating and tuning your own behavior. . ."[39]

Not only are political colleagues watching for a weakness, so are the media and, through them, the public. Sarah Weddington, who replaced Margaret Costanza as the president's special assistant for women's issues, is very aware of the media dimension. Women have a higher visibility because there are so few of them in political office. "We're all scrutinized more closely, especially in our private lives, where the double standard definitely prevails."[40]

Women have been socialized to a sex-role stereotype that is antithetical to the role of the ideal politician, who is expected to be tough, logical, independent, aggressive. Some find it difficult to approach all-male groups, show off their expertise, and fend off hecklers. They sometimes have lower self-esteem and devalue their experience. U.S. Senator Nancy Landon Kassebaum of Kansas (the first woman to be elected [1978] to the Senate without first being appointed to fill the unexpired term of an incapacitated or deceased husband) says that it took her a long time to realize that she could be qualified for the Senate without years of experience running for political office. "I believe you bring the same qualities to the Senate as you do to service on a school board," she now says.[41]

A woman who manages to develop the well-modulated style and tough confidence required of a female candidate still faces the problems of securing campaign funds and the support of the male political establishment. Party organizations tend to put women up for suicide missions when there is little chance of winning. Special-interest groups, and corporate and labor-union Political Action Committees (PACs) are reluctant to believe a woman is likely to be elected. Women can't fall back on the old-boy network for funding, and they are less likely to have affluent business contacts. There is sufficient wealth in the hands of women to support female candidates, but they are reluctant to use their money to wield power. A rich man signs a hefty check made out to the candidate of his choice. His wife, or widow, is likely to make a small contribution, anonymously.[42]

Insofar as women lack a sense of group identity, they fail to perceive that they have interests which are different from those of men. So long as women's issues are seen as relatively unimportant, they have no critical bearing on an election. In these circumstances, a female candidate has nothing to gain by supporting those issues.

Jane Byrne (elected mayor of Chicago in 1979) was told by a news reporter that the leadership of the women's movement had determined that they would help her candidacy most by not working for her and not pressing her for a statement on ERA. (Illinois had not ratified the amendment.) If that, in fact, was what happened, Byrne responded, "That was very nice of them. . . " Being followed to the beauty parlor by reporters and described as a "spitfire" was handicap enough.[43]

A female leader who identifies herself with the dominant male-group interest may not be particularly sympathetic to women's concerns. Although most women holding elective office are supportive of women's issues, a 1978 study found one congresswoman (Marjorie Holt, Republican, Maryland) who favored only two out of eight pending legislative actions supported by the women's movement.[44]

There are presently 16 women in the House and one in the Senate.* Women now vote in approximately the same proportions as men, but many of them simply do not believe that members of their sex should hold high political office. In a 1972 survey conducted in a large urban area, 23 percent of the respondents felt that there should not be more women in public office. The reason that 60 percent gave for this belief was that women's place is in the home.[45] By current estimates, at least 10 percent of the population wouldn't vote for a woman for any office.[46] Among that 10 percent are those women who accost female candidates with accusations that they are neglecting their husbands and children.

Family responsibility restrains many women from seeking high public office. An attractive wife and attractive children are important assets for male candidates, but, for a woman, a family must be considered a handicap. A husband's career is another priority consideration. Many women simply wait until the children are grown up, or run for local office. Martha Keys, congresswoman from Kansas, married a congressman from Indiana during her term of office. Her marriage became a major issue during her

---

* Women have done better politically at the local level. There are now two governors: Dixie Lee Ray of Washington and Ella T. Grasso of Connecticut. Women hold 700 seats in state legislatures, which is double the 1970 total. Seven hundred women serve as mayors, and more than 9,000 hold seats on city councils. There is hope that some of these women will move up, in time, to higher office.

reelection bid in 1976. How could she represent Kansas if her husband represented Indiana? She lost the race in 1979, when the opposition charged that "Martha doesn't shop here any more." The marriage was not raised as an issue in her husband's campaign.[47]

President Johnson believed that women should participate in the highest levels of government.[48] He was ready to appoint them to positions in his administration, but when qualified women were found, they frequently rejected the offer. This occurred not only because of family commitments, but because women in senior corporate positions found it difficult to take a leave of absence. "Like union leaders or Negro leaders, women executives often lack 'job security.'" President Johnson appointed women to 73 top positions, and 371 were appointed by executive agencies.[49]

President Carter, who encountered similar problems, had succeeded by January 1980 in placing women in about 21 percent of his appointive posts. (A number of these are unpaid advisory positions.) In 1979 for the first time, there were two women serving in the Cabinet: Juanita Kreps as Secretary of Commerce, and Patricia Harris at the Department of Housing and Urban Development.* Eleanor Holmes Norton was in an important position as chairperson of the Equal Employment Opportunity Commission. Anne Wexler, assistant to President Carter, said that while she felt individual women officeholders had been treated fairly by the press, the fact that there has been a high proportion of these appointments did not receive "sufficient coverage."[50]

WOMEN IN THE PICTURE

Women in high public office are prominent indicators of change. Their impact is greatest when the public sees them in action. Media coverage could make the powerful, authoritative woman an image familiar to all of us, if there were more of them.

Government officials and public figures dominate television-news broadcasts. Most individuals who appear in television-news reports do so in some official capacity. These important people are almost all men.

In 1977 the U.S. Commission on Civil Rights published a report titled *Window Dressing on the Set: Women and Minorities in*

* Before the end of 1979 Juanita Kreps resigned her post. Judge Shirley Hufstedler was appointed Secretary of the new department of Education in late 1979.

Television. An update of that study was published in January 1979.[51] This research showed that in 1977, the proportion of network news stories related in some specific way to women and minorities had actually declined by more than half since 1975. Only about 7 percent of broadcast newsmakers (individuals who were presented visually and mentioned by name) were women. More than half of all newsmakers were government officials. Of this group, 94 percent were men and a mere 2.3 percent were women. Clearly, the failure of women to achieve senior elective office and administrative posts on a larger scale is a very significant factor in determining their news image. There were nine male experts for every female who appeared in that capacity.

Women did a bit better in the public-figure category, which is defined as newsmakers who are either celebrities or married to well-known government officials. There were two women for every eight men. The appearance of the wife of an important man usually has little to do with her personal achievements. She is regarded as important only as an extension of her husband's image. In the 1972 Harris poll of women's opinions, 41 percent of the respondents agreed that "women are better off married to public leaders than holding political office themselves; then they get all the pleasure and few of the problems of public life."[52]

News broadcast stories which did concern women were about one-half the length of the average story. They were usually placed in the final third of the broadcast and frequently in the last seconds. The near absence of women from news reports and the poor placement of stories which do involve them conveys a more important media message than any well-meant stories about the feminist issues which might be included on slow news days.[53]

The Action Plan adopted by the Houston National Women's Conference (1977) includes a media plank urging the adoption of the international Women's Year guidelines by all of the nation's media. These guidelines suggest that "the present definition of news should be expanded to include more coverage of women's activities" at all levels. "General news stories should be reported to show their effect on women." Further, the media should "seek out news of women," and these stories should be treated adequately and not placed in a segregated or inconsequential position."[54]

It is true that broadcast-news editors, the gatekeepers of national and local news shows, are predominantly white and male. But the choices they make are largely predetermined. Any news editor must make judgments on the basis of established professional journalistic standards and principles. A number of recent independent studies indicated that women journalists make news judgments similar to those of men. "Professionalism limits the possible presentations and defuses radical critiques."[55] With the added strictures of budgets, schedules, the established procedures of news gathering, the need to satisfy the expectations of viewers and affiliates, a network news editor has few options.[56] A woman who achieves the position of editor might well be more careful about augmenting the normal balance of women's news because of her sex.

Traditionally, most female employees in commercial broadcasting have worked in clerical and secretarial jobs with little or no authority. In 1971, 600 of the 900 women employed at the National Broadcasting Company (NBC) were secretaries. These women were graded not on the basis of their skills or length of experience or value to the company, but according to the position their male bosses held. Many of these secretaries had college degrees and ambitions. They originally took secretarial and clerical work because this was presented as the only way to get into the company, and because they were promised that such jobs would lead to advancement. Usually, they did not. Occasionally, women moved into more demanding jobs without receiving the same salary or titles that men doing the same work received. Women constituted 30 percent of the total population at NBC, but they held only 10 percent of all technical, managerial, and professional positions. Some male employees thought it was cute when women initiated a job action in 1972 and confronted the corporation's senior executives.[57]

Evidence of discrimination in employment was sufficiently strong at each of the three networks to enable women to win either lawsuits or out-of-court settlements against all of them. Women have made significant advances in the lower and middle echelons of broadcasting, although very few have been promoted to upper-management positions. Some training programs have been established and steps laid out for advancement from one level to another.[58] Women continue to find many obstacles in technical job areas.

So far as the public is concerned, the precedent-setting, image-making jobs in broadcasting are on camera as correspondents and as news anchors. Female correspondents accounted for only about 10 percent of the appearances of news reporters on network broadcasts in 1977.[59] Barbara Walters appears occasionally with special reports and interviews on ABC. Women regularly anchor the news desk on weekends on CBS and NBC.

A female anchor type has emerged. The ideal anchorwoman is attractive, in her thirties, crisp, firm, professional. Marlene Sanders (ABC), the first woman to anchor a network evening newscast, says, "You want to look like Brenda Starr, . . . casual, straightforward, not phony."[60] Broadcast-news executives seem to have difficulty imagining other possibilities. Dorothy Fuldheim was the first woman to anchor a news show 32 years ago. At 86, still brilliant, ebullient, and provocative, she provides daily news commentaries for WEWS-TV in Cleveland.[61]

There was a time when television-news executives routinely claimed that women correspondents weren't aggressive or tough enough to go out and get difficult stories. They argued that women weren't dominant and authoritative enough to hold down the anchor desk. Furthermore, they insisted, the public would never accept them in these roles. Proof that they were wrong is steadily developing on all three counts.

The women's movement has produced a climate of awareness that has made women more acceptable in the broadcasting profession. The emphasis, in recent years, on the entertainment values of news shows is another factor that has resulted in hiring women whose primary qualifications were good looks and personality. News shows are now cast with an awareness that contrasting character types add excitement and diversity to performances. A woman reporter is a valuable element of variety. Some of the women who were hired on this basis had no professional background or training as journalists. Some of them learned quickly and performed well. But the policy, and to some extent the women themselves, were an affront to serious broadcast journalists.[62] With this perspective, it is easy to see why some of Walters's colleagues overreacted when she was hired by ABC-TV's network news division. Although Walters was a respected journalist, the unusually high salary she was offered suggested that ABC management valued her as a personality.

Both the NBC and ABC morning-news programs have customarily emphasized entertainment values. CBS, on the other hand, has run a fairly straight news show. There was a notable exception to this policy in 1973 when Sally Quinn was hired away from the *Washington Post* to work as coanchor with Hughes Rudd on "The CBS Morning News." Management expected Quinn, who had no previous experience as a performer, to add glamour and a sassy wit to the show, along with her talents as a writer and interviewer. CBS had been running last in the morning-news-show ratings with distressing consistency, but the new show was meant to change all that. Network promotion that preceded the opening of the show indicated management intended to exploit the show-biz values of Quinn's performance. It apparently didn't occur to them that by publicizing her sex appeal, they damaged her credibility as a journalist.

Quinn reports that she was never adequately rehearsed, and that the style of performance she was expected to give was never clearly delineated. The producer, who apparently failed to understand her situation, made impossible demands on Quinn for extensive ad libs. It is not surprising that her foot was in her mouth more often than a bon mot. It is interesting that Warren Beatty (film actor, director, producer) called to warn her: "CBS is doing a terrible thing to you"; whereas, she reports, an executive news producer, working with her on a special-coverage assignment, offered to show her how to look good on camera, if she would just relax the night before the show—in his bed.[63]

It is unfortunate that the two ideas of woman and show business are so fused in the minds of some media critics, and an even greater number of producers, that they can't seem to conceive of a woman journalist without show business coming into it. Of course, when show business and journalism get together, there is a critical license to attack.[64] Walters, Quinn, and a number of others have the scars to prove it.

Realistically, performance training should be considered part of the preparation of broadcast journalists. Hugh Downs proved to be a brilliant interviewer on the NBC-TV "Today" show some years ago. Downs had previously acquired valuable experience as second banana on the Jack Parr "Tonight" show and as a quiz-show MC. With some experience as a performer, Quinn might have succeeded in spite of all her difficulties.

A NEW SCENE

Work opportunities for women in broadcasting have improved greatly over the past ten years, for a number of reasons. Lawsuits have been brought against major media corporations by female employees under Title VII of the Civil Rights Act of 1964. Also, pressures have been exerted by the Equal Employment Opportunity Commission, the Federal Communications Commission (FCC), and private-interest organizations. The old sexist arguments have been publicly discredited. Most important, a great many women are doing well in demanding jobs when they are given a fair opportunity.

Sometimes, the problem is not ill will toward women, but rather, a culturally ingrained, unconscious prejudice. A group of women employed by the *New York Times* brought a suit against that paper that was settled by an agreement filed in the U.S. District Court for the Southern District of New York, on October 6, 1978. In preliminary hearings, Harriet Raab, who represented the women, drew these remarks from A. M. Rosenthal, executive editor of the *Times*. He said that the "Hers" column, a regular feature of the women's pages, was begun because the management felt "there are such things as male perceptions and female perceptions, on occasion." Asked if he thought a woman reporter would bring any special "knowledge, perspective or experience of women . . . to the National Staff," he responded, "Not particularly that I can think of, to the National Staff."[65]

It is the senior levels of broadcast management that have proved most impenetrable to women. A woman employed by a large, urban station feels that while there has been progress at lower-grade levels, senior management continues to be dominated by white males "with decidedly sexist views." Another professional woman says, "The upper echelons of management are a closed locker room. They don't want to integrate the locker room in spite of all their tokenism, all their marvelous promises. They will do only what they are forced to do by law and certain pressures."[66]

Reports submitted to the FCC by broadcast-industry management show that women hold one-third of the positions in the top four employment categories. The Civil Rights Commission thought, on the basis of its analysis, that these figures were highly inflated. Women employees frequently had jobs with important titles, they found, but low salaries and little authority.[67] There seems no doubt that, industrywide, there are almost no women in senior decision-making positions, either in local stations or at network level.[68] An advertising executive, Jane Trahey, has analyzed the situation and reached a depressing conclusion. This is the substance of her argument: The reason women don't have the big-power jobs is that men have them. They want them, love them, and have no intention of giving them to a woman, only to another man.[69]

The settlement of the suit against the *New York Times* established an important precedent. The *Times* agreed not only to place women "in significant numbers at every level in every news and commercial department of the newspaper," but to place women in "top management jobs on the newspaper."[70] Raab felt this was a significant victory. "There has never been an affirmative-action plan in the media, and I believe there never has been one in any other industry which sets goals for filling the top offices."[71]

Will the battling city-editor role ever be portrayed by a woman? The casting of Edward Asner in the title role of ABC's "Lou Grant Show" is not likely to be challenged by a woman, since, as Walters says, "Aggressive is . . . a dirty word for a woman and an attractive word for a man." Nancy Marchand's Emmy-winning portrayal of Mrs. Pynchon (Lou Grant's publisher) is one of the few sympathetic interpretations of a female executive ever offered by network television. Mrs. Pynchon is always dignified, but she commands with great authority. Without the examples of Dorothy Schiff, former publisher of the *New York Post*, and of Katharine Graham, publisher of the *Washington Post*, it is unlikely that a woman would have been cast in the part. However, Schiff and Graham are known by comparatively few people, and Marjorie Pynchon is known to millions.

Innovative, courageous women are creating new images of womanhood by the way they live their lives. We need artists to fashion these images into dramatic roles that interpret these new women to the public. They can help us see how to take the best of the past with us into new situations, cutting the old cloth to a pattern which fits new realities.[72]

Hollywood glamorized and popularized new lifestyles for women in the 1930s and 1940s. Katharine Hepburn played a number of "superwomen" roles[73]—those of a newspaper columnist in *Woman of the Year* (1941), and a lawyer in *Adam's Rib* (1949) were outstanding. Rosalind Russell was an aggressive news reporter in *His Girl Friday* (1940). Ginger Rogers recreated Gertrude Lawrence's role as a magazine managing editor in *Lady in the Dark* (1944). In the last reels of these films, the ladies were generally shown the error of their ways, and gave up their careers to find fulfillment as wives and mothers. Somehow, the lesson was often negated by the style of these women. "The panache, determination and self-esteem of their personae were not overwhelmed or submerged."[74]

WORKING WOMEN: THE DOUBLE LIFE

Most women marry and, from that point, they are likely to identify themselves first as wives and mothers, even if they also work. We do not think of the average woman as a person with a job, yet two-thirds of all women between the ages of 20 and 64 are employed. Ninety percent of the country's women will work at some time during their lives. Forty-three percent of these working women support themselves and, often, their dependents. Millions of them work for wages which place them below the poverty line.[75] Many intact families manage to get along, and cope with inflation only because the wife provides a second income. As a result, 60 percent of the mothers of children between the ages of six and 18 are at work while only 9 percent of mothers with children under the age of six were employed in 1948 40 percent of them are at work today.

By not facing up to this situation, we are allowing serious inequities to persist in the labor market, and are sowing the seeds of serious problems for the future. In fact, women are very far from achieving equal pay for equal work. The median wage for women is only 60 percent of men's median wage, and the gap is actually widening.[76] A major reason for this inequity is that 80 percent of working women are concentrated in the pink-collar ghetto of clerical, sales, and service jobs, which offer very little satisfaction in terms of status, self-fulfillment, or salary.

We continue to channel women into educational programs "appropriate for their sex."[77] Usually this means secretarial courses. Women are not sufficiently provided with adequate career counseling. Because they are ignorant of the realities they face, they lack the motivation to prepare themselves for the future. Many young women expect to work only briefly before marriage, and they don't see the point in preparing themselves to enter desirable fields dominated by men. The majority of these jobs require technical and mathematical skills that women have been conditioned to think of as unfeminine.

Some women have entered fields strongly associated with masculine characteristics, such as the armed forces, police, and engineering. At first, they encountered ridicule, outrage, and hostility from the public and a number of their coworkers. Where they succeed, these pathbreakers force a change of attitude, but, in spite of the publicity this group has received, women have made little progress in breaking into fields traditionally dominated by men. Most people think no woman in her right mind should consider such physically demanding and hazardous jobs as coal mining, dockwork, and firefighting, but women have sought all these jobs. If we consider that it is possible to earn $7.50 an hour in a coal mine, but only $1.60 an hour working in a diner, their reason is apparent.[78]

Unions have neglected women and their interests. Only one in five union members is a woman, and women have only half of the leadership positions they need to achieve proportionate representation in organized labor. Although 80 percent of the Garment Workers' rank and file are women, they hold only two places on the 26-member executive board.[79]

Public opinion supports women's demands for equal opportunity and equal pay in principle, but their position in the labor force is likely to remain marginal and insecure unless they are accommodated by structural changes in the system. This means not only access to better jobs and opportunities for training and advancement, but support for mothers with young children.[80]

Working women who are married are usually doing double duty. A survey made by the University of Michigan's Institute for Social Research revealed that 86 percent of the working wives in their sample believed that a job and the demands of family life interfered with each other.[81] These women consistently report that they have little or no time for recreation, or for educational programs that might help them advance in their work.[82]

Although younger men are more likely to share housekeeping responsibilities with their working wives, the average husband does not. In one survey, only 12 percent of the men shared housework equally with their wives.[83] In another study, working women averaged 4.2 hours a day spent on household tasks, while their husbands worked an average of 1.8 hours per day, not on laundry and cleaning, but on upkeep tasks such as yard work and repairs.[84]

The provision of satisfactory day care for her children is the most serious problem faced by the daytime working mother. Many women already feel guilty about not being with their children, and these feelings are intensified when they cannot find or afford adequate day care. In spite of the rapid increase in the number of working mothers, there has been no commensurate increase in day-care facilities, nor has there been a significant growth in government expenditures for child care.[85] Urie Bronfenbrenner, professor of psychology at Cornell University, feels that the needs of the nation's children are met "less and less effectively each year."[86]

Some corporations have introduced flexible work schedules for women. An experimental program in Sweden granted paternity leaves to new fathers, so that they might share the responsibility for very young children and allow their wives to return to work on a reduced schedule. The program proved unsuccessful when fathers who were taking time off were expected to do the same amount of work as before.[87]

Equal responsibility in parenting is an unfamiliar concept for most men and women. Margaret Mead felt that men should have the opportunity to play a more intimate family role, "that men and children [would be] enriched by it."[88] In fact, the time spent by the average father in primary child care is estimated to be about 12 minutes a day.[89] He probably had about the same amount of attention from his father. We are all influenced by our own childhood experience, and also by the pictures in our heads of those television family scenes showing mother taking a batch of cookies out of the oven before father came home from work.

The rigidity of sex-role attitudes in our culture increases the difficulty of shared parenting. "Social institutions and professionals resist recognizing the father as a primary day-to-day parent." A father who calls a pediatrician about a child's health problem may well be instructed, "Have your wife call me."[90]

A great deal of feminist pressure has been focused on the jobs at the top, in business and professional fields. In an article titled "Being a Woman," Midge Decter says she believes that only a handful of the girls pursuing higher education "are powerfully motivated by the idea of a professional future." They simply find college "a more interesting and carefree way of whiling away the time before marriage."[91] To feminists, this attitude seems to imply that women lack the capacity for commitment to a professional discipline, that personally achieved status and power mean nothing to them, and—the ultimate devaluation—that they would not have produced important work anyway.

Women's standing in the professions is presently rather poor. They hold only 13 percent of senior, tenured faculty positions in colleges and universities. Nine percent of our lawyers are women, .2 percent of our judges, 11 percent of our physicians, and 3 percent of our dentists.[92] But professional schools are now accepting more women, which sometimes means enforcing their entrance standards more rigorously. Department of Labor projections indicate that by 1985, 18 percent of all professionals will be female.[93] Women hold only 6 percent of the nation's top management and administrative positions. They are doing best in big corporations, which have more high-level jobs available. In the past year, there was a 28 percent increase in the number of women in management positions in the 1,300 largest companies.[94]

The role of female executive is a cynosure of nonstereotypic behavior. She has undertaken a part which is the antithesis of the sex role she has probably been conditioned to since childhood. She has entered an environment still considered an exclusive male birthright in some quarters. Prejudice in this area has at least become more covert. Flagrant noncompliance with Title VII of the Civil Rights Act of 1964 could lead to threats of a splashy lawsuit and corporate embarrassment. Some observers have recently noted a positive change of attitude on the part of senior corporate executives in their relationships with women.[95]

Even more encouraging, Rosabeth Kanter's research for her book *The Men and Women of the Corporation* seems to indicate that women respond to jobs offering power and opportunity in much the same manner as men do. As the individual shapes herself to the job, the effects of sex-role socialization become less significant.[96] However competent a woman may be in her job, she must be very careful about the style in which she exerts her authority. Consider the comments of five women who were interviewed on an occasion celebrating their appointments as directors of some of the ten largest corporations in America. Questioned as to how they had made it to the top, all five women kept repeating the same word: "luck." Thus, they maintained a certain feminine modesty and avoided the risk of inciting the chauvinists among their male colleagues.

All five women maintained that they "could speak frankly and provocatively in a board room dominated by men." "But on the other hand," one added, "you have to be politic and say what you have to say so you achieve your objective without destroying yourself."[97]

Female managers are well advised to be circumspect in their behavior with male colleagues. Data from recent sex-role studies suggest that "interaction with competent women, especially in competitive situations, may well stimulate some sort of fear in men, leading to hostility."[98] Subordinate males often find it difficult to take orders from a female superior, and most women would also prefer to work for a man.

The male corporate executive enjoys particular advantage over his competition of the opposite gender: he has a wife. A recent survey by Maryanne Vandervelde, herself a psychotherapist and a corporate wife, revealed that 85 percent of the chief executive officers and 70 percent of the wives interviewed did not feel that they had changed their attitudes about corporate wives in the past few years. Thirty-eight percent of the executives and 50 percent of the wives disapproved of those corporate wifes who were often unavailable for entertaining because of career conflict. She did find some evidence of a growing awareness that the corporate wife deserves some consideration of her own identity.[99]

Eugene E. Jennings, professor of management at Michigan State University, estimates that one-third of all executives' wives already have full-time careers of their own. The two-career family faces special problems and tensions. It is more difficult for a woman who is absorbed with a demanding career to take time off to have children. A transfer for a husband may mean that the wife must sacrifice her job, or the reverse. Also, Jennings says, "There's no hell like a double-career crisis."[100]

Erica Abeel, in an article for "Hers" in the *New York Times*, suggests the kind of dramatic material that all this experimentation with lifestyles and sex roles has created. She sketches a remarkable cast of characters. To paraphrase:

Abby, the editor, stayed in New York when her husband was transferred to Houston, because she liked her job. She is now divorced.

Marlys made the best-seller list with an astrological cookbook. She enjoyed all the hoopla, but it annoyed Malcolm, her husband. They got an "open separation," which is working out better for Malcolm and Marlys. She thinks therapy might be the answer, but he has discovered there are a lot of unattached and adventurous young ladies about, and for the moment he opts for "open opportunity."

Susan's husband Harry always said he disdained conventional housewifely types. But while Susan poured all her attention into preparing a brief for a "landmark case," Harry found someone more attuned to his needs.

Sam's wife June is a contented homebody and mother. How comfortable but dull, Sam discovers—this life in the velvet trap.

The elaborate wedding cake that illustrates these scenarios has developed serious structural defects and is crumbling at the base.[101]

TELEVISION: A CONSERVATIVE PICTURE

Abeel's portraits of women struggling with new roles and self images suggest the dramatic conflicts, the comedy and tragedy of their lives. Thus far, television has done very little to capitalize on these dramatic possibilities. The portrayal of women in television still has more to do with the traditional stereotypes and worn-out dramatic and comedic conventions than with the new realities of women's lives. This material is either reassuring to conservative viewers or, in some cases, titillating. In neither case does it have much artistic value.

Writing in 1954, Sidney W. Head said, "Television as a medium appears to be highly responsive to the conventional conservative values. . . . It will add tremendously to cultural inertia."[102] Television may well be a powerful normative force in society. Two characteristics enhance this effect. First, television is ubiquitous. Second, most programming takes the form of dramatic entertainment.

Television is a presence in 71 million American homes. The average individual views 6½ hours of programming a day. Children are exposed to it from early childhood. The numbers and letters taught by "Sesame Street" are only a small portion of what they learn. Television images and structures feed the ideational process as the toddler grows and develops. Fred Flintstone, Superman, and Captain Kangaroo are part of a common vocabulary of experience he shares with his cohorts. As he grows older, he merely substitutes Johnny Carson, Walter Cronkite, and Mary Hartman.[103]

The television viewer who settles down for an evening's entertainment usually relaxes and puts his critical faculties aside. Drama theorists call this the suspension of disbelief. The viewer becomes emotionally and intellectually involved in the action of a story, insofar as he identifies with the characters and projects himself into their situations. There may be no profound emotional catharsis or ecstasies involved in most television viewing (outside of the Superbowl games), but there is some sort of vicarious experience involved. Most television entertainment is routinely formulated and homogenized. But however shallow the average viewer's attention may be, he does expose his mind to a great many hours of programming. It would be unrealistic not to consider television a potent instrument for "modifying consciousness and organizing new modes of sensibility."[104]

We should not exaggerate the power of the medium. Most viewers seem to ignore material which doesn't fit in comfortably with their personal values, or they find explanations which make it fit. On the other hand, television producers and writers are craftsmen who control a communication process. They know that their relaxed audience is open to new ideas and new ways of seeing things. They understand how to use novelty and suspense to grip his attention. These creators have some confidence that it is possible to relate a theme to widely accepted, traditional values, in such a way that the viewer finds points of insight and sympathy that were previously unrecognized.

Television writers and producers have values and convictions. They believe a properly enlightened public would share those values and convictions. Fortunately, most of them are fairly well educated and moderately liberal. Also, they are restrained by the commercial nature of the medium. Their first objective is to entertain, not to teach. The risk of offending a large audience segment must be avoided at all costs. The media expert Robert L. Hilliard offers this advice to the tyro television author: "Realistically, the most well-intentioned writer is still under the control of the network and advertiser, whose first loyalties seem to be directed toward their own interests and not necessarily toward those of the public."[105]

During periods of rising social consciousness, it is easier to present relevant themes. Very often, this is done in a self-conscious and patronizing manner. Even so, if the entertainment values are sufficiently strong and the message is not too offensive, the show may succeed.

CBS's long-running "All In The Family" is a good example. This program frequently took up feminist issues. Edith Bunker's character made her the perfect spokeswoman. Her husband Archie was an offensive bigot and male chauvinist. The son-in-law, Mike Stivic, annoyed some traditionalists with his liberal viewpoint. Edith offended no one; she was climbing over the fence and had a foot on each side. On the one hand, although aggrieved far beyond what most housewives might have to bear, Edith was selflessly devoted to her family. On the other hand, she was growing and liberating herself in a positive way. Edith had the wisdom and strength not only to change herself, but to change Archie as well. In fact, as the series wore on, we had seen Archie learn so much from Edith that his ability to incite outrage became practically defused. It is only fair to say that much of the effectiveness of the Edith Bunker character rested on Jean Stapleton's sensitive and touching performance.[106]

Audience, Players, and the Advertising Nexus

The first priority of network executives is not the quality of the television product, nor its educational or entertainment values. They are in the business of delivering massive audience segments to commercial advertisers. That is the source of their revenue and the measure of success or failure. The most desirable segment of the mass audience, and the target of most television advertisers, are women between the ages of 19 and 49. They are the major purchasers of advertisers' products. Not only do housewives comprise the major daytime viewing audience, but broadcasters believe that there are more women than men watching in all prime-time periods. They are thought to make 60 percent of the program selections. Not surprisingly, programs which are designed for women are thought to draw a larger audience than programs designed for men.[107]

Since women are the primary audience television must attract, we might expect to see largely female casts and stories celebrating women's achievements and leadership roles. The reality is quite different. The U.S. Commission on Civil Rights studies cited earlier also provide facts and statistics describing the portrayal of women in adult dramatic programming offered on commercial television.

The percentage of white female characters appearing in the sample studies of prime-time dramatic programs, from 1969 through 1977, remained under 25 percent and showed very little variation. (The actual proportion of majority females in the U.S. population is 41.6 percent.) Minority females were even less well represented.

The manner in which women were portrayed in the 1969-77 period is even more disappointing. Women consistently appeared in roles in which they were likely to be dominated by white males simply because the men had superior occupational status. Women turned up in 60 percent of the clerical roles and 90 percent of the household-service roles. Only 6.6 percent were seen in managerial positions, and 6.5 percent appeared as craftsmen. Virtually all the nurses, but only 5 percent of television's doctors, were played by women. Males were executives; females were secretaries. Men were engaged in law enforcement; women appeared as victims. Women appeared in 20 percent fewer job categories, and half of all female characters had no clearly specified job or professional employment.[108]

This is a very depressing picture. But, when we compare the proportionate employment statistics and the types of female employment with the statistics cited on women's actual participation in the labor force, they match very well. Television is conservative as claimed. It continues, in general, to portray women in traditional roles. But, in spite of the necessity of staying in the midstream of public opinion, popular programming must appear to be topical and fashionable. Like all art and entertainment media, TV must at least seem to be predictive in some respect, or it will very shortly be considered irrelevant and dull.

By watching television, we would not learn that more women are working in a greater variety of jobs, that they are getting more education and moving into management and the professions and politics. Some roles suggest a greater independence and self-esteem in women, but we almost never see an aggressive or authoritative woman who is not ridiculed.

Television actresses, eager for stronger, more interesting parts, are sorely disappointed with this situation. Norma Connolly, cochair of the women's conference committee of the Screen Actors' Guild (SAG) says, "In real life you find women lawyers practicing, but if the script doesn't specify that the role must go to a woman in casting, they'll ask for men."[110] SAG's president, Kathleen Nolan (elected on a write-in vote), calls women's television roles "disgraceful."[111]

Age is even more rare than power in female television roles. Programmers and producers are more fascinated with girlish nubility than ever before. Close to 40 percent of all female roles are now in the 21-30 age bracket.[112] The least pleasant consequence of this is that a television actress is virtually forced into retirement at age 40. As casting opportunities decline, she loses her livelihood at the very time she has become the master of her craft and has the most to offer an audience.

Men, who are cast in authoritative roles, make 60 percent of their appearances between 31 and 50 years of age. Only by submitting to cosmetic surgery do most women over 40 continue to work. Connolly describes herself as so angry she "could kill" over the situation. "It isn't vanity," she says. "It's sheer economics. It's adding 10 working years."[113] As the braless look becomes commonplace, plastic surgeons will probably be doing more body work as well.

The basic themes and prototype characterizations of today's television were first developed in the 1950s and early 1960s. Network executives who harbor male-chauvinist sentiments today are not outspoken about them, but in 1964, Friedan was able to get some candid responses to her questions about the portrayal of women in television that help explain some current characterizations.

Norman Felton could find no reasonable justification for serious, dramatic roles for women: "After all, it's housewives we are appealing to, and marriage is their whole life." Wives don't identify with unmarried women. "Most women are dominated by men, and they would react against a woman who succeeded in anything." But, you can't really have a drama about a married woman. Who could imagine her doing anything interesting or exciting? "In comedy, it's alright. You're not supposed to take her seriously; you laugh at her." Madelyn Martin, a longtime writer of the "I Love

Lucy" show, said, "You can't package a dramatic show around a woman, because women only want to look at a man. . . "[114]

The consequence of these opinions was that most television shows were built around male characters. Women were featured only in domestic comedies that presented either a female clown or an idealized version of a housewife. These happy homemakers kept perfect houses, raised adorable children, and never had a curl or a stocking seam out of place.

Throughout the 1950s and early 1960s, the experts, the media, and advertisers found themselves in happy agreement. The only satisfactory role for a woman was marriage, motherhood, and a career of family togetherness. Articles by pediatricians, psychologists, and sociologists appeared in all the women's magazines, where they set forth their rationale for female domesticity.[115] Benjamin Spock, whose book *Baby and Child Care* sold in the millions, encouraged women to believe that raising children was a full-time job that could not be safely delegated.[116] The suburban housewife might feel isolated, dissatisfied, and bored, but advertisers soothed her with idealized and glamorized images of her life. They suggested products which would help her solve almost any housekeeping problem. "Daily life was expected to be carried out according to the conformities of consumption."[117]

Television commercials for household products have scarcely changed in 20 years. They are like voices from the past. Feminists see them as so anachronistic, so blatant and odious that they are felt to actually serve as consciousness-raising devices. The average viewer now sees an estimated 500 commercials a week. A National Organization for Women (NOW) survey showed that 36.5 percent of the women in those commercials were portrayed as "unpaid household workers," or, in other words, housewives. Many 30-second commercial dramas, they said, showed housewives as "stupid" and "obsessive," and in need of male advice in the form of voice-overs or the help of magical assistants. (Mary Hartman [*Mary Hartman, Mary Hartman*, CBS] exhibited this syndrome in her exaggerated concern about "yellow, waxy buildup" on her kitchen floor.) Three-quarters of the housekeeping problems presented occurred in the bathroom and kitchen.[118]

Carroll Carroll, a columnist for *Variety*, provides a column of witty commentary on television commercials titled "And Now A Word From . . . " Carroll reports receiving a letter from a gentleman in New Orleans, complaining about a commercial which was being tried out in his area. In this minidrama, a lady, identified as a local resident, uses brand X in her laundry at the behest of an interviewer. She is thrilled with the results, amazed to discover the product is Oxydol, and vows to go on using it. Outraged on behalf of the New Orleans area, the author of the letter feels that this commercial is an "unfair stereotyping of regional gullibility."[119] The format, demonstrating the trend of using real people in order to enhance viewer identification, is familiar.

A number of commercials approach women with emotional appeals. For example, the housewife who feels guilty about not baking can find love and appreciation by serving Sara Lee baked goods: "I'm gonna Sara-Lee-love my family, and they're gonna Sara-Lee-love me back."

Among the most objectionable television commercials are those which exploit women as sex objects. One of the most famous examples is the "Fly me!" commercial for National Airlines. *Time* magazine reported that the stewardesses who participated were told by the director to pretend "you're standing there stark naked."[120] The Underall commercial fits in the same category: "It looks like you're not wearin' nuthin.'"

A television actress, Susan Barrister, describes the humiliation of a commercial audition from the viewpoint of the performer. On one such occasion, she was shown a bicycle, standing in for the product (an automobile), and was directed to respond to it with "sensuality" and "passion."[121]

Among the most pernicious television advertisements are those for over-the-counter drugs and medications. Many of these are specifically urged on women with promises of instant relief of symptoms or of improved health. A number of multimillion-dollar, nonprescription-drug companies spend 90 percent of their advertising budgets on television commercials.[122] The value of some of these products is dubious. The quantity in which they are consumed is certainly excessive. American women are considered the most overmedicated group of people in the world, and much of that medication is self-prescribed on the basis of earnest advice from the manufacturers.[123]

Ad men have succeeded in manipulating female consumers so well that it is not surprising that they still occasionally address them in a manner clearly suggesting that they think the girls may not be too clever. A woman advertising executive says, "Most men in advertising think of women as having low intelligence. They believe that across the country, women are really children. You can't say anything too fancy to them."[124]

NOW's Media Reform Task Force has organized letter-writing campaigns and suggested product boycotts. They have also tried conducting workshops on sexist advertising for members of the Broadcast Standards and Practices Departments of the networks. Women in senior executive positions in advertising, including Mary Wells and Jane Trahey, are an ameliorating influence.

Thus far, however, all concerned parties are passing the buck. The agencies say they would like to use better ads, but their clients are behind the times. Sponsors blame the agencies for a lack of creativity. Market researchers claim that the consumers aren't negatively influenced by patently sexist ads—the products still sell.[125]

Meanwhile, network advertising volume is expected to be up 15 percent in 1979, and a big increase is expected in 1980. An estimated 20 percent of the nation's ad budget goes into television advertising, in spite of rapidly rising costs. Thirty-two second spots on the "Laverne and Shirley" (ABC) show sold for $120,000 in 1979; the price for "Charlie's Angels" was $100,000. Advertisers who were frightened away by increasing costs, a year or two ago, have tried other media and are returning to the fold. Business is booming at all three networks.[126]

Unfortunately, commercials can be irritating and insulting and still sell the product effectively. Because people think they are ignoring the commercials, their annoyance is suppressed. But there are signs of growing consumer resistance among housewives, and some sponsors are becoming concerned. As Carroll puts it, viewers are "'wising up'. . . . They're getting bored with being talked down to, insulted by innuendo and, as a result, are prepared to respond quickly and positively to what they perceive to be the straight of anything."[127]

The most significant change is that television commercials have finally begun to address working women. Female airline pilots and physicians have appeared in some 30-second vignettes. Women who are providing their own income have a new perspective on themselves that makes some sales appeals meaningless. Perhaps there was some prophecy as well as confusion involved when Mary Hartman held up a bar of soap, instead of a dish, and said, "I can't see my reflection," instead of saying, "What a nice reflection on me!"[128] There may eventually be a vogue for commercials featuring bright housewives who keep laundry problems in perspective, women who obviously have dignity and alternatives.

Some of the women in the new ads have only changed their costumes, not their personalities. For example, the woman carrying a briefcase can't summon the courage to ask the druggist for a breath freshener. (She used to announce she was on her way to try her first case in court. Was there a complaint from the bar association?) In general, these working-woman commercials address women in more flattering and respectful terms. Indeed, Eleanor Holtzman, vice president of DKG Advertising, and Harriet Bloch, associate research director at the same agency, conducted a study which established that ads showing working women had more appeal for housewives as well as jobholders.[129]

Daytime and Prime Time

Historically, the women's movement has suffered from disunity and the lack of group consciousness. Today, leaders are more aware of the necessity of broadening the base of the movement, and of the need to establish bonds of understanding with all those women who would be outraged by identification with women's libbers.[130] Through participation in team sports, boys learn to tolerate differences in one another and work together toward mutual goals; but girls seldom have this experience.[131] Feminists are now making new efforts to find common chords for themselves, and for those women who see them as threats to traditional values and lifestyles. (Eleanor Smeal, president of NOW, describes herself as a housewife. She has attempted to find some areas of agreement between both sides in the abortion issue.)[132]

Daytime television could provide an arena in which women could express their diverse viewpoints and discover points of common interest. Unfortunately, the large monetary stakes involved are a deterrent. Daytime programming accounts for roughly 75 percent of network income. It is also a lucrative source of station income. A conservative approach, therefore, is the order of the day. Station management sometimes responds to pressure from the local NOW organization by putting on a half-hour show with a feminist orientation at about 7:00 a.m. on Saturday or Sunday. This helps the station fulfill its public-interest responsiblities, and no one is too concerned about how stylish or effective the program is. Typically, there is also a daily, hour-long magazine/entertainment program for women, with a large budget and staff, which attracts numerous advertisers. Here is a female employee's description of her station's show: "It is geared to housewives with a diapers and dishes content. . . . It talks down to women and sees them as mindless drudges."[133]

Some of these shows have followed the same repetitive, noncontroversial formats for years. There are many other stations that have allowed sensitive and intelligent writers and producers to create women's programs that have made important contributions. They have helped to widen women's perspectives, sharpen their awareness of issues which concern them, and develop understanding among divergent women's groups that may have more in common than they realize.

Women's programs do not have to be parochial. Walters, who originally presented "Not for Women Only" on NBC, believes that producing a show for women only puts women down.[134] Daytime programs should provide a testing ground for the argument that news features and documentary studies on women's and minorities' subjects can be sufficiently interesting and important to warrant inclusion in the evening schedule. Women have a stake in a great number of community activities and issues that have no sexual priorities. Art/crafts, housekeeping, and parenting are a little less exclusively female concerns than they used to be, and they are certainly enriched by male involvement—as participants, not just as authorities. There is a potential male audience segment for daytime programs among men who are retired or work irregular hours. Women's shows have been ghettoized entertainment less because of the daytime scheduling than because they were obviously addressed to a stereotyped housewife.

Programmers are mistaken to believe that housewives are put off by professional women or women of high achievement. They are repelled by arrogant, contemptuous attitudes, and by people who condemn the domestic lifestyle without understanding its values. "The Phil Donahue Show" is a good example of what can be achieved with an intelligent, free-wheeling discussion program using listener call-ins.

Daytime game shows elicit feminist despair and critical condemnation. The shows are popular, but the viewer isn't offered too many alternatives in daytime television. The dominant form, filling the daytime schedule from 11:00 a.m. to 4:30 in the afternoon, is the soap opera. This venerable genre has been part of American life for 50 years. There are now 13 serials broadcast on the three networks in half-hour or hour-long segments.

These afternoon dramas, more than any other type of television-drama program, are by, about, and for women. Women writers largely developed and dominated the form. It continuously provides a large number of dramatic roles for women, and is largely concerned with issues which are considered likely to interest women.

For a time it was feared that the large number of women who have returned to work in recent years would deplete the audience for daytime serials. A recent study conducted by National Television Research, for CBS, restored confidence. More women, men, and teenagers are tuning in than ever before. Research studies estimate that an audience of 10 million women and 2 million men watch daytime serials. Network executives consider them the key to daytime programming. Nielsen figures indicate that about 60 percent of the women who watch soaps are in the 19-40 age bracket—the very group which buys 75 percent of the products advertised during the day.[135]

The old radio soaps were considered hopelessly lowbrow and unsophisticated. Only housewives, bored to distraction, were considered an appropriate audience for them. The quality of television serials is much higher. There is also a new realism and frankness in the dramatic themes. The generation gap, mastectomies, abortion, and narcotics addiction are now among the problems which beset characters in daytime serials. Sexuality is dealt with more honestly than in most evening programs.

A great many high school and college students are aficionados, and producers are encouraging their interest. More young people have been introduced to soap-opera casts, and they are presented in situations which concern young people. A high school girl in Chicago said, "When I'm watching a story, I always put myself in the position of a teenager and figure out how I would handle some of the situations and what I'd say to my mother."[136]

The primary focus of the soaps, however, is the housewife, the good woman. They sympathize with her, flatter her, and reassure her. They uphold conventional morality with a sentimental fervor. The literary historian Ann Douglas sees an "intimate connection between critical aspects of Victorian culture and mass culture."[137] However superficially stylish and relevant it may seem, the contemporary soap opera has strong roots in the sentimental Victorian novel.

The feminine heroines of today's soap operas embody the same qualities as their Victorian predecessors. They have moral superiority, intuitive understanding, and skill in human relations—which they discuss endlessly. They are also more self-reliant now and capable of taking on glamorous jobs. A woman must never put her own achievements before her family and her responsibility to her husband. The career opportunity she has always dreamed of may open up in another town, but, if her husband has his reasons for not moving, then she must give it up. Traditional ideology is firmly reinforced.

Viewers identify strongly with soap-opera characters that are developed fully; they come to know them intimately over the years. These characters have frequent troubles; there is a new catastrophe and suffering behind every turn of the plot. Theoretically, this has some therapeutic value. The housewife has the satisfaction of observing someone who has even more troubles than she does. Unlike conventional drama, there is always a tomorrow in the serials. Characters persevere and find solutions. Writers and producers are becoming more aware of a responsibility to suggest positive means of coping with common problems, but entertainment values still come first.

Soap operas develop slowly, but they are full of events. When the situation is blackest, there is still hope because tomorrow, something entirely unexpected will happen. The best thing it could be is a new, romantic love. In soap opera, with unrealistic frequency, that's just what it is. Fans seem to accept these events with eager credulity. Daytime serials may well have the effect of making life within the stereotype more tolerable through romantic fantasies and unrealistic optimism.

The characters in soaps are almost exclusively white, professional, middle-class residents of small towns, people who are involved with their families. The better-than-average standard of living is thought to make identification a bit more attractive to the viewer.[138]

Network competition is sharpest in the evening hours, the prime time. There the programmers fight for a competitive edge. They require material which is inoffensive, but novel, amusing, or exciting. It should reflect popular interests and respond to changing attitudes.

At the height of the publicity for the women's movement in 1970, the "Mary Tyler Moore Show" (CBS, 1970-77) was introduced. Its producers considered it quite daring at the time. Mary was old enough to be experienced, and not obsessed with catching a husband. She was self-supporting and cared about her job and her friends. Although the show was undeniably topical, it was rooted in traditional ideals and values. Mary was modern, but also responsible, self-reliant, and decent. She assured the audience, the critic Paula S. Fass says, "that what is solid in the American character, male or female, will never by overpowered by fickle fashion."[139]

The "Mary Tyler Moore Show" successfully ignored Felton's objection that women would be bored by a program centered on a single, unmarried female. Feminists' complaints were minor. Mary seemed very insecure and tentative for a successful career woman, and why should she be the only person in the office to call the boss Mr. Grant? In a way, the program dodged the problem of a female producer. Mary could manage with those incompetents at WJM, but how would she stand up against serious competition? Mary wasn't quite a submissive, self-deprecating girl, nor was she a masculinized, aggressive boss lady. Basically, she was the good woman, but she was in tune with evolving cultural standards. She adapted the stereotype.

In the course of time, the show dealt with a number of issues raised by the women's movement. Top-flight women writers, such as Charlotte Brown and Tricia Silverman, made contributions. Joan Darling and other women directors worked on the series. Once the water was tested, others jumped in. The role of single women was explored further through the exploits of Rhoda and Phyllis (offshoots of the "Mary Tyler Moore Show" on CBS). Norman Lear's Maude (CBS) was as aggressive and dominant a female personality as television has ever seen. Lear's "One Day at a Time," with some daring, featured a divorced woman in the central role.

With the growing concern over law-and-order issues in the early 1970s, crime stories replaced westerns as the dominant form of the action-adventure drama series. One of the problems in plotting these shows was the difficulty of using women in some role other than sex object and victim. But, in real life, women were joining some police forces in small numbers. With the introduction of "Police Woman" (NBC, 1974-78), starring Angie Dickinson as Sgt. Pepper Anderson, it became possible to take an approach to crime stories that was fresh and topical. The producers felt they were bucking the tradition that women would not accept a female in an authoritative male profession. The other innovation was that Pepper used her gun. Julie in "MOD Squad" (ABC, 1968-72), and Emma Peel in "The Avengers" (ABC, 1966-69) relied on their skill in judo and karate.

In some respects, Sergeant Anderson was used in very traditional ways. She frequently worked undercover, sometimes in very provocative circumstances, in which she could approach the criminal or act as a sexual lure. This would lead to a tight spot and rescue by her male colleagues. She would use her sensuality to entrap criminals, her feminine intuition to crack a case.[140]

At least Sergeant Anderson suggested a new perspective on women's role in society. Dickinson said she received numbers of letters from young women who told her the show had provided them with models which helped them deal with situations in their own lives.[141]

The dramatic programs that caused most concern for the authors of the Civil Rights Commission *Update* report were those which centered on violence and the so-called jiggle shows.[142] Foremost among these is "Charlie's Angels" (ABC), which was introduced in 1976. It has placed consistently in the top ten in the Nielsen ratings since then. Some 20 million households view "Charlie's Angels." The show was not just a success, but a phenomenon, a trend setter. As Sergeant Anderson, Dickinson was beautiful in a mature, sultry, provocative way. Charlie's Angels are what Karl Meyer, television critic for the *Saturday Review of Literature*, has described as a "triumph of product engineering that enables the pre-teen consumer to move from the playroom to the living room." The Angels are Barbie-doll sex goddesses, good girls, but spicy girls, braless but virtuous.[143] Fred Silverman, the ace programmer, variously described as a *wunderkind* or a *schlock meister*, saw the show as a means of attracting the heavy viewers, as something novel enough to attract the most jaded appetites. The movement of women into untypical jobs made it possible to cast girls as picaresque crime fighters. With the addition of dollops of sex and mild violence, ABC had the perfect light entertainment for the late 1970s, a concoction even the overdosed television addict found hard to resist.

The Angels' appeal to men is obvious, and most women haven't found the show offensive. It is a kind of comic-book sexual fantasy made glamorous. Some feminists have criticized the show as sexist. Charlie, who gives the Angels their orders, is remote and unseen, but so much better informed than the people on the spot that he seems clairvoyant. But the Angels are not just automatons. They are self-reliant, daring, assertive—distant, pedestrian relatives of James Bond. Like the British secret agent, they use their good looks just as it suits them, and relish the impact they make with some detachment. The Angels have machisma.[144]

Farrah Fawcett-Majors scored the greatest impact in the original cast of "Charlie's Angels." Dolls, posters, T-shirts, and a line of cosmetics have been marketed with the Farrah name and image. It was reported that a group of midwestern schoolgirls, in a jealous fit, threw lye on a classmate who showed up with the first Farrah hairdo.[145] Farrah Fawcett-Majors, in a poll of more than 14,000 junior and senior high school students conducted in 1977 by

Scholastic Magazines was elected their "no. 1" personal hero. Only one national or international leader was in the top 20: President Jimmy Carter was in sixteenth place.[146]

MOVING RIGHT ON

Critics found the 1977-78 season remarkable for the abundance of what they described variously as "trash" or "drivel." ABC was the clear leader in the ratings. "Mork and Mindy," the runaway success of the year's new programs, was lightweight, escapist fantasy. The manic improvisational genius of Robin Williams, as Mork, won the show first place on the Nielsen chart. Eight of the top ten shows in the Nielsen list were situation comedies throughout the year. "Laverne and Shirley" and "Happy Days," both nostalgic comedies, continued to appear in top positions. A risqué comedy, "Three's Company," placed well on the charts.

"Television . . . has the right to do what the public wants it to do," Russel Nye argues in his study of popular culture, *The Unembarrassed Muse.*[147] Today the public has a clear preference for comedy and diversion,[148] and the networks plan to satisfy their taste. Anthony Thomopoulos, president of ABC Entertainment, says the public wants "laughter brought into their lives," shows that make them "feel good." Programmers at all three networks were reported to be concentrating on the development of more comedy formats with eccentric and fantastic qualities for the 1979-80 season.[149]

The most fascinating entry discussed for 1980 was described as "a sophisticated comedy about a woman who is married to a kind of boring man"; he just likes to watch television.[150]

The "Mary Tyler Moore Show" and "All in the Family" were innovative. They changed the television stereotype of women in useful ways. But, there is much more to be said. On television, women are absent from many of the roles they play in life, not just in terms of jobs and a variety of lifestyles, but in sheer numbers. The stereotyped behavior and attitudes TV is teaching children today may mean they will have problems of overcoming conventional role-model limitations, just as their parents do today. We do not need a didactic or propagandistic approach, nor would all the comedies be replaced with serious drama. What programmers are overlooking is that comedy with a contemporary, realistic base could be more satisfying to audiences than nostalgia and fantasy.

Neil Simon's film *The Goodbye Girl* was such a story. When situation comedies have taken up problems such as divorce, the material is so hyped with gags and slapstick that the story becomes meaningless. If producers would deal honestly and humorously with the subtle revolution that is changing our lives, suppliers and audiences would benefit.

Three sets of circumstances would have a favorable effect: a wave of public consciousness regarding women's rights, similar to the one which rose in the early 1970s; a serious attempt to produce original, excellent dramatic shows; and the presence of women as writers, producers, and directors, and in senior decision-making positions in the industry.

The first of these is unpredictable, but there is a vast tide of aspiration on which a new wave will ride. The scope of the women's movement indicates a broad interest in new roles and new identities for women. Also, the lower-middle class audience, which is the major audience for commercial television, is more fragmented and changing more rapidly than ever before.[151] There is little reason for confidence in familiar, stereotyped formulas.

The second circumstance is less encouraging. The public statements of senior network executives are high minded and assert the best intentions. It is their express purpose to produce important television, not programming, which merely satisfies "the vagrant wants of an audience,"[152] but programming that "says something or creates viewer awareness of social ills or injustices."[153] This has a somewhat paternalistic ring. There is a suspicion that programming with these goals would very quickly get out of its depth.[154]

There are restraints on this policy, however. Just one rating point in prime-time television means around $30 million in pretax profits, per year, to the networks.[155] Furthermore, the network which does poorly in the ratings tends to lose affiliates to the network which leads the race. In this situation, management must select the "least objectionable" program.[156] Frederick S. Pierce, president of ABC Television, has articulated what might be described as a copout in his "voting theory" of television management. He says that programming decisions are made on the basis of votes from three sources: the viewers, the advertisers, and the creative community.[157] The goal of network management and of the advertisers is the same: the delivery of the target audience in massive numbers. The audience has "vagrant wants" for laughter and escapist nonsense. The only voice in this hierarchy that is likely to speak for quality is the least powerful, the creative community. As professionals, they have some stake in doing respectable work, but the negative factors that influence their performance are very great.

First, it's hard to be honest. Christopher Knopf, veteran TV writer and a past president of the Writers' Guild, is quoted as saying that writers are forced "to feed Middle America all the pap we know as lies and nonsense; we are feeding things we personally resent, which have no resemblance to real life."[158]

The networks deal with a very limited number of producers and writers who are tried and true. The accelerated ratings war means that shows are tried out, quickly cancelled if they don't immediately succeed, and replaced. Hollywood producers are struggling to adapt their operations. They frequently complain that they are not given sufficient lead time to prepare a new show, but the networks offer little sympathy. There are reports that prime writing and creative talents have grown increasingly disillusioned, and have chosen to leave the business before their ulcers start to bleed.

The movement toward lightweight entertainment has meant the virtual abandonment of the 60- and 90-minute dramatic form. "Roots" (ABC, 1977) made the long-form, miniseries format a great popular success. Three-hour made-for-TV films are also presented frequently. Unfortunately, the dramatic quality of these productions is seldom high. They are often dragged out to a boring length. Stories seem to be chosen for their potential as melodrama or soap opera rather than for serious quality. *Variety* critic Bob Knight says, "Exploitation potential is becoming more important to the choice of mini-series material than a work's substance."[159] Still, it is usually the long-form presentations that are pointed out by executives as evidence of quality productions. Television standards of excellence do not aspire to a level which might be considered elitist.

William S. Paley has suggested that something more might be necessary for the continued well-being of television. He sees "a responsibility to do a certain amount of high-quality programming that is not aimed at a mass audience." With the goal of improving network broadcasting, he proposes all three networks produce two hours a week of the finest-quality, frankly elitist programs they can create. They would not be subject to rating. His suggestions have not been greeted with an enthusiastic reception.[160]

The high-minded, elitist approach of the Public Broadcasting System has emphasized alien culture in the form of British imports. There is only one way to get at the dramatic realities of the emerging role of women in our society—or of any other aspect of contemporary life. The hierarchy of the voting theory of network management must be revised to give the creative community a stronger voice and more latitude to work in, and that community must be expanded and become more diverse.

Some male writers are achieving breakthroughs in their perception of women. The Broadway playwright Bruce Jay Friedman (*Scuba Duba* [1968] and Steambath [1971]) says, "I could always write female characters, but they were dingalings or had to be in a nightgown. . . . I was the last to realize that if you have something interesting to say, you can let a woman say it. . . . Now, I could actually write a play with a woman in the lead."[161] There are probably a number of those resilient writers and producers out on Sunset Boulevard thinking along the same lines as Friedman. They could give a woman something interesting to say if they were encouraged to do so.

Surely it is reasonable to suppose that women writers and producers would have even more insight and incentive to deal with the problems of women in TV. The networks would find rewards by investing some of their profits in writer workshops with a special emphasis on developing writing talent in women and members of minority groups. Experienced women writers and producers of proven talent should be encouraged. Alex Rose and Tamara Asseyev, a two-woman production team, in 1979 released the film *Norma Rae* (20th Century Fox), the story of a woman labor organizer. They are reported to have six more productions under way, all based on the stories of strong assertive women.[162]

Jane Cahill Pfeiffer, chairman of the board at NBC, holds the highest position of any woman in broadcasting. She is too visible a target. Also, feminism and altruism were not relevant qualifications for the job. But, just as marketing goals and changing demographics led the networks to develop programming designed to attract youthful audiences, the real changes in the roles women now play suggest that it would be wise to make some alterations in the image of the woman on the tube. There is a steadily increasing number of prime time programs which attempt to present women's issues and create positive portrayals of women who have moved outside of conventional stereotypes. The overwhelming weight of television programming, however, still presents women in a retrogressive and demeaning manner. Hopefully, Pfeiffer, and eventually many other women in senior management positions, will have special insights that will help bring those changes about.

NOTES

1. Elizabeth Janeway, *Between Myth and Morning, Women Awakening* (New York: William Morrow & Co., 1974), p. 170.

2. Gunther Grass, *The Flounder* (New York: Harcourt Brace Jovanovich, 1977), p. 34.

3. Francine du Plessix Gray, "Friends—A New Kind of Freedom for Women," *Vogue* 168, no. 8 (August 1978):190, 257.

4. Juanita H. Williams, *Psychology of Women, Behavior in a Biosocial Context* (New York: W.W. Norton & Co., 1977), pp. 1-15.

5. Ann Douglas, *The Feminization of American Culture* (New York: Avon Books, 1978); see chap. 3, "Ministers and Mothers: Changing and Exchanging Roles," pp. 94-143; and chap. 7, "The Periodical Press: Arena for Hostility," pp. 273-313.

6. Gunnar Myrdal, *An American Dilemma* (New York: Harper, 1944), app. 5, "A Parallel to the Negro Problem," p. 1073.

7. Douglas, op. cit., also see Julia Cherry Spruill, *Women's Life and Work in the Southern Colonies* (Chapel Hill: University of North Carolina Press, 1938).

8. On the subject of women's health in the period following the Civil War, Catharine Beecher wrote: "During my extensive tours in all portions of the Free States, . . . the more I traveled, . . . the more the conviction was pressed on my attention that there was a terrible decay of female health all over the land. . . " She offered her opinion as to the cause of the problem: "A 'perfectly healthy' or 'a vigorous and healthy woman' is one of whom there are *specimens* remaining in almost every place; such as used to *abound* when all worked, and *worked in pure air*." Catharine Beecher, *Woman Suffrage and Woman's Profession* (Hartford, 1971), cited in *The Oven Birds: American Women on Womanhood*, 1820-1920, ed. Gail Parker (New York: Doubleday, 1972), pp. 165-67.

Douglas, in op. cit., p. 109, writes on the same problem: "'Attention' to a problem in a given period is as telling as its actual 'incidence,' which may be almost impossible to determine. . . . To stress their ill health was a way for women punitively to dramatize their anxiety that their culture found them useless and wished them no good; it supplied them moreover, with a means of getting attention, of obtaining psychological and emotional power even while apparently acknowledging the biological correlatives of their social and political unimportance."

9. Mary Roth Walsh, *Doctors Wanted, No Women Need Apply: Sexual Barriers in the Medical Profession, 1835-1975* (New Haven: Yale University Press, 1977).

10. Barbara Ehrenreich and Deirdre English, *For Her Own Good, 150 Years of the Experts' Advice to Women* (New York: Doubleday, 1978), p. 99. In Charlotte Perkins Gilman's story "The Yellow Wall-Paper," she describes a woman who suffers what is diagnosed as "a temporary nervous depression" and is "absolutely forbidden to 'work' until she is well again." The woman speculates that what she really needs is "more society and stimulus." The fact that her husband is also her physician may be "the one reason I do not get well faster." *The Oven Birds*, op. cit., pp. 315-34.

11. Traditionally, women, particularly lower-class women, have constituted a reserve labor pool to be drawn into the economy only as required. Turning a blind eye to wage discrimination was only simple prudence in these circumstances. Overall, awareness of discrimination is increasing rapidly. In 1962 a Gallup survey showed that most American women did not see themselves as victims of discrimination or unequal treatment. By 1970 over 50 percent of women surveyed did have this

perception of themselves. See Laurie Larwood and Marion M. Wood, *Women in Management* (Lexington, Mass.: D.C. Heath and Co., 1978), p. 14.

12. Irene H. Frieze, Jacquelynne E. Parsons, Paula B. Johnson, Diane N. Ruble, and Gail L. Zellman, *Women and Sex Roles: A Social Psychological Perspective* (New York: W.W. Norton and Co., 1978), pp. 287-88.

13. Alice Ross Gold notes that studies conducted prior to 1970 indicated that women as well as men typically perceived women to be less intelligent and competent than men. A number of studies conducted after 1970 demonstrated that women were making many more egalitarian judgments of other women's achievements and abilities. See Alice Ross Gold, "Reexamining Barriers to Women's Career Development," *American Journal of Orthopsychiatry* 48, no. 4 (October 1978):691-93.

14. I. K. Broverman, S. R. Vogel, D. M. Broverman, F. E. Clarkson, and P. S. Rosencrantz, "Sex-Role Stereotypes: A Current Appraisal," *Journal of Social Issues* 28, no. 2 (1972):59-78.

15. Helen Mayer Hacker, "Women as a Minority Group," in *Masculine/Feminine*, ed. Betty Roszak and Theodore Roszak (New York: Harper & Row, 1969), p. 141.

16. Gordon Allport, *Psychology of Prejudice* (Boston: Beacon Press, 1954). See Frieze et al., op. cit., pp. 287-90. Also, see Jo-Ann Gardner, "The Psychology and the Psychological Effects of Discrimination," in *Women's Role in Contemporary Society, The Report of the New York City Commission on Human Rights, September 21-25*, (New York: Avon Books, 1972), pp. 95-96. Also see, Phyllis Chesler, *Women and Madness* (New York: Avon Books, 1972), pp. 38-49.

17. Hearst Corp. advertisement for *Cosmopolitan* magazine, in *New York Times*, March 7, 1979.

18. Sandra L. and Daryl J. Bem, "Training the Woman to Know Her Place: The Power of Unconscious Ideology," *Women's Role In Contemporary Society*, p. 102.

19. Frieze et al, op. cit., p. 298.

20. Betty Friedan, *The Feminine Mystique* (New York: W.W. Norton & Co., 1963).

21. Marion K. Sanders, "The New American Female, Demi-feminism Takes Over," *Harper's*, 231, no. 1382 (July 1965):39.

22. Harriet Van Horne, "The Feminine Mistake," *New York Post*, February 14, 1969.

23. Marabel Morgan, *The Total Woman* (Old Tappan, N.J.: Fleming H. Revell Co., 1973).

24. Phyllis Schlafly, *The Power of the Positive Woman* (New York: Harcourt Brace Jovanovich, 1978), p. 171.

25. Ibid., p. 224.

26. Ibid., p. 176.

27. "Housewives for ERA," Membership Brochure, (Urbana, Ill.: Housewives for ERA, n.d.).

28. Letter to the author, from C. Jordan, for Anne Follis, president, Housewives for ERA, April 17, 1979.

29. Judy Klemesrud, "Most Women Want Status Improved, Poll Finds," *New York Times*, October 3, 1974.

30. William H. Chafe, *Women and Equality, Changing Patterns in American Culture* (New York: Oxford University Press, 1977), pp. 139-40.

31. Elizabeth Hardwick, "Domestic Manners," *Daedalus* 107, no. 1 (Winter 1978):10.

32. Leslie Bennett, "Bella Abzug: Picking Up the Pieces," *New York Times*, December 1, 1978.

33. Alice Bonner, "21 Abzug supporters quit panel," *Boston Sunday Globe*, "U.S. & World," January 14, 1979. Also, see Martin Tolchin, "Women's Leaders Cancel Meeting With President," *New York Times*, November 23, 1978; Terence Smith, "Carter, in Angry Exchange, Ousts Bella Abzug From Women's Unit," *New York Times*, January 13, 1979; Donald G. McNeil Jr., "Three More Resign From Women's Unit," *New York Times*, January 15, 1979; "Sensitivity will hurt Carter, Abzug says," *Boston Globe*, January 15, 1979; Terence Smith, "Bella Abzug's Ouster and the Limits of Dissent," *New York Times*, January 16, 1979; "Excerpts From Panel Statement," *New York Times*, January 17, 1979.

34. Martin F. Nolan, "Jordan and Abzug and abrasiveness," *Boston Globe*, January 16, 1979.

35. Susan & Martin Tolchin, *Clout, Womanpower and Politics* (New York: Coward, McCann & Geoghegan, 1974), p. 169.

36. "TAT Sells 'Onward' For CBS' Midterm," *Variety*, November 29, 1978.

37. "*Mister Dugan* is Voted Out," *Time*, March 19, 1979, p. 85.

38. Martin Tolchin, "White House Bars Woman Aide's Senate Appearance," *New York Times*, February 1, 1979. Actress Marlo Thomas was one of number of committee members who resigned from the National Advisory Committee on Women, in a gesture of support for Abzug after she was fired. Thomas observes that "the government has been reluctant to recognize that the economy is a woman's issue." News coverage has played up the "so-called personality clash," she says, and obscured this point. Testimony presented by Marlo Thomas on "The Coming Decade: American Women and Human Resources Policies and Programs," before U.S. Congress, Senate, Committee on Human Resources, Washington, D.C., February 1, 1979, xerograph copy.

39. Leslie Bennetts, "On Aggression in Politics: Are Women Judged by a Double Standard?" *New York Times*, February 12, 1979.

40. Ibid.

41. Hank Whittemore, "A Kansas Landon Goes to Washington," *Parade*, March 18, 1979, p. 6.

42. Frances Lear, "Clout, Women-Wise," *New York Times*, December 14, 1978.

43. Douglas E. Kneeland, "Jane Byrne Insists That Bilandic is Silent on Transition in Chicago," *New York Times*, March 7, 1979.

44. "How Women in Congress Use Their Power," *Redbook* 150, no. 5 (March 1978):114.

45. A. Wells and E. Smeal, "Women's Attitudes toward Women in Politics: A Survey of Urban Registered Voters and Party Committee-Women" (Paper presented at the meeting of the American Political Science Association, Washington, D.C., 1972), quoted by Irene H. Frieze et. al., op. cit., p. 347.

46. Steven V. Roberts, "A Woman's Place Is. . . " *The New Leader*, November 20, 1978, p. 9.

47. Sharon Percy Rockefeller, "Women in Elected Politics," testimony presented before U.S. Congress, Senate, Committee on Human Resources, January 31, 1979, see especially p. 9.

48. Peter Lisagore and Marguerite Higgins, "L.B.J.'s Hunt for Womanpower," *Saturday Evening Post*, June 27-July 4, 1964.

49. Martin Gruberg, *Women in American Politics, An Assessment and Sourcebook* (Oshkosh: Academia Press, 1978), p. 133.

50. Letter to the author from Anne Wexler, assistant to President Carter, March 13, 1979. Also see Leslie Bennetts, "Women, Comparing Carter and Rivals" New York *Times*, Nov. 11, 1979.

51. *Window Dressing on the Set: Women and Minorities in Television, A Report of the United States Commission on Civil Rights* (Washington, D.C.: Government Printing Office, August 1977); and *Window Dressing on the Set: An Update, A Report of the United States Commission on Civil Rights* (Washington, D.C.: Government Printing Office, January 1979).

52. Louis Harris and Associates, *The 1972 Virginia Slims American Women's Opinion Poll.* As reported in Judy Klemesrud, "Do Women Want Equality? A Poll Says Most Do" New York *Times*, March 24, 1972.

53. *Update*, op. cit., chap. 3, pp. 23-32.

54. National Commission on the Observance of International Women's Year, *The Spirit of Houston: An Official Report to the President, the Congress and the People of the United States*, (Washington, D.C.: Government Printing Office, 1979), "10 Media Guidelines," p. 69.

55. Gaye Tuchman, "Women's Depiction by the Mass Media," *Signs: Journal of Women on Culture and Society* 4, no. 3 (Spring, 1979):535.

56. Edward Jay Epstein, *News From Nowhere* (New York: Random House, 1973), p. 9.

57. Mary Scott Welch, "How Women Just Like You are Getting Better Jobs," *Redbook* 149, no. 5 (September 1977): 176.

58. Judith S. Gelfman, *Women in Television News* (New York: Columbia University Press, 1976), p. 85.

59. *Update*, op. cit., p. 25.

60. Marlene Sanders, quoted in Gelfman, op. cit., p. 50. "Brenda Starr, Reporter," is the syndicated comic strip by Dale Messick. Jane Fonda describes her portrayal of Kimberly Wells, a television news reporter, in Columbia Pictures's *The China Syndrome* (1979) as her "Brenda Starr fantasy." Interview on "The Dick Cavett Show," Public Broadcasting System, April 1979.

61. Nancy K. Gray, "Before Barbara Walters There Was Dorothy Fuldheim," *Ms.* 5, no. 6 (December 1976):40-45.

62. See Gelfman, op. cit., pp. 110-24; she presents material on the expectations and motivations of male news executives and the responses of women news reporters.

63. Sally Quinn, *We're Going To Make You a Star* (New York: Simon and Schuster, 1975).

64. Ron Powers, *The Newscasters, The News Business as Show Business* (New York: St. Martin's Press, 1977), pp. 163-82.

65. "Deposition recorded in the conduct of a sex discrimination suit brought against the New York *Times* by its women employees," *Media Report to Women* 6, no. 13 (December 31, 1978):16.

66. Mary Jane Aldrich (Broadcast Standards, WMAQ/TV, Chicago) quoted in Anita Klever, *Women in Television* (Philadelphia: The Westminister Press, 1975), p. 103.

67. *Update*, op. cit. pp. 31-36.

68. Ibid., pp. 33, 41.

69. Jane Trahey, *Women and Power* (New York: Avon Books, 1977), p. 15.

70. *Media Report to Women*, op. cit., p. 1.

71. "The Times Settles Sex-Bias Suit Filed by Female Workers in U.S. Court," *New York Times*, November 21, 1978.

72. Janeway, op. cit., pp. 174-81.

73. Molly Haskell, *From Reverence to Rape, The Treatment of Women in the Movies* (New York: Holt, Rinehart and Winston, 1973).

74. Joan Mellen, *Women and Their Sexuality in the New Film* (New York: Horizon Press, 1973), p. 17.

75. "Women are 63 percent of the 16 million Americans living below the poverty level. . . . Women are 42 percent of the labor force, but 50 percent of the unemployed. Two-thirds of all 'discouraged' workers—the hidden unemployed—are women." Bella Abzug, testimony presented before U.S. Congress, Senate, Committee on Human Resources, February, 1, 1979, p. 4.

76. "Currently a male with a seventh-grade education earns more than a woman with a college degree." Marjorie Bell Chambers, testimony presented before U.S. Congress, Senate, Committee on Human Resources, January 31, 1979, p. 12.

77. A report written by the National Advisory Council on Women, entitled "Neglected Women," states that 26 million American women (one out of every three) lack the basic educational and job skills needed to get along in today's society. "1 in 3 women untrained for job market," *Boston Globe*, October 11, 1978.

78. The comparative figures on hourly wages are cited by Alexis Herman, director, Women's Bureau, U.S. Department of Labor, in testimony presented before the U.S. Congress, Senate, Committee on Human Resources, January 31, 1979, p. 4. Other facts cited in the preceding three paragraphs are largely based on material presented in those same hearings. See, particularly, testimony offered by Willard Wirtz, Joan Goodin, Sarah Weddington, January 31, 1979.

Helen Lawrenson discusses women's attitudes toward paid employment in her book *Whistling Girl, Candid Confessions of a Chameleon*. She takes to task the "vociferous feminists" who complain that "women get all the shitty jobs." Most of these feminists, she says, "are white, middle-class, well-educated women who have never known backbreaking manual labor themselves or anyone who has been close to it." She feels they should give a thought to "the millions of men . . . who work in coal mines or clean sewers or operate pneumatic jack drills. . . . What these women want is to be The Boss." The main interests of a majority of women are "home, husband and children," she argues, and they "enjoy taking care of their own homes." Lawrenson is a former managing editor of *Vanity Fair* magazine, a newspaper reporter, and the author of numerous magazine articles and two books.

79. Joann S. Lublin, "Getting Organized, More Women Enroll in Unions, Win Office And Push for Changes," *Wall Street Journal*, January 15, 1979.

80. Jill Conway, testimony presented before the U.S. Congress, Senate, Committee on Human Resources, February 1, 1979, p. 3.

81. *Quality of Employment Survey*, (Ann Arbor: Institute for Social Research, University of Michigan) cited by Wirtz, op. cit., p. 4. Jan. 31, 1979.

82. Wirtz, op. cit., p. 5.

83. A Harvard University-based project on human sexual development, conducted in Cleveland, cited in "Working Women: Joys and Sorrows, Impact at Home When Mother Takes a Job," *U.S. News and World Report*, 86, no. 2 (January 15, 1979):70.

84. J. R. Robinson and P. E. Converse, Summary of the U.S. Time Use Survey, May 30, 1966, cited by Gwendolyn L. Lewis, "Changes in Women's Role Participation," in Frieze, et al., op. cit., p. 144. Also, Joseph H. Pleck estimates men work an average of 1.6 hours per day on combined household and child-care tasks. *Men's New Roles in the Family: Housework and Childcare* (Ann Arbor: Institute for Social Research, University of Michigan, 1976), quoted by Nancy Press Hawley, "Sharing Parenthood," in *Ourselves and Our Children, A Book By And For Parents*, by the Boston Women's Health Book Collective (New York: Random House, 1978), p. 142.

85. Conway, op. cit., p. 4.
86. "Impact at Home When Mother Takes a Job," *U.S.News and World Report*, op. cit., p. 69.
87. Eric Morgenthaler, "Dads on Duty, Sweden Offers Fathers Paid Paternity Leaves, About 10% Take Them," *Wall Street Journal*, January 29, 1979.
88. Margaret Mead, "Can the American Family Survive?" *Redbook* 148, no. 4 (February 1977).
89. Pleck, quoted by Hawley, op. cit., p. 142.
90. Hawley, op. cit., p. 132.
91. Midge Decter, *The Liberated Woman and Other Americans: On Being a Woman, On Being a Liberal, On Being an American* (New York: Coward-McCann & Geoghegan, 1971), pp. 32-33.
92. Mary F. Berry, testimony presented before the U.S. Congress, Senate, Committee on Human Resources, p. 4. (Feb. 1, 1979).
93. Statistical projection by the Labor Department, quoted in "Working Women," U.S. News and World Report, op. cit., p. 67.
94. "Working Women," op. cit., p. 66.
95. Jacqueline Wexler, former president of Hunter College, New York City, states that she believes "that there has been a marked change in leading corporate executives in their attitude toward peer relationships with women." Letter to the author, February 26, 1979.
96. Rosabeth Moss Kanter, *Men and Women of the Corporation* (New York: Basic Books, 1977), especially chaps. 6 and 7.
97. Judy Klemesrud, "Women Executives: View from the Top," *New York Times*, March 11, 1979.
98. Gold, op. cit., p. 694.
99. Maryanne Vandervelde, "A Position Report on Corporate Wives," *New York Times*, March 11, 1979.
100. "The New Corporate Wife Goes to Work," *Business Week*, (April 9, 1979), pp. 88-91.
101. Erica Abeel, "Hers," *New York Times*, March 1, 1979.
102. Sydney W. Head, "Content Analysis of Television Drama Programs," *Quarterly of Film, Radio and Television* 9 (Winter 1954):192-93.
103. Tuchman, op. cit., p. 540.
104. Susan Sontag, *Against Interpretation, And Other Essays* (New York: Farrar, Straus & Giroux, 1966), p. 296.
105. Robert L. Hilliard, *Writing for Television and Radio* (New York: Hastings House, 1976), p. 29.
106. Kathryn Weible, *Mirror Mirror, Images of Women Reflected in Popular Culture* (New York: Doubleday, Anchor Books, 1977), pp. 71-72. Also, see Spencer Marsh, *Edith the Good* (New York: Harper & Row, 1977).
107. Les Brown, *The Business Behind the Box* (New York: Harcourt Brace Jovanovich, 1971), p. 119.
108. *Update*, op. cit., chap. 2, pp. 7-22.
109. J. L. Aranguren, *Human Communication* (New York: McGraw Hill, 1967), pp. 122-24.
110. Bill Mayer, "Is There a SAG in Minority Hiring for TV Roles?" *Variety*, August 24, 1977.
111. "SAG's Nolan Blasts TV Portrayal of Women," *Broadcasting*, June 5, 1978, p. 55.

112. *Update*, op. cit., pp. 10-11.

113. Will Tusher, "Facelift Panic Among Actresses Traced To Male Chauvinism," *Variety*, November, 15, 1978.

114. Betty Friedan, "Television and the Femine Mystique, Part I and Part II, in Jay Harris, ed., *TV Guide: The First 25 Years* (New York: Simon and Schuster, 1978), pp. 93-98.

115. Alice S. Rossi, "Equality Between the Sexes: An Immodest Proposal," in *The Woman in America*, ed. Robert Jay Lifton (Boston: Houghton Mifflin, 1964), p. 102.

116. Benjamin Spock, *Baby and Child Care* (New York: Duell, Sloan & Pearce, 1946). Also, see Philip Slater, *The Pursuit of Loneliness, American Culture at the Breaking Point* (Boston: Beacon Press, 1976), chap. 3, pp. 62-87.

117. Stuart Ewen, *Captains of Consciousness: Advertising and the Social Roots of the Consumer Culture* (New York: McGraw-Hill, 1977), p. 216.

118. Lucy Komisar, "The Image of Women in Advertising," in *Woman in Sexist Society: Studies in Power and Powerlessness*, ed. Vivian Gornick and Barbara K. Moran (New York: Basic Books, 1971), pp. 207-18.

119. Carroll Carroll, "And Now A Word From. . . ," *Variety*, January 24, 1979.

120. Quoted in Hilliard, op. cit., p. 82.

121. Susan Barrister, "The TV Commercial Audition," *TV Book: The Ultimate Television Book*, ed. Judy Fireman (New York: Workman Publishing Co., 1977), p. 297.

122. Peter Barry Chowka, "Television: A Medium beyond Control? Part 1," *New Age* 4, no. 10 (April 1979), p. 38.

123. Jacqueline H. Hall, chief, Mental Health Education Branch, National Institute of Mental Health, reports: "The number of women who use 'pills' to cope with stress increased almost 30 percent from 1972-1974; among males there was no similar increase." Testimony presented by Hall before the U.S. Congress, Senate, Committee on Human Resources, February 1, 1979, p. 16.

124. Frankie Cadwell, advertising executive, quoted by Komisar, in op. cit., p. 213.

125. "Sexist Ads," *Media Report to Women* 6, no. 12 (December 1, 1978):2.

126. Larry Michie, "TV Riding Surprise Bonanza in '79," *Variety*, March 28, 1979, p. 1.

127. Carroll Carroll, "And Now A Word From. . . ," *Variety*, December 6, 1978.

128. Stephanie Harrington, "Mary Hartman, The Unedited All-American Unconscious," *Ms.*, 4, no. 11 (May 1976):53.

129. Philip H. Dougherty, "Advertising," *New York Times*, March 31, 1978.

130. Lois Gould, *Not Responsible for Personal Articles* (New York: Random House, 1973), p. 160.

131. Margaret Hennig and Anne Jardim, *The Managerial Woman* (New York: Doubleday, 1977); see, particularly, chap. 2, "Patterns of Difference and Their Implications," pp. 11-34.

132. "Both sides of abortion issue sit and talk," *Boston Globe*, May 16, 1979.

133. This description came from a female employee of a station in an eastern, metropolitan location, who did not wish to be identified by name. She responded to a questionnaire sent to a random sample of 75 women whose promotions were reported in the pages of *Variety* during 1978.

134. Barbara Walters, quoted in Hilliard, op. cit., p. 296.

135. Frank Beermann, "After 20 Years, ABC Daytime Is (Relatively) Secure As No. 1," *Variety*, October 23, 1978. Also, see Robert Lindsey, "Soap Operas: Men Are Tuning In," *New York Times*, February 21, 1979.

136. Lindsey, op. cit.

137. Douglas, op. cit., p. 3.

138. See Manuela Soares, *The Soap Opera Book* (New York: Crown Publishers, 1978); Dan Wakefield, *All Her Children: The real life story of America's favorite soap opera* (New York: Doubleday, 1976); Madeline Edmondson and David Rounds, *From Mary Noble to Mary Hartman: The Complete Soap Opera Book* (New York: Stein and Day, 1976); Raymond William Stedman, *The Serials: Suspense and Drama by Installment* (Norman: University of Oklahoma Press, 1971).

139. Paula S. Fass, "Television as a Cultural Document," in *Television as a Cultural Force*, ed. Richard Adler and Douglas Cater (New York: Praeger, 1976), p. 44.

140. Sue Cameron, "Police Drama: Women Are on the Case," *Ms.*, October 1974, pp. 104-8.

141. Dickinson read a number of letters she had received from young women on a Johnny Carson "Tonight" show interview, February 1979.

142. *Update*, op. cit., pp. 5-6.

143. Karl E. Meyer, "The Barbie Doll as Sex Symbol," *The Saturday Review of Literature*, November 10, 1977, p. 45.

144. "TV's Super Women," *Time*, November 22, 1976, p. 67.

145. "Farrah Fawcett-Majors Makes Me Want to Scream," *Redbook*, September 1977, p. 102.

146. Bill Davidson, "The Farrah Phenomenon," May 21, 1977, in *TV Guide, The First 25 Years*, op. cit., p. 261.

147. Russel B. Nye, *The Unembarrassed Muse; The Popular Arts in America, Two Centuries of American Life, A Bicentennial History* (New York: Dial Press, 1970), p. 416.

148. Respondents in a *TV Guide* poll responded most frequently (23 percent), that they preferred situation comedies and wanted to see more of them. Myles Callum, "What Viewers Love/Hate About Television: An Exclusive TV Guide Poll," *TV Guide*, May 12, 1979, pp. 6-12.

149. Les Brown, "Situation Comedy Still Most Popular TV Staple," *New York Times*, April 4, 1979.

150. "Where's the Magic," *Newsweek*, March 19, 1979, p. 98.

151. Herbert J. Gans, *Popular Culture and High Culture: An Analysis and Evaluation of Taste* (New York: Basic Books, 1974), p. 88.

152. Richard S. Salant, "Broadcast News: What People Need, Not What They Want," *Variety*, January 3, 1979.

153. Tony Thomopoulos, president of ABC Entertainment, quoted in Bob Knight, "Tony T Charts Direction Of New ABC Programs," *Variety*, February 14, 1979. Also, see "Tony T Claims ABC Projects Are 'Important,'" *Variety*, January, 24, 1979.

154. Philip Terzian, "Now, Moral Issues, Homosexuality as Chic Malady, etc." *Commonweal*, February 16, 1979, pp. 82-83.

155. Aljean Harmetz, "CBS Moves 'Paper Chase' in Effort to Raise Ratings," *New York Times*, January 16, 1979.

156. Paul L. Klein, former vice president of NBC, is responsible for the least-objectionable-program theory of programming. See, Paul L. Klein, "Why you watch, what you watch, when you watch"; TV Guide, The First 25 Years, op. cit., pp. 186-88.

157. John J. O'Connor, "TV Executives: 'The Buck Does Not Stop Here,'" *New York Times*, December 17, 1978.

158. Quoted in Peter Barry Chowka, "Television: A Medium beyond Control? Part 1," *New Age*, April 1979, p. 40.

159. Bob Knight, "Padded, Formula Minis May Wear Out Credibility," *Variety*, December 22, 1978.

160. Les Brown, "Paley Bids Rivals Cooperate to Offer Quality Programs During Prime Time," *New York Times*, February 19, 1979.

161. Carol Lawson, "A Spate of Shows Awaits Cue to Enter," *New York Times*, February 7, 1979.

162. "Strong, Assertive Women Central To Rose & Asseyev, Gal Partners," *Variety*, March 14, 1979. Jane Fonda is one of a growing number of established professionals newly interested in television projects. Fay Kanin, who wrote and co-produced "Friendly Fire" for the 1979 season, has been signed to a contract by ABC. Esther Shapiro, ABC entertainment vice-president, is a writer who has brought a new emphasis on women's concerns to the program schedule.

NINE

IMAGES, IMMIGRANTS, AND THEIR PRESS

Lawrence M. Martin

AMERICAN MELTING POT: MYTH OR REALITY?

Daniel Boorstin, in his *The Image: A Guide to Pseudoevents in America*, says that American journalists are preoccupied with carefully planted pseudoevents masquerading as exciting news. The rising tide of these pseudoevents is one of the explanations why life among ethnic minorities is underreported in the American press. They can't offer, and don't have the inclination, to stage events in order to attract the attention of the press. Just as pseudoevents tend to overshadow spontaneous events, so do celebrities (Boorstin calls them human pseudoevents) tend to overshadow heroes.[1]

The Czech, German, Polish, or Italian ethnics—the focus of this study—don't have much to offer to the drama-oriented press, and neither their problems nor their culture are much in evidence in the U.S. media. By reading the Boston newspapers, for example, one wouldn't assume that Boston has a large Italian and Polish community. An American journalist, if he wants to succeed in the highly competitive business of print and broadcast journalism, has to "see the whole national picture, and to escape mere regional, ethnic, or denominational views."[2] The Polish, Czech, German, or Italian ethnics, with their ordinary profile and silent-minority life style, do not stimulate American journalists to pay systematic attention to their problems.

Ethnic neighborhoods usually do not like interviewers. They resent the media, because they feel that almost all spokesmen they meet from the worlds of intellect have disdain for them. If something dramatic happens in the ethnic neighborhood, the press reports seem to be consistently unfair. They print not only their side and perception of the story, but even popularize the view of the villain. The Anglo-American cult of press freedom and objectivity, something the ethnics would be willing to accept in a friendly, theoretical discussion, appears ridiculous and unjust in a real situation in which they have been victimized.

Very few stories then, in the daily press or in the broadcast media deal with life and problems of the European ethnics—unless, of course, they have the dimension of the extraordinary. The outbreak of the racial violence in the 1960s gave the blacks media exposure they had never received before. After all, racial violence made big news. The mass media suddenly discovered that under the surface of social harmony, there were 20 million blacks, mostly undereducated and underemployed. The growing number of Hispanics, a great many of whom enter the United States illegally, offer the press the opportunity to investigate the potential threat of a foreign element spreading quickly throughout the body with an Anglo-Saxon brain. Again, it is a delicious food for the action- and drama-oriented press.

During the past ten years, American broadcasters have become more careful in their portrayal of ethnics. Understandably, television, as a profit-making enterprise financed by commercials, doesn't want to offend potential buyers with derogatory remarks or pictures. The stigma of a German war criminal or an Italian gangster still survives, but stereotyping of major villains has tended to be switched from blacks, Chinese, or Indians to white Anglo-Saxon types.

According to the *Statistical Abstract of the United States, 1978*, listing the number of immigrants by country of last permanent residence, the United States admitted, from 1820 to 1977, 6,968,000 immigrants from Germany, 5,285,000 from Italy, 510,000 from Poland, and 137,000 from Czechoslovakia. In 1976, for example, the Immigration and Naturalization Service reported 398,613 new immigrants. Out of the 73,035 Europeans, only 267 came from Czechoslovakia; 3,192, from Poland; 6,642, from Germany; and 7,993, from Italy. Great Britain, with 11,444 imigrants, remained the major European country of origin.[3]

Soon after his arrival, the new immigrant faces the barriers of a different language, outlook, food, family pattern, and morality.

American culture, emphasizing objectivity, and technical and scientific proficiency, is afraid of instincts, emotions, and imagination. The dominant principles of American democracy and social life have their roots in the Anglo-Saxon traditions. The nativist American expects newcomers to approve of, and adapt to, the existing social rules, and most immigrants try to fulfill that expectation, although it is a painful process.

Indeed, Europeans, particularly those coming from a Communist society, have to learn rules they have never before been exposed to: how to find a job or an apartment; how to buy a car or an insurance policy; even where and how to buy their own burial plots. An American feels responsible for himself. He wants to be left on his own, to cultivate his individuality. For an Eastern European—at least in the beginning—it is a frightening experience.

Mass media, in the adaptation and assimilation process, play an important role, but they do not necessarily make it easier. The national and local media—especially television—provide the immigrant with his first glimpses of a society rife with violent confrontations, kidnappings, murders, and psychopathic mayhem. Very few entertainment or even news heroes have positive appeal. Mass media, by revealing, with great relish, every mistake or blunder of the federal, state, or local government, contribute to the immigrant's chaotic state of mind. He is looking for permanent values he can respect, adopt, and stick to. Instead, he gets a picture of a society constantly on the move, abandoning, from one day to another, policies and practices that didn't work; attacking politicians today who yesterday were hailed for their wisdom; and glorifying individuals who make headlines only because of notoriety earned as criminals.

The American press, subscribing to the adversary relationship with the government, is willing and ready, with few exceptions, to publish any secret or politically sensitive governmental document, regardless of the possible consequences for the United States abroad. In the United States, the Polish and the Czech-language press follow a totally different journalistic concept. With a clearly detectable patriotic undertone and pro-American bias, they have been zealous protagonists of the American way of life, and vigilant guardians of American national security. The writers and editors of the Czech and the Polish ethnic press went through historical experiences that made their anticommunism an integral part of political consciousness.

Starting with the first ehtnic publication, *Die Philadelphia*

Zeitung (*Philadelphia News*), a German bimonthly established by Benjamin Franklin in 1732, the ethnic press has gone through several stages directly related to the immigration process. During the eighteenth century and the first half of the nineteenth century, there emerged a relatively small number of ethnic publications. Toward the end of the nineteenth century and the beginning of the twentieth, with large immigrant groups coming from Central, Southern, and Eastern Europe, there was a rapid growth of ethnic periodicals, reaching a peak in 1917, with 1,323 titles. After World War I, the number of ethnic journals declined, and the process continued after World War II. By 1960, only 698 titles were published. As of 1975, Lubomyr and Anna T. Wynar, the authors of the *Encyclopedic Directory of Ethnic Newspapers and Periodicals*, registered 960 ethnic publications, with a total circulation of 9,063,362 copies, of which 386 were published in non-English languages, 246 were bilingual, and 328 were in English. The rise in publications between 1960 and 1975 may be accounted for by higher levels of ethnic consciousness in the country.

Of the four European ethnic groups under study, the Polish ethnic press in 1975 had the largest circulation (583,650), followed by the Italian ehtnic press (482,176), the German (437,484), and the Czech (164,302).[4]

These newspapers and periodicals are the spiritual force behind the ethnics; they help a newcomer to understand the new, unfamiliar environment, and they are the major binding factor helping each ethnic community to preserve its identity and cohesiveness.

THE POLISH ETHICS: AWAKENING GIANT OF AMERICAN POLITICS

Cruel Images

Once a very powerful country expanding from the Baltic to the Black Sea, Poland had been several times eliminated from the political map of Europe, occupied by Germans, Russians, and Austrians. This tragic experience forced many Poles to leave their country. In the late nineteenth century and the first two decades of the twentieth, most Polish immigrants came from the agricultural and rural, lower economic, classes, areas of Poland with little formal education. They were the last Europeans who came to the United States in large waves. The communities they built were homogeneous and relatively self-sufficient. Their reclusive lifestyle in part explains the prejudice and discrimination from other ethnic groups. An inseparable part of the Polish ethnic culture is the religion. Polish-Americans—overwhelmingly Catholic—worship their own saints and give the religious ceremonies a definite Polish slant. An in-depth look into the complexity of the Polish ethnicity reveals another interesting quality, namely, a strong sense of individualism and competitiveness, as well as high motivation. There is obvious determination, in the second and third generations of Polish-Americans, to break the isolationism and succeed in the competitive, achievement-oriented American society.[5]

Helena Znaniecki Lopata, the author of the *Polish Americans* (1967), estimated that some 12 million Americans of Polish descent live in the United States today, making them the country's largest Slavic group. A series of informal interviews with functionaries and members of the Polish group, done by the present writer in Boston in February and March 1979, revealed a vibrant community that has been largely ignored by the mass media, in part because of low visibility. Although only a fraction of those interviewed actively participate in the Polish community's life and read the Polish ethnic press regularly, all interviewees look with pride at their cultural heritage, and all of them feel offended by Polish jokes.

According to ethnic-humor expert Alan Dundes, of the University of California Folklore Department, Polish or Polack jokes embodying the lower-class white stereotypes originated in Germany. On the lists of Nazi extermination victims, during World War II, the Poles—perceived as poor, dirty, stupid, inept, and vulgar by Nazi propagandists—were on the top of the list of "inferior" persons, next to Jews, gypsies, and homosexuals.[6]

Although the volume of the Polish jokes has visibly decreased in recent years, they still circulate, even among intellectuals who wouldn't dare to utter an anti-Semitic remark or antiblack joke. As late as September 1978, a group of writers who put out a parody, *Not The New York Times*, during the printers' strike, didn't hesitate to include a few anti-Polish jokes. Poles are still vulnerable. The *New York Times* reported, on February 5, 1979, a confrontation that happened at a public meeting of the selectmen's finance committee in Deerfield, Massachusetts, the previous day. When the police chief, John Skronski, asked for a pay increase, one of the selectmen said: "Do you expect a Polack to make as much as an Irishman?"

When dealing with prejudice, many ethnic Americans simply withdrew from competition with the rest of the society, and this was for a long time the case with Polish-Americans. Like many Czechs, they didn't have a highly positive self-image. Instead of fighting the prejudice through positive action, they hid in the safe environment of their communities and angrily criticized the hostile outside world. The Polish ethnics charge that what television presents as the American family and way of life is a fabulous fantasy of the dominant culture, an elaborate delusion, cultural conditioning, and media manipulation.[7]

Some detectable anti-Catholicism, another barrier the Polish ethnic community has to fight, involves class as well as religion. It has been characterized as the anti-Semitism of the intellectual, and it has become more pronounced in recent years as the groups have lined up on the opposite sides of such issues as abortion and desegregation.

Alexander Janta, a Polish writer, explains the original inferiority complex of many Polish-Americans as a result of their own ignorance of Polish cultural heritage, and widespread antiintellectualism: "In spite of the efforts of a few national intelligentsia, . . . an overwhelming majority of Poles in America can express their Polonism in relation to the American background by little more than costume, dance or food."[8]

In order to change the status and image of Polish-Americans, several Polish ethnic organizations (including the American Council of Polish Cultural Clubs, the Polish-American Congress, and the Kosciuszko Foundation), starting in 1970, undertook a well-concerted, systematic, long-term campaign, called Project POLE, against the Polish jokes disseminated by American mass media. By ridiculing their peasant culture and presenting Polish-Americans as dumb and ignorant, the mass media were spreading the message of prejudice. The Kosciuszko Foundation asked the public to send it information about examples of Polish jokes, including names, dates, and places involved, and descriptions of the events, and made it clear that newspapers and broadcast media disseminating anti-Polish jokes would have to face countermeasures, including economic boycott. The Polish business community joined the effort. Edward J. Piszek, president of Mrs. Paul's Kitchens, Inc., of Philadelphia (manufacturing frozen foods), donated $500,000 in 1973 for an advertising campaign explaining to the American public why Polish-Americans were "every bit as good as other Americans."[9]

The election of the Polish Karol Cardinal Wojtyla as the 265th pope, in 1978, gave the Polish community in the United States a fresh surge of pride, and the American press an opportunity to explore not only the life in Communist Poland, but also the Polish minority in the United States.

Wojtyla visited the United States in September 1969, and again in 1976, to attend the bicentennial celebration. The press coverage of his visits was rather scanty. When he became Pope John Paul II, the event had a galvanizing effect on the Polish-American self-image and on the Polish public image in the United States. National and local mass media published a great amount of materials about Polish cultural, literary, and scientific achievements, and contributions to American national well-being. Zbigniew Brzezinski, President Carter's national security advisor, who was born in Poland reportedly said: "I am aware that my cultural, religious and literary past is very much connected with the 1,000-year-old history of a people who have fought very hard to maintain their identity. . . . The choice of a Polish Pope was a thrilling event especially since I know and admire the man deeply."

There is no doubt that the era of the Polish Pope will stimulate greater assertiveness by the American press in regard to the problems and life of the Polish ethnic group, and greater sensitivity toward the Polish ethnic pride so often, in the past, offended by vulgar Polish jokes.

Polonia (the title describing all Poles living abroad) has mixed feelings about Poland. A peak in Polonia's identification with Poland occurred in the years surrounding World War I. The Yalta Treaty of 1945, which gave a substantial part of the Polish historical territories to the Soviet Union, provoked many protests by Polish-Americans. When the Communist regime was firmly established a few years later, the official contact between American Polonia and Poland nearly ceased for more than a decade. Since the early 1970s, the Polish Iron Curtain was gradually lifted, making the human contact between families in Poland and America possible. Economic progress in Poland is usually mentioned by Polish-Americans as a positive achievement, but the community remains distinctly anti-Communist, objecting to the paucity of political, economic, artistic, and religious freedoms. Leaders of the Polish-American community do not oppose limited contact with Polish cultural institutions, or growing human contact between Poland and Polonia, but their ultimate goal remains the recovery of Polish political independence and freedom.[10]

The Communist government in Warsaw realizes the growing visibility and influence of the Polish ethnic community in the United States, and, undoubtedly, would like to use it for its own political purposes. The Polonia Society of Warsaw, for example, is officially a nonpolitical institution uniting Polonians around the world. While supporting and organizing cultural and educational cooperation between Poland and Polonia, it hopes that the ethnic ties will gradually transmute into support for the Communist regime. The political, and to a degree, the cultural gap between Polonia and Poland is too wide today to make the potential threat a reality.

The Polish-American Press

The origin of the Polish ethnic press goes back to 1843, when the first periodical, called *Poland Historical, Literary, Monumental and Picturesque*, was established. The first publication in Polish—*Echo z Polski* (Echo from Poland)—appeared 20 years later in New York. In 1892 the number of titles rose to 50; by the turn of the century it increased to 75; and after World War I, the Polish community supported 82 publications claiming over 1.2 million readers.

After World War II, the number of publications slowly decreased. In 1960 it was still proportionately higher than that of other ethnic groups. While the Polish-Americans formed 12 percent of the non-English-speaking population, they were responsible for 22 percent of the foreign-press circulation.[11] By 1975, Lubomyr Wynar registered 53 Polish-American journals, with a total circulation of 583,650—the third highest, next to the Jewish and the Spanish ethnic press.

Before World War II, the Polish-language press reflected the heterogeneity of the community as well as of language. Many newspapers addressing the lower classes slipped into a "combination of regional, lower class, and Americanized language."[12] For the new immigrant, it was an unpleasant surprise, and in the following years there has been a visible improvement in the purity of the language. Several publications now print articles in both Polish and English, as a service to the old, Polish-speaking generation, and as a stimulant for the young.

Polish-American publishers offer their readers a variety of publications, starting with papers addressing the general public, and ending with those directed at a specialized audience like doctors or farmers. Like the publications of other ethnic groups, the Polish ethnic press is characterized by short-lived papers. Newspapers started by individual without experience or training in business management usually survived only a few years or even months and attracted only a limited number of readers.

Among the most popular and influential Polish ethnic publications at this writing in 1979, are three daily papers: *Dziennik Polski* (Polish Daily News) of Detroit, with a circulation of 16,000; *Dziennik Zwiazkowy* (Polsih Daily Zgoda) of Chicago, circulation 20,000; and *Nowy Dziennik* (Polish Daily News) of New York, circulation 6,500 serving the needs of Polish-Americans in the eastern United States.

Gwiazda Polarna (Northern Star) is a bilingual weekly paper claiming a circulation of 22,000, and is published in Stevens Point, Wisconsin. The front page of a typical issue (March 3, 1979) shows heavy emphasis on international news ("Chinese Invasion of Vietnam"; "Tragedy in Kabul"; "Pope John Paul II in Mexico"; "Private Operation To Free Americans in Iran"), and ethnic news ("Polish Demonstration in front of the Polish Consulate in New York"). The newspaper prints a variety of well-written human-interest stories ("Prehistoric Animals"; "The Mediterranean Is Ill"; "Natural Medicine"), and cultural and historical pieces ("The Chopin Cult"; "Number of Polish Kings"). One page is devoted entirely to "News From and About Poland." The March 3 issue also reveals that *Gwiazda Polarna* is serializing books by Polish authors (in this issue, Maria Dobrowska: Nights and Days). One and a half pages out of the 16 are devoted to answering readers' letters.

ZGODA (Unity), a semimonthly printed in Chicago, is the largest Polish publication in the United States, claiming a circulation of 160,000. It is an official organ of the Polish National Alliance, covering Polish ethnic social, cultural, and sports activities, and general news. The newspaper emphasizes, according to its editor, "Polish-American participation in the mainstream of American life."

Polish journals reflect the continuing effort of the Polish-American community to uplift the Polish image and paralyze the Polish joke syndrome. The monthly *Polish-American Journal*, for example, printed on December 8, 1978, a front-page story, "Free Speech Doesn't Cover Ethnic Slurs," explaining the implications of a decision by Florida's Third District Court of Appeals, that "although the freedom of speech is a cherished civil liberty, . . . it is by no means an absolute right." The case involved a dietary supervisor at Jackson Memorial Hospital who had been making anti-Semitic wisecracks.[13] The following issue of the *Polish-American Journal*, on January 8, 1979, criticized Senator Henry Jackson for a joke he made about Pope John Paul II, during a National Restaurant Month banquet on October 23, 1978, in Vancouver ("The Catholic Church, now that it has a Polish Pope, might substitute vodka for wine in an attempt to increase church attendance"), and printed also Senator Jackson's apology saying: "I can only say that this was all done in jest."[14]

A month later, the *Polish-American Journal* printed another front-page story about a high school teacher in Brownesville, Pennsylvania, who prepared a historical test comprised of anti-Polish jokes ("What happened to the Polish National Library?—Someone stole the book!"). The newspaper also reported that a spokesman for the Polish Heritage Club petitioned the Pennsylvania State Human Relations Commission to pursue the matter, on the grounds that it is "a form of child abuse."[15]

The primary functions of the Polish-American press today are to record community life, help develop Polish culture, and build role models in the highly competitive American society. The press reflects the status competition among Poles of all classes and proudly describes the stories of Polish-Americans who succeeded in attaining political, financial, scientific, and societal prestige.

AMERICANS WITH A SLAVIC ACCENT: THE CZECHS

According to Vera Laska's *The Czechs in America, 1633—1977*, 452,812 people claimed the Czech mother tongue in 1970, and barely 80,000 Czechs born abroad live in this country.[16]

In comparison with the Polish, Italian, and even German topics covered by the U.S. national and, for example, the local Boston press, the Czech problem received, in 1978 and during the first three months of 1979, the least attention.

The Czechoslovak experiment with democratic socialism, the Soviet invasion of 1968, and the following prosecution of the liberal elements in Czechoslovakia, with strong aspects of human tragedy, were natural stories for the American press. Starting in 1970, the interest in Czechoslovak affairs rapidly declined. American correspondents stationed in Prague were either expelled or transferred to other, journalistically more interesting countries. What American readers now get from the press on Czechoslovakia are occasional stories about the continuing persecution of human-rights activists, the intellectual stagnation of the country, or the nostalgic beauty of Prague.

Despite the Anglo-Saxon neglect of Eastern Europeans, the prevailing feeling among Czech ethnics favors total absorption into the American mainstream, rather than extensive cultural pluralism. Josef Martinek, in an article published in *Stolet Jednoty*

CSA (One Hundred Years of the Czechoslovak Society of America) in Cicero, Illinois in 1955, explained why Czechs do not feel that they live in a foreign country, and by and large consider themselves "indivisible and a natural component of the American nation," not a "national minority in the European sense." In addition: "They feel that America is their homeland, that it belongs to them because they helped in building America, they fought for their new country and died for it—in all wars that the last century had brought upon America."[17]

Few Czechs came to America during the colonial period. They started arriving in large numbers following the defeat of the 1848 revolution against Hapsburg absolutism. Around the turn of the twentieth century, there were some 150,000 first- and second-generation Czechs living in the United States, two-thirds of them in the northwestern part of the country. Only 1.2 percent of the newcomers were illiterate. Regardless of their political and ideological beliefs—and quite a few subscribed to radical political doctrines—they became deeply loyal to their new homeland. Thomas G. Masaryk's campaign for Czechoslovak independence, enthusiastically supported by Czech and Slovak ethnic organizations in the United States, resulted in the establishment of the Czechoslovak Republic on October 28, 1918. The new country, grateful for the American sympathy and support, adopted many principles of the American democracy. The fact that the first president of the new republic, Masaryk, was married to Charlotte Garrigue, an American, symbolized a special bond between the two countries.

During World War I, the number of Czech immigrants rapidly declined. In 1917, for example, only 327 Czechs came to the United States, even though many Czechs were outside their homeland. The restrictive Emergency Quota Act adopted by the Congress in May of 1921 further limited the number of Czech immigrants. Between 1920 and 1930, the number of Czechs living in the United States declined from 234,000 to 201,000. One of the 20,000 refugees who fled the country under the threat of Nazi occupation, only a few thousand found refuge in the United States.[18]

The post-World War II immigration from Czechoslovakia came in two waves: the Communist takeover in February 1948 initiated political refuge for many non-Communist politicians, scholars, and professionals; and the Soviet invasion of Czechoslovakia in 1968, crushing the dream of democratic socialism, forced several thousand Czechoslovak political refugees—including former Communist Party members—to find a new home in the United States. All three last waves of refugees (in 1938, 1948, and 1968) were politically motivated and characterized by a high percentage of intellectuals, professionals, and skilled workers who found jobs with relative ease. Just like other post-World War II newcomers from Eastern Europe, most of the Czech immigrants are distinctly anti-Communist. For them, communism is not a theoretical, potential threat; it has, rather, a repulsive, earthy smell of the physical experience they went through.

What do Americans think about Czechs? Travel guides, with their simplistic explanations of foreign cultures, teach the traveler what to expect, and, to a degree, reflect and support existing stereotypes and images among nations. *Fodor's Czechoslovakia, 1971* is an illustration of the American image of Czechs. The author finds them rather complex, "highly sophisticated," but not "merry." They are not amusing, although they have the ability to laugh at themselves. But the author warns the reader not to be fooled, because every Czech has something of "Good Soldier Schweik" in himself; you can never be sure whether he is an idiot or a genius. Czechs supposedly have "passive aggressiveness"; they are "eager to help," but only if everything is done their way. As for relations between Czechs and Americans, he makes an observation that Czechs and Slovaks understand the "down-to-earth, practical ways of Americans."[19]

And how do the Czechs perceive the Americans? The Audience and Public Opinion Research Department of Radio Free Europe, in Munich, published, in September 1970, results of a research study exploring the Czech and Slovak self-images and the Czech and Slovak images of the Americans, Germans, Russians, and Chinese. Prior to the Soviet invasion of Czechoslovakia, Czechs saw themselves as "peace-loving," and to a lesser extent, "intelligent," "hard-working," and "advanced." Surprisingly, they didn't consider bravery as an essential element of their national character, probably because, since the Battle on the White Mountain (1618), they have not had any occasion to fight wars as independent nations. "In the course of history," the authors of the study state, "Czechs had to learn to live under the rule of other nations for hundreds of years." They did not indulge in "wishful thinking as is often evidenced in exaggerated national self-appraisals.

The results of the survey further revealed that the Czech and Slovak self-images had a high positive correlation only with their image of Americans. Actually, Czechs and Slovaks had a more positive emotional image of Americans than was true of their self-images. Among Czechs, Americans scored high in regard to being "practical" (74 percent), "intelligent" (68 percent), and "generous"

(66 percent). Only 22 percent of Czechs and Slovaks thought of Americans as "domineering," and 36 percent, as "brave."[20] The remarkable correlation between the Czech self-image and the Czech image of Americans, to a degree, explains why many Czechs in the United States, after a relatively short adjustment period, don't have a feeling of living in a foreign country.

The Czech-American Press

The Czech ethnic press spontaneously reflects this feeling of sympathy. The origin of the Czech ethnic press on the American continent goes back to January 1860, when Frantisek Korizek started publishing a semimonthly (later a weekly) called *Slowan Amerikansky* (American Slav) with some 450 subscribers. Fifty years later, the Czech ethnic community, with some 150,000 members, supported about 90 regular publications across the country, with the political slant ranging from conservative to distinctly socialist.[21]

Since then, the number of Czech publications has been gradually decreasing. Vojtech Duben, in his study *Czech and Slovak Press Outside Czechoslovakia in 1978*, lists 45 Czech periodicals published in the United States, most of them monthlies and quarterlies.[22] The only daily newspaper is *Denni Hlasatel* (Daily Bohemian Herald), published in Chicago. With its origin going back to 1891, *Denni Hlasatel* is the oldest continuing Czech daily in the world. Over the past 20 years, *Denni Hlasatel* has lost 54,000 subscribers, and as of May 1979, its circulation was 6,800 on weekdays and 50,000 on Sundays.[23]

The weekly paper *Americke Listy* (American Newspaper), printed by Universum Sokol Publications in New York, traces its origin to 1874. Its circulation has dropped from 14,450 in 1970 to 1,600 in 1979. It pays attention not only to the major affairs affecting the life of the Czech ethnic group in the United States, but also to the situation in Czechoslovakia, international relations, and the continuing competition between the Soviet Union and the United States. The content analysis of four consecutive issues, between March 9 and March 30, 1979, reveals that each front page contains a lengthy editorial dealing with a major international issue ("Chinese Involvement in Vietnam," March 9; "Italian Election," March 23; "Austrian President Visiting Czechoslovakia," March 30), or a domestic U.S. issue ("Is the Next Mayor of Chicago to Be a Woman?," March 16). All 19 front-page stories published during the period under investigation covered international issues, with an emphasis on American foreign policy toward the Soviet bloc ("American Foreign Policy," March 9), the Middle East negotiations ("The Victory of Reason," March 16), and American-Czechoslovak relations ("U.S. Embassy in Prague Celebrating the Memory of T.G. Masaryk," March 23).

Pages 2 and 3 are usually devoted to the latest developments in Czechoslovakia, including the regular short-news column "About Czechoslovakia." Another regular column, "International Survey," on page 4 summarizes major international developments. Rather than following the American journalistic tradition of factual, straightforward reporting, *Americke Listy* presents news mixed with editorial comment. The paper also carries sports, culture, an ethnic-news column, and a few ads offering mostly products and services of business enterprises owned by Americans of Czech origin. *Americke Listy* is distinctly anti-Communist, politically conservative, and deeply patriotic. It favors a strong military presence in trouble spots around the world, and more effective support for Israel against the growing power of leftist Arabic regimes and movements. Among the American politicians who didn't find enthusiastic support by the Czech ethnic press in 1978 were Senator George McGovern and the U.S. delegate to the United Nations, Andrew Young—McGovern, for the conciliatory tone of his speeches delivered in Cuba during his visit there in 1978; Young, for his comment on the jailing of Soviet dissident Anatoly Scharansky, when he said that the United States has its own "political prisoners." "The latest controversy around Andrew Young," *Americke Listy* wrote, "is not the first and certainly not the last one in his political career. This black politician from Georgia—the state of Jimmy Carter—who is Carter's personal friend, acts in his present role, as a high diplomat, rather undiplomatically. Maybe he does it on purpose. Quite often he has been criticized for it here in America as well as abroad. He said a few times that he would resign if President Carter is not satisfied with his performance. It is on the President now to decide whether he will tolerate Young's views."[24]

The regular reader of the weekly *Americke Listy* would find that, although the paper reports on the growing visibility of the European ethnic groups and calls the bloc of their voters "the sleeping giant of American politics," the most distinctive and surprising observation he would make is the total absence of any criticism of the Anglo-Saxon majority and its policy toward minorities. Judging from the Czech ethnic press, the Czech element in the United States sees itself integrated and absorbed into the national fabric.

ITALIANS: VERSUS THE MAFIA IMAGE

The Italian tradition in American culture is a relatively young phenomenon. In 1850, only about 4,000 Italian-born people lived in America; in Boston, for example, it was a few hundred people. For the most part, Italians immigrated in the late nineteenth and the early twentieth century, 85 percent of them from southern Italy.

By the late nineteenth century, many members of the Northern and Western European minorities improved their economic status to such a degree that they started a noticeable movement out of the worst slums. Their places were filled by such as the Irish and by Polish, Russian, Italian, and other newcomers from Southern and Eastern Europe.

The Italians were the largest of all new-immigrant groups. Extremely poor and largely illiterate, they lived on a small portion of their income, and either saved the rest or sent money back to relatives in Italy. They did have a high return rate, much higher than other ethnic groups.

The "birds of passage," as they were called, faced an unhospitable reception. They were willing to work for the lowest wages, stayed away from the incipient organized labor movement, and had an inherent distrust of police. Their lack of experience in public affairs and political apathy separated them from immigrants from other parts of Europe. They always thought of themselves as Neapolitans, Sicilians, or Venetians, rather than Italians. Clustered in little-Italy sections in California or eastern cities, they maintained their cultural closeness as a self-protection against the hostile Anglo-Saxon world.

The family, rather than any social gathering or community organization, was the center of life. Though the family provided a great amount of security, it did not stimulate the younger members to venture out too far from the family circle. Education and personal achievement were hesitantly recommended only to the male members of the family, and parents sometimes felt that too much formal education would place children above them.

The exposure to the American way of life resulted in a visible gap between the first-generation Italians and their children, particularly in the decades following the "100 percent Americanism" movement of the 1920s and the experience of World War II.[25] Many aspects of the family-oriented Italian culture were changed in favor of Americanism. On the whole, the young were brought up with Italian traditions, but either with a greater or lesser knowledge of the language. But Italy was a country they did not know, and their loyalties, like those of most second- and third-generation Americans, were directed toward the land of their birth rather than the land of their ancestors.

America prides itself as a pluralistic society of tolerance, with many ethnic groups preserving their cultural heritage, yet coexisting and molding with others. For an Italian-American, however, the cultural difference from mainstream America is a handicap. He has been too often portrayed by mass media in a relatively fixed character, as a lover type or a greasy, uneducated individual, usually involved in organized crime. The casting is not new. Robert J. Ward, the author of a study analyzing 118 works of American fiction between 1890 and 1919, found that many figures of Italian background were pictured usually as cowardly, treacherous, and violent.[26] The pre-World War II radio programs and films adopted this stereotype, and it survived even in the 1970s. While the "dumb Swede" has faded away; while the American Jewish community, through well-organized measures, has driven most anti-Semitic portrayals out of the public arena; and while middle-class America is unwilling to listen to jokes ridiculing racial minorities, America still indulges in defamatory Italian jokes.

In an article published in the *New York Times Magazine*, under the title "It's Still Hard to Grow Up Italian," on December 17, 1978, Elizabeth Stone, who is half Italian and half Jewish, recalls an incident when a man who assumed she was entirely Jewish, in view of her academic achievement, expressed surprise to find out she was half Italian. When she interviewed an Italian investment banker, he admitted that "if I want certain things in life like a college education, I have to be almost emotionally distant from my family, consciously independent."

National media reinforce the image of Italians as people who are not too bright, or who make pasta all their life. Authors of television commercials portraying a fat, emotional Italian mama serving spicy meatballs or spaghetti may not be discriminating in their minds, but it is a subtle form of negative stereotyping. While Jews are considered to be into books, working-class Italians are perceived as a part of the Mafia, and a small minority do not object. It gives them at least some sense of power.[27]

A comprehensive survey to gather demographic, economic, cultural, and attitudinal indicators among Italian-Americans, sponsored by the national Italian-American Foundation and conducted from September to November 1977, revealed very strong and consistently negative relationships between the respondents' Italian identification and their socioeconomic status. For example, 59 percent of those making less than $10,000 a year are married to full-blooded Italian-Americans, while only 41 percent of those making over $40,000 are. The most important part of the survey, dealing with the preservation of the Italian culture and the Italian-American image, revealed that 56 percent of the respondents or members of their families, including college-educated professionals, had experienced discrimination because of their ethnic background. They particularly were concerned with fair portrayal of Italians on TV and in the movies. The authors of the survey were able to conclude that the respondents felt most strongly on the following five areas of concern: maintenance of ethnic heritage (55 percent); Italian-Americans' image portrayal (34 percent); Italian-American representation in government (31 percent); recognition of Italian-American contributions (20 percent); and diversity of ethnic groups in neighborhoods (13 percent).[28]

The resurgence of Italian ethnic pride—a phenomenon of the last decade or so—seems to affect the third generation, usually totally absorbed in mainstream America. They oppose the Mafia-spaghetti-meatball image and strive for full acceptance in the political, economic, or cultural life of the country.

Without inferring distortion in the press, but recognizing how sparsely foreign affairs are covered, apart from sensational matters, one realizes that Italian-Americans are not enhanced by many items. News stories dealing with Italy, published in prominent journals like the *New York Times*, *Time* magazine, or in local Massachusetts newspapers like the *Boston Globe* or the *Herald-American*, during the period between October 1, 1978, and March 1979, painted a picture of a country troubled by continuing strikes, political terrorism by the Red Brigades, babies killed by a mysterious disease in Naples, financial scandals; and governed by political acrobats who were just able to form the country's 41st post-Fascist government.

The Italo-American Press

Since 1849, when the first Italian journal, *L'ECO d'ITALIA*, appeared in New York the Italian-American press has gone through several stages, reaching a peak in the beginning of the twentieth century and slowly declining afterward. Most papers became weeklies and specialized in folksy advice and comprehensive coverage of local news. With the progress of integration, the press was carrying more and more features in English. American-born children of immigrant families, educated in English, preferred

American journals, and when their parents died, subscriptions to ethnic newspapers—particularly those printed in Italian—were not renewed.

Just like the journals of other ethnics, the Italian-American publications today function as a unifying element, reflecting political, cultural, social, and, to a degree, economic interests and activities of the community.

Out of the existing 48 Italian journals, only one—*Il Progresso Italo-Americano* (Italian American Progress) of New York—is a daily. Established in 1880, *II Progresso Italo-Americano*, with a circulation of 69,735, today provides readers with international, national, as well as local New York news and stresses also the news coverage of events in Italy.

The Italian press around Boston is still quite active. The largest publication is the *Post Gazette* (formerly, *Gazetta del Massachusetts*), an 83-year-old weekly printed in English. The newspaper claims a circulation of 14,900. It comes with 16-20 pages of international, national, and local news, including sports, travel, culture, Italian-society news, and a column dealing with Italian cooking. Content analysis of four subsequent issues published between April 6 and April 27, 1979, reveals that the paper systematically emphasizes positive achievements of Italian-American politicians, writers, artists, and businessmen. Out of the 23 front-page stories, 11 belong to that category. Even the inside pages are filled with many stories of Italian-Americans who were appointed to important positions or received awards—reflecting the motto of the editorial, "They Make Us Proud," published in the April 27, 1979, issue.

A series of interviews done by this writer among members of the Italian community in and around Boston confirmed growing cultural self-awareness and a positive outlook. Most interviewees thought, however, that Italian-Americans do not always get the fairest shake in the media. "Organized crime involves people of various ethnic backgrounds, but we have to pay the bill," was a typical reaction.

Italian ethnic newspapers, including the Boston-based *Post Gazette*, expressed their indignation when they found out how the federal Urban Development Action Grant (UDAG) deals with individuals of Italian origin. UDAG, a $400-million-a-year program, operating under the jurisdiction of the Department of Housing and Urban Development, provides funding for urban-area projects. According to the information leaked to the press, UDAG considered running an FBI check on any applicant from New

Jersey, or anyone with an Italian surname, who would apply for a grant.[29]

In recent years, many Italian-American publications became actively involved in an antidiscrimination campaign. Among them is a national monthly called *I-AM Magazine*, which was established in 1976 as a rallying force for dissatisfied Italians who feel that they have been unfairly treated because of their origin. The editor, Ron de Paolo, points out that "many cases of discrimination are hard to pin down and almost impossible to eliminate through legal channels." *I-AM Magazine* exerts public pressure on the parties whom the community considers guilty of discrimination, and tries to insure that mass media, including television and motion pictures, portray the Italian-American community realistically without bias or slander.[30]

Another journal, called *Italia Magazine*, was expected to appear in Boston in the fall of 1979. The brainchild of Tony Cucchiara, a third-generation Italian-American who is not pleased with the way mass media cover Italian events, the projected magazine, with a planning staff of seven located in Boston and New York, intends to help Italian-Americans to rediscover their cultural identity. "When I visited Italy in 1973 I was impressed, astounded, and surprised at the treasures and brain power," Cucchiara says. "Many Italian-Americans do not realize what Italy has given to Western men in the past 500 years. . . . Yet, the anti-Italian bias persists."

GERMANS: THE INVISIBLE MINORITY

The German element has played a significant role in America's ethnic, cultural, scientific, economic, and journalistic history. After all, even the term Anglo-Saxon (according to Webster, a member of the Germanic, Ingwinian peoples: Angles, Saxons, and Jutes living in England before the Norman Conquest) indicates their ethnic closeness to the British. In that sense, it may be a contradiction to call Germans an ethnic minority. But they also showed remarkable peculiarities that clearly separated them from mainstream America.

Germans were for a long time considered the most independent, separatist, and the most disdainful of American culture, of all immigrants. According to John Arkas Hawgood, the author of *The Tragedy of German America*, they demonstrated "determined and conscious resistance against assimilation or Americanization."[31]

The first major wave of German immigrants, which arrived in America in the 1830s and after the unsuccessful revolution of 1848, consisted of a mixture of dissatisfied intellectuals, artisans, scholars, journalists, and laborers—a group with a relatively high level of education. They were proud of their German heritage and tended to create distinct German colonies preserving their culture and language. This period of the so-called hyphenated German-Americans, with demonstrative ethnic pride, lasted up to World War I.

In the words of Hawgood, they were hardly frontiersmen. They followed the American frontier at a "respectable distance," consolidating and improving what others had won.[32] The German settler encouraged his children to marry within the German community in order to paralyze, or at least to slow down, their assimilation process, and supposedly looked with disdain at the customs and mores of his native American contemporaries.

The relative quietness of the German America of the first decade of the twentieth century was interrupted by the eruption of World War I. Torn between their sympathy for Germany and the United States, many of them favored American neutrality, and until 1917 it was not a crime even to defend Germany's position. Several German ethnic organizations showed support for Germany's policy, and the German-American Alliance opposed any participation of America in the war.

The progress of the war, and particularly the U.S. declaration of war in 1917, dramatically changed the situation, and the growing anti-German mood silenced the isolationist voices. Everything German was publicly attacked, including names, literature, music, language—even frankfurters. Sauerkraut was renamed victory cabbage in many places. The German element was exposed to considerable official and public-opinion pressure equaling "the greatest trial that any foreign element in a country ever had to face."[33] Feelings of isolation and even many personal tragedies followed, like suicide cases, in the draft camps, among ethnic Germans.

The German immigrants who arrived after World War I became either quickly Americanized—and that was the majority—or remained visibly German. The anti-German mood disappeared, but the nineteenth-century ethnic pride and feeling of cultural superiority was gone, and by 1930 the hyphenated-German-American era was definitely over.

When Hitler came to power in 1933, he didn't find many enthusiastic supporters among the 6 million people of German descent in America—with the exception of a small group of recent immigrants and some economic victims of the Great Depression. The few admirers established the nationalistic Deutschamerikanischer Volksbund (German American National Union), propagandizing a close relationship and alliance between the United States and Nazi Germany. They helped to create the periodical *Das Neue Deutschland* (New Germany) and even emulated the Nazi SS troops by forming the so-called Ordnungs-Dienst units (Security Service). All this effort was in vain. The outbreak of the war in 1939, and America's entry into the war in December 1941, convinced the German-Americans that their place was firmly on the side of the Allies. But the experience of the war had undoubtedly a traumatic impact on them. When the Nazi regime collapsed and new immigrants started pouring into the United States, willingly or unwillingly, they kept a low profile, becoming a part of the invisible minority.

The German-American Press

In comparison with its Italian, Czech, or Polish counterpart, the German ethnic press has maintained much higher professional journalistic standards, but just like the press of these other ethnic communities, it has been essentially an American press published in a foreign language. With few exceptions, it remained financially and editorially independent from the influence of the mother country, and adopted the style, pattern, and commercial methods of the American press.[34]

No other ethnic group, except Jews, has been more interested and involved in journalism than the Germans. Three decades after the birth of the first continuous American newspaper, Benjamin Franklin established the *Philadelphische Zeitung* (Philadelphia Newspaper), which was addressed to the local German community in Philadelphia. It survived only a few issues, but the German-American press was now firmly established. It was the beginning of a remarkable history involving hundreds of publications, some of which lasted for more than a century.

The number of titles accelerated with the arrival of political refugees in the 1830s, and after 1848. The period between the end of the Civil War and the end of the nineteenth century witnessed the fastest expansion of the press, coinciding, of course, with the greatest influx of German immigrants. From its peak of 800 publications in the 1880s, the German ethnic press steadily declined, particularly after 1917, when the golden age of ethnic German journalism was over. In 1930 approximately 172 publications were still in existence, and by 1950 the number dropped to 60. Out of the five daily newspapers published in New York at that time, only the *New Yorker Staats-Zeitung und Herold* (New York State Herald) has survived. A similar trend developed in Texas, Ohio, Illinois, and Minnesota.

World War II left deep traces on the orientation and further development of the German ethnic press, pushing it away from controversial issues and political activism and toward reporting mainly social gatherings, and historical articles. After the war, the declining process continued. Many German immigrants, some of whom were able to learn English in less than a year, didn't have to lean on the German ethnic press for moral support, but, rather, started reading the English-language papers. As of 1975, the German-American community supported 60 publications, including three dailies and 26 weeklies.

The most influential German-language newspaper in the United States today is the *New Yorker Staats-Zeitung und Herold*, claiming a circulation of 29,350. The paper's origin goes back to 1835, and although its journalistic standards, in comparison to many other ethnic newspapers, are high, the number of staff members and the circulation have been declining. The *New Yorker Staats-Zeitung und Herold* carries major international and national stories, particularly those dealing with European affairs, and, of course, the bulk of information articles and features are concerned with social activities of the German ethnic community in the United States. The weekend issue of February 17/18, 1979, contained a 14-page news section and a 14-page weekend magazine, both illustrating the emphasis placed on international and ethnic news. Here are the front-page headlines: "The Problem of Oil," "President Carter Visits a Neighbor," "U.S. Ambassador in Kabul Murdered," "Mass Evacuation of Americans From Iran," "Democracy With Islamic Identity," and "Prince Sihanouk in Peking." Pages 2, 3, and 4 contained mostly feature articles with these topics: vacations in 1979, dangers of winter sports, the West German delegation in the United States, driving under the influence of alcohol, unemployment in Canada, the new trans-Canada highway, and Gottfried Wilhelm Leibnitz—thinker and diplomat. The following six pages were devoted to German ethnic news, and the remaining two pages covered sports. The weekend magazine of the same issue carried feature articles on a variety of cultural, scientific, and human-interest topics, including a few short stories and the 21st installment of the novel by Elisabeth Gurt, "When Are You Going To Have Time for Me."

Once the most prestigious and independent element in American ethnic journalism, the German newspapers today illustrate clearly the tendency of speedy assimilation and Americanization.

After the racial disturbances in major U.S. cities, and the growing self-awareness among blacks, American mass media, and television networks in particular, became more careful in picturing blacks in the traditional second-rank-citizen roles. Since the mid-1970s, under pressure by Hispanics and organized campaigns of the Polish and Italian ethnic organizations, most of the derogatory jokes and remarks concerning these minorities disappeared from the television screen.

The Germans, however, have been in a different situation. While the press, including the broadcast media, doesn't publicize any controversial, openly biased materials or entertainment programs that are against German-Americans per se, the negative German image is surviving in all sorts of media products.

When the press reported and commented on the collapse of the Nixon administration, and names like Haldeman, Ehrlichman, and Ziegler became symbols of the political chicanery in the country, some authors found direct connecting lines between their German names and the deviousness of their actions.

The persisting feeling of shame and guilt for the brutal crimes committed by Nazis in World War II is probably the major reason why the German-Americans are a silent minority. Reports on West German affairs in the major American daily papers only reinforce the persisting stereotype. In the six months between October 1, 1978, and March 31, 1979, most stories on West Germany published in the *New York Times*, *Boston Globe*, *Boston Herald-American*, and *Time* magazine dealt with political terrorism in West Germany, the neo-Nazi movement, the controversial reaction to the American television series "Holocaust," espionage affairs, and the Nazi past of the Christian Democratic presidential candidate Karl Carstens.

The German past is a constantly reappearing theme in American mass-media reporting, documentaries, and even entertainment programs. Of course, American journalists, just like the public at large, are not trying to condemn German people or to make all of them responsible for Hitler's crimes. What they find surprising, for one example, is the ignorance many Germans showed about war crimes, or their ability to bury these crimes in an undefined area of their minds, as if they had never existed. Many stories dwelt upon the rebroadcasts of the American-produced Holocaust dramas in the Federal German Republic in 1978. The traumas of many Germans and the ignorance of many others provided much grist for the journalistic mills.

DOES THE AMERICAN MELTING POT INDUCE A UNIFIED, TRULY AMERICAN VALUE SYSTEM?

Regarding the question of whether America induces a unified value system, the answer is not clear. Many symbols, cultural rituals, and images appear to be the same, but under the surface, many ethnic differences remain. It seems that we are entering a new era of raising ethnic consciousness, and even the ethnic Americans from Europe—the sleeping giants of American politics—are awakening and moving toward full participation in every field of this multiracial and multicultural society.

It is in the interest of the material and cultural advancement of the country to preserve the delicate balance between necessary and minimal uniformity and the preservation of ethnic differences. Cultural conformity would deprive the nation of one of its major sources of vitality and enrichment.

Immigrants from non-English-speaking countries are seriously handicapped when they arrive without knowledge of English, and some favor extensive bilingual education for their children. The immediate benefit may be outbalanced by a long-term disadvantage. Children who speak a native language at home and at school, without mastering English, enter their adulthood seriously handicapped. In a specialized, highly technological and competitive society where language skills are more important than at any other time in history, it may prove a fatal handicap. A large subculture with little or no skill in English could lead to a nation-within-a-nation, something that the United States has managed to avoid so far.[35]

What role does the ethnic press play in the life of European ethnic groups today? Similar to its position a century ago, it is concerned with maintaining the cultural ties with the immigrant's country of origin, and at the same time helping him to find his place in the new society and to understand its political, economic, and social patterns. The ethnic press, in a way, is a bridge between the past and the future. Naturally, the mortality rate among ethnic papers has been high. The ethnic press blossomed at the high tide of immigration, and found its most loyal readers among the first-generation immigrants. Successful integration among the second- and third-generation ethnics has been accompanied by the loss of interest in the ethnic press. Only a few Polish, Czech, Italian, or German ethnic publications address young readers, leaving the majority of young ethnics dependent on American mass media.

The history of the ethnics and their press is an integral part of American cultural history. Despite declining circulations, the ethnic press will survive and continue reflecting the pluralism of the American society. Since the early 1970s, the European ethnic organizations—particularly the Polish and the Italian—and their press have become more vocal and visible on the American national scene, making some journalists and historians believe that the United States is entering a historical era of distinctive ethnicity. But the Southern, Eastern, or middle European ethnics are striving for fair treatment rather than advocating total change of the traditional American system.

One of the distinctive features of the European ethnic press is the close attention paid to international news. The ratio of international versus domestic news is much higher with ethnic papers than it is with domestic American publications. The new immigrants, many of whom are homesick, want to maintain contact with the country they decided to leave. Gradually, during the adjustment period, when the newcomer acquires knowledge of the new country and its language, and the nostalgic memories of the past lose their intensity, his self-esteem rises, and with it, the interest in domestic American news.

And even here, the ethnic press plays a role in helping the immigrant to learn more about the new environment, the culture, traditions, customs, and norms of the new society. In the long run, however, by performing this second role of smoothing the assimilation, the ethnic press deprives itself of a stable, loyal constituency. The forces of assimilation always prove stronger, each year taking away from the ethnic press substantial numbers of readers. In the words of Carl Wittke, the author of *The German-Language Press in America*, the better the ethnic press performs its integration role, the sooner it signs its own death warrant.[36]

NOTES

1. Daniel Boorstin, *The Image: A Guide to Pseudoevents in America* (New York: Harper Colophon Books, 1964), pp. 9-16.

2. Michael Novak, *The Rise of the Unmeltable Ethnics* (New York: Macmillan, 1973), pp. 41-42.

3. Bureau of the Census, *Statistical Abstract of the United States 1978* (Washington, D.C.: Government Printing Office, 1978), pp. 88-89. See also *Information Please Almanac, Atlas and Yearbook 1978* (New York: Information Please Publishing, 1978), p. 764.

4. R. Lubomyr and Anna T. Wynar, *Encyclopedic Directory of Ethnic Newspapers and Periodicals in the United States* (Littleton, Colo.: Libraries Unlimited, 1976), p. 24.

5. Helena Znaniecki Lopata, *Polish Americans: Status Competition in an Ethnic Community* (New York: Prentice-Hall, 1976), pp. 2-4.

6. Dianne Dumanoski, "Getting Serious About Ethnic Jokes," *The Boston Phoenix*, November 21, 1978, pp. 10-11.

7. Lopata, op. cit., p. 64.

8. Ibid., p. 86.

9. *Wall Street Journal*, October 12, 1973, p. 1.

10. *Polish American Congress Newsletter*, July 20, 1970, pp. 7-8.

11. Frank Renkiewicz, "Language, Loyalty and Ethnic Culture," *Polish American Studies* 26, no. 2 (August 1969):57-61.

12. Lopata, op. cit., p. 64.

13. "Free Speech Doesn't Cover Ethnic Slurs," *Polish-American Journal* 67, no. 12-C (December 8, 1978):1.

14. "Senator, Government Head Slur Polish Pope," *Polish-American Journal* 68, no. 1-C (January 8, 1979):1.

15. "Teacher Fired for Bigotry in History Test," *Polish-American Journal* 68, no. 2-C (February 9, 1979):1.

16. Vera Laska, *The Czechs in America 1633-1977, A Chronology and Fact Book* (Dobbs Ferry, N.Y.: Oceana Publications, 1978), p. 62.

17. Ibid., p. 122.

18. Ibid., p. 54.

19. *Fodor's Czechoslovakia 1971* (New York: David McKay, 1971), pp. 13-15 106-8.

20. *The Czech and Slovak Self-Image and the Czech and Slovak Image of Americans, Germans, Russians, and Chinese* (Munich: Audience and Public Opinion Research Department, Radio Free Europe, 1970), p. 7.

21. Laska, op. cit., p. 43.

22. Vojtech Duben, *Czech and Slovak Press Outside Czechoslovakia in 1978* (New York: Oceana Publications, Occasional paper No. 4, 1978).

23. "Journals of Czechs in U.S. Are Lagging," *New York Times*, May 13, 1979.

24. "Does the President Really Agree?," *American Listy*, no. 38 (September 22, 1978):2.

25. J. Joseph Hutchmacher, *A Nation of Newcomers, Ethnic Minorities in American History* (New York: Delacorte Press, 1967), p. 40.

26. Arcangelo R. T. D'Amore, "A Psychological Commentary of Italian Americans" (Paper delivered and published as part of the proceedings of the Ninth Annual Conference of the American Italian Historical Association, Georgetown University, in October, 1976).

27. See Elizabeth Stone, "It's Still Hard to Grow Up Italian," *New York Times Magazine*, December 17, 1978, pp. 42-43, 86-104.

28. Paul J. Asciollo, "Setting Priorities," *Washington Newsletter* (published by the National Italian American Foundation) 2, no. 3-4, (March-April, 1978).

29. See "Maguire Demands Discrimination Investigation," *Post Gazette* (Boston), no. 7 (February 16, 1979):1.

30. See *Washington Newsletter* 1, no. 3-4 (March-April, 1977):3.

31. See John Arkas Hawgood, *The Tragedy of German American* (New York: Arno Press and New York Times, 1970), p. 37.

32. Ibid., p. 23.

33. Ibid., p. 295.

34. Carl Wittke, *The German-Language Press in America* (Lexington: University of Kentucky Press, 1957), p. 6.

35. See "It's Your Turn in the Sun," *Time*, October 16, 1978, pp. 50-51.

36. Wittke, op. cit., p. 7.

PART V

APPLYING PRESSURE: ORGANIZED MEDIA ADVOCACY WORK

TEN

ADVOCATING THE MINORITY INTEREST: ACTORS AND CASES

Emil Ward

INTRODUCTION

The electronic media constitute the nervous system of America. Yet, blacks and other minorities have traditionally been excluded from the media, leaving it predominantly in the control of white males. To be excluded from the mass media is to become less and less a part of the society. One has no voice with which to speak. The minority person may only listen to what others say to him or about her, while still lacking the means to reply. But, only black and other minority people can adequately present themselves in the mass media. The abuses of "Amos 'N' Andy," the exclusion of minority news events, the absence of minority viewpoints, the lack of minority station owners, the prevalence of misinformation about minorities, the dearth of control over information gathering and disseminating sources—these have long been understood by those historically excluded from the mainstream of American life.

The media-reform movement began in 1955, when blacks in Jackson, Mississippi, decided that their local television station had discriminated against them for too long, and began complaining to the Federal Communications Commission (FCC). This writing is an attempt to describe only a few of the many actors and cases that have come to the forefront, inadvocacy work for minority interests.

THE OFFICE OF COMMUNICATION OF THE UNITED CHURCH OF CHRIST

Background

The United Church of Christ (UCC) is a coalition of Protestant denominations that existed prior to their merger in 1957.*

Since its inception, the United Church of Christ has had a deep and continuing commitment to the eradication of racial injustice both in America and in foreign countries, such as Angola, Rhodesia, and South Africa.

The organization has long recognized that today's communication society demands that the church teach and preach to mass audiences. Indeed, to that church, mass-media communication is a missionary field.[1]

In 1954, the Office of Communication (OC) was formed as an offshoot of the separate predecessors of the church that had previously cooperated to braodcast religious programs. The Office of Communication involves itself in many areas. It broadcasts all of its own internal news and affairs. It participates actively in the planning and production of network television and radio shows. It produces radio and television programs that focus on moral and ethical problems of all strata of contemporary society.

The Office of Communication is the unit of the church having primary responsibilities in the field of media reform.[2] At its inception, the Office of Communication adopted a mandate to see that the media function would be handled in the best Judeo-Christian manner possible. It was early recognized that the new medium of broadcasting had very profound effects on society and that, therefore, the United Church of Christ should be involved in shaping those effects.[3] The Office of Communication has carried over the church's vehement opposition to racial injustice into broadcasting. Employment and programming are two areas of discrimination in which it continuously works to bring about the equality it views as essential to the fulfillment of the church's purposes.[4]

Funding

The Office of Communication has been funded by a variety of

*The Congregational Church (one of the principal churches that eventually merged with the evangelical and reformed churches to form what has become the United Church of Christ) has traditionally been involved in the fight for racial justice, as far back as Civil War days. Often its efforts were directed at funding and founding black colleges like the one at Tougaloo, in Jackson, Mississippi.

sources. The Ford Foundation, in 1968, gave it a substantial grant ($100,000 per year for ten years), to establish "A Program To Combat Racial Discrimination in Broadcasting." The funds from this grant are used to support many general activities, such as license challenges, rule makings, appellate-court activities, publications, and so forth. Other grants are given for more specific purposes. The AFL-CIO has funded fairness-doctrine activities. Funds from the Rockefeller Brothers Foundation and the Veech Program (a church group in the Long Island, New York area) have been applied to the conducting of workshops in different parts of the country, wherein local groups come together with representatives of the Office of Communication to increase their knowledge of the skills required to properly deal with media issues and with station management. The Markel Foundation has given support for the production and distribution of publications. The church itself supplies some funding, but its principal aid is given in the form of in-kind services, such as making available personnel consultants, accountants, and printing facilities.[5]

Dr. Everett C. Parker is the director of the Office of Communication. Parker has been involved with media reform since the 1940s. This nationally recognized media reformer has worked for the Congregational Christian churches and with early coalitions of radio groups, seeking reserved channels for educational stations, and defending the fairness doctrine.[6] A representative survey of key OC programs follows.

Community Assistance and Followup Activities

Dixie National and WLBT-TV of Jackson, Mississippi

In the WLBT case, the Office of Communication asked the FCC to reopen the case because it had uncovered information concerning the management of the Dixie National Broadcasting Corporation, to whom the license had been tentatively awarded. The OC charged that the chairman of the board concealed, from the FCC and the Securities Exchange Commission, (SEC), his relationship with a modular-home-building company that went bankrupt, losing millions of dollars for thousands of stockholders.[7] Its evidence included flight logs showing the officer provided the use of an airplane to the former attorney general, John Mitchell, five U.S. senators, and a Watergate figure. The OC sought to show possible violations of the Federal Corrupt Practices Act, which forbids corporate contributions of cash or services to political compaigns.[8]

The OC's action, and that of one of the companies vying for

WLBT's license, Civic Communications, Inc., resulted in the FCC's staying the tentative grant to Dixie National and scheduling new hearings on the matter.[9] We see that exposure of one type of bad license management helped open the door for the OC's interest in minority issues.

Native Americans and KELO-TV and KPLO-TV, Rosebud, South Dakota

Members of the Sioux nation, living on the Rosebud Reservation in South Dakota, and represented by the Television Radio Improvement Association (TRIA), were supplied with legal and technical assistance in their fight against KELO-TV and KLPO-TV dominance of television stations that together reached 90 percent of the listening audience in South Dakota.[10]

Midcontinent, the owner of KPLO-TV, presented a particularly egregious situation. Its owner "told the people of central South Dakota that the only way they could ever have television would be to build a television station for him to operate."[11] Curiously, the area residents, including 40,000 Native Americans living at or near the poverty level, raised $250,000 and gave it to Midcontinent.[12] Since 1956, when the KPLO venture began, it has declined to the lowly role of being a satellite to station KELO-TV. It had not fulfilled most of its duties and commitments to promote localism, one of the basic requirements of the Communications Act of 1934.[13] KPLO offered no local programming, no local news, no coverage of important tribal events, no programming interpreting the problems, culture, life history, or future of the Sioux nation.[14]

The Office of Communication aided attorneys of the Sioux in filing a petition to deny license renewal, against KELO-TV, with whom the Sioux had also had their grievances. The mere existence of the petition against KELO caused Midcontinent to open negotiations with TRIA concerning both stations.

The result was an agreement between TRIA and Midcontinent that included the following terms: ten minues of news and weather, and 30 minutes of local programming from the Reliance, South Dakota, area; the hiring of five Native Americans, full time; regular meetings with the TRIA advisory unit; and a contribution of $30,000 to anyone wishing to construct another broadcast outlet in the KPLO-TV service area.[15]

Publications

Efforts to educate and prepare the public and public-interest lawyers have been undertaken by the OC with the distribution of several widely circulated publications, including *How to Protect Citizen Rights in Television and Radio*, and *Parties in Interest*. They provide an analysis of the American communications scheme, and of the public's rights, and instruction on how to acquire access to the airwaves.

Legal Actions

The most glamorous and far-reaching activities are to be found in the three United Church of Christ cases that follow. There are others, however, which were brought for policy reasons, and those in which the Office of Communication became involved to vindicate the rights of specific individuals or public-interest groups.

The Equal Employment Opportunity Petition

In 1967, the Office of Communication petitioned the FCC, asking it to require all of its licensees to "furnish satisfactory evidence . . . that they do not discriminate in employment practices on the basis of race, color, religion or national origin."[16] Further, the petition requested the FCC to refuse to grant a license to any station which discriminated.[17] That position derived from the Office of Communication's interpretation of the Civil Rights Act of 1964, which prohibits discrimination on the basis of "race, color, religion, sex, or national origin," and from its conviction that discrimination against personnel appearing in the electronic media, or who participate in programming, "sets a conspicuous public example of unfairness."[18]

Pressures such as this, coupled with pressures from the Justice Department and numerous other parties, resulted in the eventual promulgation of a series of equal employment opportunity (EEO) rules.

Comments, Rulemakings, and Petitions

The Office of Communication has entered comments in the following FCC proceedings (circa 1975): the proposed rulemaking concerning the clarification of the policy regarding broadcaster-citizen agreements;[19] and (a petition and comments) in the VHF drop-in rulemaking.*

The Office of Communication assists in bringing challenges, and intervenes in cases where it feels its presence is necessary to vindicate an interest of the office that is being infringed.

---

*Drop-ins are newly discovered frequencies on the TV band that pose no electrical interference to one another.

The office moved to intervene in *The Honorable Shirley Chisholm, et al., v. FCC* (Nos. 75-1951 and 75-1994, October 28, 1975). It sought to overturn the FCC order exempting political debates and press conferences from the equal-time provisions of the Communications Act.[21] The provision requires that any station which allows one candidate for public office to use its station "shall afford equal opportunities to all other such candidates for that office in the use of such broadcasting station. . . ."[22] The church argued that the change would hurt minorities, women, and other third parties who were candidates for public office, since the station would then be able to simply deem its favored candidate's appearance to be "on the spot coverage of a bona fide news event," and thereby be exempt, at will, from the requirement to air such appearances of opposing candidates that the station might not favor.[23]

Testimony

When important issues are before the Congress, the Office of Communication appears to testify. For example, Parker offered testimony in the 1978 hearings held by the House of Subcommittee on Communications, of the Interstate and Foreign Commerce Committee, on HR 13015, concerning, among other broadcast-deregulation provisions, that which removes EEO regulation from the FCC's direct authority.[24] Parker also testified at the 1975 Senate oversight hearings held by Senator John Pastore, upon the request of the United Church of Christ and others, to investigate the FCC's deregulation of broadcasting through its rulemaking powers.[25]

Key Office of Communication Cases

Office of Communication of the United Church of Christ v. FCC, 359 F. 2d 994 (1966) *United Church of Christ I*

The *UCC I* is a seminal one in the field of public-interest communications law. It is the case in which citizen-consumers (members of the listening and viewing audience) were given "standing," which enabled them to participate as "parties in interest" in FCC proceedings. This enabled the public to file petitions to deny renewal of station licenses, and to petition to deny the transfer of a license which would not serve the public interest. Prior to this landmark case, standing in FCC proceedings was conferred only upon those having a direct, usually financial, interest in FCC matters, which meant only other broadcasters, to the exclusion of the public.

In the late 1950s and early 1960s, the civil-rights movement was fast beginning to take hold, and it attracted more and more of the attention of the United Church of Christ. During those civil-rights days, the United Church of Christ placed the cause of racial justice among its top priorities.[26] The church was very sensitive to the events surrounding the discriminatory programming practices of WLBT-TV of Jackson, Mississippi, for several reasons. The church had an affiliate at Tougaloo, and many members of the congregation were members of the educational community there as well. Blacks also comprised a significant segment of the church's congregation. As the movement for civil rights gained momentum, the racial climate in and around Tougaloo became tense, causing political unrest in this small southern city. Some of the charges were that WLBT-TV had cut off a network show on race relations on which the general counsel for the NAACP was appearing—the station having flashed to viewers, in place of the show, a "Sorry, Cable Trouble" sign; that WLBT had aired programming urging continued racial segregation without allowing time for opposing views of this controversial issue, a violation of the fairness doctrine;[27] that blacks had been referred to as "nigger[s]" or "negra[s]" on the air, by station commentators; that black people, comprising 45 percent of the local service area, and black institutions had received slight and unfavorable treatment by the station.[28] Discrimination against the Catholic Church and overcommercialization were also charged.[29]

Although the United Church of Christ did not usually engage in such conflicts directly, the church was drawn into the developing conflict for several reasons. The members of the local community who wanted to take action against WLBT were many, but the fear of physical, political, and economic reprisals made it a very discouraging and risky proposition. The local complaining audience did not have the national clout necessary to overcome traditional small-southern-town power structures. In addition, much community organizing and civil-rights activity had been carried out in conjunction with the church and Tougaloo College, between which there were affiliations. When the station began attacking their civil-rights activities as being radical left-inspired, the United Church of Christ was placed directly under fire.[30] Therefore, the church had to enter the conflict—first, to vindicate its own name, and second, in order to provide the necessary national visibility and support with which to oppose the station management's discriminatory practices. In addition, the church had long believed that it should become involved with influencing the medium which so undeniably influenced the public. The WLBT situation offered that opportunity. It was under these conditions that the United Church of Christ at Tougaloo, R.L.T. Henry, president of the Mississippi NAACP, and Aaron Smith, a local resident, filed a petition to deny WLBT-TV's license-renewal application in 1964.*

Legal Existence or NonExistence

"Standing" is the term describing the legal right of status to enter a forum such as the FCC or a court, and to avail oneself of its powers. Courts generally require the parties to have a direct and substantial interest (generally of a financial nature) in the issues at hand, to meet the standing requirements. Otherwise, a party will not be heard. For example, as between the reader of this study and this author, if the reader's car were damaged by a vandal, the author would not have standing to enter a court and make a complaint, for damages to the car, against the vandal, because the author would have no direct or substantial interest in the car. Only the reader would have those interests, and therefore, only the reader would have standing to ask the court to make the vandal repair the damage or to pay for the damage.

In the *UCC I* case, the FCC denied the church and the other challengers standing to come before it, and did not even listen to their grievances as contained in their petition to deny the station's license. The commission merely renewed the license. The FCC interpreted the law to say that only those parties who could allege economic or electrical interference had standing; and to say further, that these petitioners were not harmed to any greater degree

---

*A license to broadcast is a privilege, not a right, granted by the FCC. All licensees are granted a license to operate, which must be renewed every three years. The licensee is a public trustee of the public owned electromagnetic spectrum. In return for the right to use such a license for profit, the licensee is burdened with only a duty to the public. The licensee may keep its license only as long as it continues to operate in the public "interest, convenience and necessity." See the Communications Act of 1934, 42 USC § 309. In passing upon a license, the FCC must make an affirmative finding tha tthe renewal or transfer will be in the public interest, before it can renew or approve a transfer of a license. At renewal time, once every three years, "a party in interest" may petition the FCC to deny renewal of the license, alleging, for example, discrimination in employment practices, electrical interference, fraudulent business practices, discriminatory programming practices. If upon the basis of the allegations in the petition to deny, the FCC finds that a "substantial and material question of fact" exists, or if the FCC is "for any reason unable to find" that the renewal is consistent with the public interest, convenience, and necessity, then it must designate a full evidentiary hearing and resolve the issues at hand, before it can renew the license or approve its transfer. If after the evidentiary hearing, the FCC still cannot find it in the public interest to renew the license or to approve the transfer, it must deny renewal or transfer. See the Communications Act of 1934, 47 USC § 309 (d).

than were other members of the listening public, so how could they assert an injury direct enough or substantial enough to confer standing on them?[31]

There were other issues as well, but the standing issue was the crucial one. On appeal, the U.S. Court of Appeals for the District of Columbia reversed the commission, granted the challengers standing, and sent the case back to the FCC for a full evidentiary hearing. The court failed to see how members of the consuming public audience could not have at least as great a claim to standing to protect their interests in their publicly owned airwaves as broadcasters had.[32] Public participation was found to be a necessary part of the broadcasting system. The FCC, unassisted by the public, could not adequately protect the public interest.[33] Since the broadcaster had to operate in the "public interest, convenience, and necessity," in order to be granted renewal,[34] public input was essential. The court held: "In order to safeguard the public interest in broadcasting, therefore, we hold that some 'audience participation' must be allowed in license renewal applications."[35]

The case is, of course, more involved than the above analysis would appear to make it. The crucial practical impact, however, is the obvious one, that now the public had standing to intervene in or to initiate proceedings, and to vindicate its own interests. The courts, at least, welcomed the public intervenors.[36] The ability of minorities, especially, to be able to enter formal proceedings and to potentially influence the treatment the media accorded them became very powerful and inspiring. Many minority groups immediately recognized the open door and entered. The majority of petitions to deny in the 1970s were brought by minorities "seeking increased coverage, outlets, access, employment and advisory roles . . ."[37] Although almost all of these petitions were rejected,[38] they have had their effect.

Office of Communication and the United Church of Christ v. FCC, 425 F. 2d 543 (1969) (*UCC II*)

Having been granted standing before the commission in *UCC I*, the petitioners were now obliged to go back before the FCC to request the relief they had originally sought.

The petitioners' grievances still had not been heard by the FCC even after several years in the appellate courts. The commission was no more hospitable to the petitioners at the renewal hearing than it was when it had previously denied them standing. The WLBT license application was renewed, although on a one-year probationary basis, after a full evidentiary hearing.[39]

The United Church of Christ and the local petitioners were dismayed by, what seemed to them the blatantly improper procedures and subsequent improper decision of the FCC, and returned once again to the U.S. court of appeals for relief.

In 1969, 14 years after the original complaints were filed, an exasperated appeals court again overruled the commission and itself revoked the renewal first granted by the commission.

It appeared to the court that there had been much hostility displayed toward the petitioners, and a great deal of improper procedure. The appeals court was outraged by both the long delay and the favoritism shown to the industry over and above the public.

The court stated that the commission had placed burdens of proof on the wrong parties. The FCC wrongly required the petitioners to show that Lamar Life Broadcasting Company, the licensee, should be denied a license, rather than requiring Lamar Life to prove that despite all complaints against it, the public interest would still be served if its license were renewed. The law, said the court, requires the latter allocation of burden, and not the former.[40] The court noted that the petitioners were treated as interlopers, or as plaintiffs versus the defendant-licensee, which they were not.[41] The petitioners were members of the public supposedly on the same side of the issues as the FCC, intervening solely to vindicate not private, but rather, public interests. The court felt that the "curious-neutrality-in-favor-of-the-licensee,"[42] the FCC's improper procedures, and shoddy treatment of the petitioners so tainted the case that the petitioners could not have received a fair hearing at the commission: "[I]n our view the entire hearing was permeated by similar treatment of the efforts of intervenors, and the pervasive impatience—if not hostility—of the Examiner is a constant factor which made fair and impartial consideration impossible."[43]

The court severely rebuked the commission for its complete ineptitude, and concluded that the "hostility" shown toward the petitioners, and the lack of substantial evidence upon which the renewal was based, would make it a useless act to remand the case once again to the commission.[44] Having said this, the court indeed took the unprecedented step of itself denying the license, and it ordered the FCC to implement an interim operation plan until a permanent licensee could be found.

For the first time, the court had taken away a license on the grounds of discrimination in programming, the fairness doctrine, and employment—grounds particularly important to minorities. It was an inspiring precedent for broadcast consumers throughout the country. It greatly encouraged traditionally underrepresented groups to take more definitive legal action to gain fair treatment both behind and in front of the camera and microphone. It was a stimulus for starting the two major communications law firms, Citizens Communications Center (*Citizens*), and the Media Access Project (MAP).

At the time, it was seen as the beginning of a great new era of reform, as many groups rushed to file petitions to deny license renewals. From 1969, when two petitions were filed, the number jumped to 50 in 1973, affecting 150 stations.[45] Yet, few petitions to deny resulted in hearings being designated, and even fewer hearings have resulted in denials of licenses. The *UCC II* case, therefore, has not proven to be as significant in the renewal-denial area as hoped. However, it was a clear signal to the industry and to the FCC that now that the door was open, licenses could be lost through efforts of the minority public. The whole industry would have to shift into a more legalistic arena—an arena of courts and procedures, vastly different from the mere letter writing to which the public had traditionally been relegated.

This was not a novel route for minorities to take, for most of their rights have been secured only through the intervention of the courts.

Broadcasters now had to listen and pay heed to the events unfolding between themselves and an aggrieved public group, no matter how insignificant the chances of losing one's license might seem. Today, when a petition to deny is filed, one can be certain that the broadcaster is at least aware of, and responding to, the group which filed it. Few licensees choose to ignore petitions to deny, and few today choose not to at least negotiate. Additionally, stations, under challenge, often upgrade their performance, e.g., in programming and employment, in an effort to avoid the expenses and risks of having to come before the FCC. So, the public challenger can actually win without winning" (the formal protracted legal contest).[46] Public groups often have problems which can be solved by the positive acts of a sensitized broadcaster. Few broadcasters will remain impervious to the plaints of its audience when a license challenge, with all of its bad publicity, risk, and expense, is hanging over its head. The leverage for a public-interest group flows from the mere existence of the possibility that a license might be lost, or that large expenses might be incurred. This is usually sufficient to sensitize a licensee to the point where it will listen to grievances of its audience.

These United Church of Christ cases, in the final analysis, did bring about the practical effects that the aggrieved blacks and church groups first set out to achieve in 1955. The interim operator finally chosen by the commission was a multiracial, nonprofit organization, which then implemented some innovative programming and management practices during its tenure.* Since the station staff was multiracial, black people had the opportunity to receive invaluable exposure to broadcasting, first-hand, at a time when few blacks were on station staffs, much less in the upper job categories.

The local audience benefited from the change in management, because of increased diversity of personnel and viewpoints, which of course meant more diverse program content—a desirable goal in itself.[47]

Taken together, *UCC I* and *UCC II* provided the beginnings of a public reform movement designed to regain control of the scarce public airwaves. Blacks and other minorities set out on the road to greater media access for the first time in their history.

Office of Communication of the United Church of Christ v. FCC, 465 F. 2d 519 (1972) (*UCC III*)

The United Church of Christ was responsible for one of the first successful citizen-broadcaster agreements. *UCC III* was the genesis for two major developments: the agreements themselves, and voluntary reimbursement grants from licensees to challenging public parties and their consultants.

In 1968, a citizens' group in Texarkana, Texas (the Texarkana Junior Chamber of Commerce and 12 local unincorporated associations), with the aid of the UCC, challenged station KTAL-TV's license on grounds that its ascertainment,† as to blacks (comprising 26 percent of the community), was defective; that KTAL failed to adequately serve Texarkana; and that the station failed to respond to public inquiries.[48]

Parker; Ralph M. Jennings, the deputy director of the Office of Communication; and UCC's general counsel, Earle K. Moore, met with the local group and advised them on general issues, programming, and employment in order to prepare a basis for impending

---

*An interim operator is a group approved by the FCC, which operates a broadcast facility on a temporary basis, until a permanent broadcast group can be found in a case where the incumbent broadcaster becomes incapacitated, or, as in this case, loses its license. The object is to provide some service for the audience, rather than no service.

†Each broadcast licensee is required by the FCC to survey leaders of significant community groups and ascertain their needs, problems, and interests, in order to develop programming which speaks to those ascertained issues. *Ascertainment of Community Problems by Broadcast Applicant*, 41 Fed. Reg. 1372 (1976); *Commission Policy on Programming*, 20 Pike & Fischer, R&R 1901, 1913—15 (1960).

discussions with station management.[49] Both sides saw the possible advantages to making an amicable settlement of grievances, rather than proceeding with a protracted, expensive, and uncertain fight through the commission and the courts.

An agreement between the challenging group and the licensee, KCMC, Inc., was signed in June 1969 and filed with the FCC as an amendment to the licensee's renewal application. The station promised in essence (see KCMC, Inc., 19 FCC 2d 109, 120-122 [1969]):

> KTAL will employ a minimum of two fulltime Negro reporters, one for Texarkana and one for Shreveport. These reporters will appear regularly on camera. . .
>
> KTAL recognizes its obligations to present regular programs for the discussion of controversial issues, including, of course, both black and white participants. The station will not avoid issues that may be controversial or divisive, but will encourage the airing of all sides of these issues. . .
>
> Network programs of particular interest to any substantial group in the service area will not be preempted without appropriate advance consultation with representatives of that group. . .
>
> KTAL is obligated to discuss programming regularly with all segments of the public. In particular, a station employee with authority to act will meet once a month with a committee designated by the parties to the petition to deny KTAL-TV's application for license renewal. Similar efforts will be made to consult with groups representing other segments of the public. . .

The members of the community group agreed to withdraw their petition, and to recommend a license renewal, based on provisions contained in the agreement. The commission renewed KTAL-TV's license, commended the parties for reaching a settlement, and noted that this form of grievance resolution was much more desirable than intervention by the commission: "We believe that this Commission should encourage licensees to meet with community oriented groups to settle complaints of local broadcast service. Such cooperation at the community level should prove to be more effective in improving local service than would be the imposition of strict guidelines of the Commission."

Having concluded negotiations, the United Church of Christ sought to collect over $15,000 in expenses, which KTAL had agreed to pay as part of the settlement. However, the FCC refused to allow such reimbursement, stating that it feared the dangers of overpayment or of encouragement of frivolous strike suits brought to extract fees, and the danger that the merits of a dispute might be compromised by the ability to recover expenses from a challenged licensee.[50] Therefore, the commission took the extreme step of barring recovery of expenses or financial benefit to any challenger in all petition-to-deny cases.[51] Two commissioners dissented (Commissioners Dean Burch and Nicholas Johnson), suggesting that implementation of guidelines to guard against such dangers would suffice, and further, that barring all reimbursement was too severe a sanction.[52]

On appeal, the court held that the FCC could not bar such reimbursement in all petition-to-deny cases. "Once these determinations [that the public group seeking to withdraw its petition, upon settlement, is bona fide, and that the terms serve the public interest] are made, voluntary reimbursement of legitimate and prudent expenses of the withdrawing group cannot be forbidden" (see *UCC III* at 527). The court noted the growing acceptance of the concept that public participation in decisions where the public interest was involved was not only valuable, but "indispensable."[53] Having concluded that the public was a necessary element in the public interest, the court espoused the following conclusion: "It seems to us that the goal of facilitating public participation is necessarily furthered by the rule we have established above."[54]

Although the court did not hold that the FCC must allow expenses here, the principle was established that "when the settlement of issues and termination of a petition to deny between the public and a broadcaster is in the public interest, voluntary reimbursement of the public group may be allowed."[55] Finally, when remanded to the FCC solely on the issue of whether the expenses in the case were "legitimate and prudent," the commission decided that they were, and allowed them.[56]

This was a very important victory for minorities and media consumers. The case again set an invaluable agreement precedent.

This resolution saved both sides time, which of course represented cost to both parties. It would have cost both sides large sums of money to litigate throughout the commission's procedural steps, hearings, decision-making steps, court appeals, possible renewals, remands back to the FCC, and finally, the new decision, which could easily have been subject to appeal by one side or the other. UCCI took two years, from the 1964 petition to deny, to the release of the appellate court's opinion in 1966. Another three years passed before WLBT's license was denied in 1969. All the while, the legal expenses to the broadcaster were mounting up. Legal fees can easily run into $100-$200 per hour. With a two- or three-person team to do the work, the fees and costs can be phenomenal. Obviously, no matter what reduced fees and costs the public challengers paid, they were still burdensome.

The consumer paid an added intangible cost. The local group had grievances which had become critical—critical enough to start legal proceedings. The costs of continuing to endure discrimination in programming and in employment practices are unascertainable, but undoubtedly enormous.

There is the advantage of avoiding the uncertainty of possibly losing, after all is said and done. Fifty percent of something is generally considered to be better than 100 percent of nothing. Citizens' groups embrace agreements for this reason.

Public-interest groups were allowed by the agreement in *UCC III* to avoid becoming entangled in the FCC's processes, which can be rather unpredictable and, at that time, were often hostile to the public.[57] The agreement amendment to the application became part of the promises given by the licensee to the FCC. As such, there were grounds for FCC enforcement and oversight.

Minorities and other public-interest groups now had a very useful tool to achieve substantial bargaining power. Both sides are usually willing to talk, to reach the advantages or to avoid the disadvantages noted above.

Finally, a reimbursement precedent was set. Public groups could now recoup at least their "legitimate and prudent" costs of furthering the public interest. A dollar in the hands of a public-interest group goes much further than that same dollar in the hands of the private litigant, simply because of the nature and structure of public-interest entities. The newfound ability to diffuse a siege-type mentality where the industry seeks to starve out or bankrupt a public intervenor, created by the possibility of reimbrusement, is a tremendous addition to public leverage. The agreement strategy has been used successfully since that time.

In 1971, Citizens Communications Center, on its own behalf, intervened in a $110-million transfer of broadcast properties between Capital Cities Broadcasting Corporation, Triangle Publications, and various third parties alleging, among other charges, violations of the FCC "top-50 policy." The result of negotiations was a million-dollar, three-year minority-program project aimed at providing programming to black and Hispanic peoples in the affected broadcast areas, and $5,000 in reimbursement to CITIZENS. In return, the public-interest groups withdrew their petitions, gave their express support of the transfer to the FCC, and allowed the broadcasters to make the FCC-required public-interest showing and thereby consummate the transfer.

The predominant fears of the commission concerning agreements eventually crystallized around the issue of improper delegation of a broadcaster's ultimate responsibility over employment, programming, improper reimbursements, and other such areas belonging exclusively within the broadcaster's control.[58] Eventually, the FCC issued certain orders attempting to more clearly define the area previously developed on a case-by-case basis.

Essentially, the FCC *Agreements Report & Order*,[59] espoused several principles which have been interpreted on a case basis ever since. The order stated, principally: there shall be no delegation by the licensee of programming, employment, and other operational duties, particularly, to any nonstation persons; the licensee shall retain the right to modify the agreement if the public interest would, in its judgment thereby be better served; the agreements would become promises to the FCC, enforceable as such; FCC review will only be made upon complaint or request; and there is no requirement imposed upon the licensee to either negotiate or to enter into an agreement with public groups.[60] The reimbursement order[61] added little to the effect of the agreements order or to the reimbursement area whatsoever.[62]

Once again, it becomes difficult to accurately assess the impact of *UCC III*, due to a lack of data. However, the use, by so many public groups, of the agreement process can be construed to show its value to such groups for achieving more responsive media. Several examples follow.

The Rochester Black Media Coalition (RBMC), a National Black Media Coalition affiliate, after filing an appeal of transfer of control of WOKR-TV, from Flower City Television Corp, to WOKR, Inc., a Post Corporation subsidiary, won concessions from the new licensee. These included promises to nominate a minority person to the licensee's board of directors; to provide financial and technical assistance to prospective minority broadcasters; to give regular notice to prospective minority broadcasters when sales of broadcast affiliates are to be undertaken; to actively seek minority station management; to reimburse RBMC's reasonable and legitimate costs; and to give $2,500 per year for five years to the Howard University Communications Conference, and other such benefits.[63]

There are of course problems, such as mutual agreement in the first place, enforcement, monitoring, and improper delegation and proper representation of legitimate issues; but on the whole, agreements appear to be a welcome addition to the few tools minorities have for vindicating their interests in the media.

FOR RESPONSIVE MEDIA: CITIZENS COMMUNICATIONS CENTER

Inside the Organization

Citizens Communications Center is one of the two major public-interest communications law firms in the country. The Media Access Project is the other. (Together, at this writing they account for virtually the entire public-interest communications bar—a total of seven attorneys.) CITIZENS is a law firm, a major resource center, and to a great degree, it is an invaluable research center for the media-reform movement. There are few other entities in the communications field, on either side, that have added so much to the furtherance of the public interest or to furtherance of minority interests in electronic media.

Since its inception in 1969, the firm has been involved in almost every principal effort for responsive electronic media. CITIZENS's history is considered a capsule history of the movement itself.[64] It has given testimony on Capitol Hill in key areas of legislation; it has appeared before every major tribunal from the FCC to the Supreme Court to hearings in the field; has advised nonclients, the Corporation for Public Broadcasting, the industry, upon request, in media matters; and much, much more.

The Beginning

Prior to CITIZENS's founding in 1969, an antitrust attorney named Albert Kramer had a chance meeting with Ralph Nader.[65] They discussed the media and related consumer interests therein. Kramer then decided to found a law firm along the lines of other consumer-oriented legal-aid and public-interest firms. CITIZENS, however, was to specialize in the problems of consumers of the electronic media.

The purpose of CITIZENS was to address the needs and problems of a growing portion of the public that the electronic media had traditionally ignored—to make the media more responsive. For years, there had been those concerned with exercising some influence over this dynamic new medium that affected people so greatly—broadcasting.[66] But as I explained earlier, in 1969, the movement was born from the *UCC I* case. Legally, the climate for a firm such as CITIZENS was now very accommodating. Ordinary citizens, all members of the audience, now had standing, the legal right to advocate their own directly affected interests. Kramer, armed with this new right, stepped quickly into a new field of law.

Kramer left the prestigious law firm of Covington and Burling in Washington, D.C., and obtained space, secretarial help, and supplies from the Robert F. Kennedy Foundation and opened the doors of CITIZENS. Most clients then were black.

As always, funding was a problem. The exercise of legal rights is an expensive process, consuming much money, time, and energy. Only after much effort was a small grant from the Midas International Foundation obtained. Several more small grants came in thanks to the farsightedness of such foundations as the Playboy, the Stern, and the Robert F. Kennedy Memorial Foundations. In 1971, a two-year grant of $200,000 per year was given by the Ford Foundation.[67] From a one-attorney situation, CITIZENS enlarged its staff, and by 1972 there were four barristers handling the work. Currently they rely heavily on the talents of law-school interns. In May of 1977, Nolan A. Bowie, a distinguished black attorney (a former naval officer, a Superior Court clerk of the District of Columbia, and a Watergate special prosecutor) was appointed executive director. He was the first black appointed to the position.

Coming on the heels of the civil-rights movement in the streets of urban centers, the movement in communications law was fueled by the pursuit of any of the same goals and lessons of community organization and diversity of participation.

The education of present and prospective clients was a primary concern of CITIZENS's early agenda. The tasks of CITIZENS were already required to be expanded beyond those of traditional law firms, because this was not traditional law. People had to be taught to monitor stations, to study their files, and to study FCC required reports and license applications. Local people were taught how to organize and how to prepare data with which to open negotiations with station management.[68]

CITIZENS assisted in starting the Media Access Project. It has produced studies,* developed instructional packages for attorneys and citizen groups, participated in conferences on national communications policy, and been active in community education.

---

* See, for example, Citizens Communications Center, *A Study of the Federal Communications Commission's Equal Opportunity Regulation—An Agency in Search of a Standard,* (1976) and *Public Broadcasting and Equal Employment Opportunity Regulation—Where Does the Buck Stop?* (Washington, D.C.: CITIZENS, 1976).

Representative Activities

KJAZ and the Alaska Renewals Case

After dismissing a petition to deny license renewal, filed against KJAZ, in California, the FCC requested the appeals court to remand the case to it, because the commission had decided upon review to designate certain issues against KJAZ, after all. Following threats by the licensee to sue the public-interest groups for abuse of process (the petition to deny), and after the *San Francisco Chronicle*, which owns KRON-TV, published a series of articles, branding the petitioners with derogatory labels, the FCC announced that it intended to designate a hearing wherein one of the issues was to revolve around an investigation into the very motives of the public-interest petitioners. CITIZENS, as of October 1978, was awaiting the official release of the order so that it could take action to assist the petitioners in opposing such industry actions, which would have a chilling effect on all such public-interest groups. CITIZENS, as of this writing, is acting as a friend of the court (advising the court on matters in which it is not a principal party, but wherein it has a substantial policy interest), on behalf of the Media Access Project and its public-interest clients in certain Alaskan license challenges where they too are being attacked by the licensees.[69]

Also, CITIZENS has urged that the FCC allow for reimbursement of public participation in all commission proceedings, not only rulemakings, as the commission itself proposes.

Alabama Educational Television Commission

CITIZENS has participated with other groups in many different kinds of cases during its brief but eventful existence.

The *Alabama Educational Television Commission* (AETC) case is examined here for several reasons. It was the first case wherein the commission, not the court, denied television-broadcast licenses. It involved a public educational network, not a commercial one. The basic issues were discrimination in employment and programming practices against blacks and improper ascertainment. It is one of those rare cases where a licensee has done all in its power to resist compliance with the law.

By way of background, the AETC was established by the Alabama legislature in 1953 for "the purpose of making the benefits of educational television available to and promoting its use by inhabitants of Alabama."[70] It was thus a public body licensed under the usual public-interest standards.

Complaints against AETC had been increasing since the 1967-70 license period. The FCC, however, resolved the informal-complaints issues by concluding that there was "no substantial problem," and then by renewing AETC's licenses.[71] The petitioners, believing this to be an inadequate resolution of the serious charges of racial discrimination in employment, programming, and ascertainment, asked the commission to review the earlier ruling. Finally, in 1975, the FCC was convinced that AETC had not acted in the public interest during its 1967-70 license term, and it denied the licenses.

At that time, Alabama had a population composed of approximately 30 percent black people. The egregious activities of AETC therefore had an effect on a significant portion of the state's viewing audience. The commission's decision to deny renewal was based on some of the succeeding findings.

The FCC found that although there was a significant amount of black-oriented programming readily available to AETC from such sources as National Educational Television, "AETC elected to broadcast virtually none of these programs."[72] AETC had paid some heed to its programming obligations and to the implications of the renewal process, in that its percentage of integrated programming (programs which show at least one black person per program) increased steadily from 1967 to 1970. However, even this apparent improvement was in actuality a farce. The case text reveals that "this additional integrated programming, . . . 46 hours and 45 minutes, amounts to only 0.5% of the over 10,000 hours of programming broadcast during the license term."[73]

AETC demonstrated no less contempt for blacks in its employment practices than it had in its programming practices. The FCC text summed up the situation:

> There were no black AETC Commissioners, no black AETC professional staff, and no blacks on the Program Board during the license period. The production centers were all located at predominantly white institutions and the record establishes that there was no significant black involvement in the preparation of programming at those production centers. . . . There were no blacks on the Curriculum Committee, an organization created by SDE for the purpose of planning and coordinating instructional programming. . . . No integrated in-school programming was produced locally.[74]

To add to the already ludicrous situation existing, in which the FCC delayed for almost ten years before finally and reluctantly denying the AETC licenses, it allowed AETC to continue to run the stations as an interim operator.[75] The commission could have procured a different interim operator, as it had done in the WLBT case. Despite the express invitation issued by the commission for different operators to apply for the recently lost licenses, AETC was not barred from reapplying immediately for its old licenses, as it should have been under normal FCC procedures. It was given a little slap on the wrist. The only detriment which AETC suffered was a denial of an incumbent's preference such as that usually afforded to incumbent licensees when they undergo a comparative challenge* for their licenses.[76] The denial of preference here is of slight consequence because "[e]ntry [into the broadcast industry] by challenge is not a viable alternative because of the lack of clear standards employed by the Commission in determining the prevailing party. . . ."[77] Obviously, the FCC levied a very small penalty on AETC for having failed to operate in the public interest, in that the commission took away something which was generally acknowledged to be of slight value in comparative hearings. The remarkable thing about AETC is that despite all the findings of unfitness to hold its licenses, it continues to obstruct proper operation of the Alabama educational television system.

The Early-1979 Status

Alabama Citizens for Responsive Public Television (Alabama Citizens), a local Alabama group, applied for three of the licenses which AETC had lost—for stations in Birmingham, Demopolis, and Montgomery. By order of the FCC, in 1976, Alabama Citizens and AETC were to enter into a comparative hearing for the three stations.

The Montgomery Citizens Advisory Committee (MCAC), a committee of diverse citizens, was formed at the express behest of AETC, to assist the statewide system to better discharge its public-interest obligations. A series of conflicts and disputes ensued between AETC and MCAC over the release of program-budget

---

* A comparative hearing is the FCC proceeding wherein the relative merits and negative factors of two or more mutually exclusive applicants competing for the same license are weighed by the commission, which then determines who the license shall be awarded to. A preference is generally awarded to an incumbent licensee on the basis of the prior broadcast experience or record of the owners.

information, lack of access to management, the scope of MCAC's activities, and other such areas. After realizing that AETC was actively opposing it, MCAC was forced to complain to the FCC's chairman, Charles Ferris. The group retained CITIZENS as its counsel because AETC unilaterally jettisoned the group after its complaints to the FCC. It was possible that strong legal sanctions would be necessary. The FCC managed to complicate matters even more, through a number of procedural actions. Meanwhile, Alabama Citizens had run into financial difficulties due to the protracted hearings and infighting. It was forced to give up its application for one of the available stations.

Alabama Citizens for Responsive Public Television, Citizens Communications Center, and its client, Montgomery Citizens Advisory Committee, have entered into negotiations to settle the matter. After four years, the Alabama Citizens group has assented to an agreement proposed by AETC, that it give up its claim to the Demopolis station license in favor of AETC, and thereby be left to apply for only one station of the three it had originally sought. AETC would in turn relinquish its claims to the Birmingham station in favor of Alabama Citizens.[78]

CITIZENS and MCAC proposed a much more result-oriented agreement. Their most important proposals were as follows:

1. Affirmative action should be carried out in employment, not merely nondiscrimination, with the establishment of goals, timetables, active recruitment, and job-vacancy notices, including information on employee sex, race, job title; and the recruitment and use of minorities and women in all job categories, especially management: The goal should be that recommended by the U.S. Commission on Civil Rights, of 80 percent parity with their representation in the labor force of the station's service area.[79]
2. MCAC should be completely reinstated.
3. Citizens' advisory committees should be created at all of AETC's stations, along with a serious commitment to give them full cooperation, access to budget information, support services, and a budget.
4. Reimbursement should be provided for CITIZENS during the pendency of the litigation.[80]

AETC responded, and CITIZENS and MCAC replied as follows. CITIZENS notified AETC that, first, its suggestion of merely sending job notices only for engineering positions, and not for all positions, including management, was an erroneous position for it to take.[81] CITIZENS took the position that the FCC's EEO rules and the federal antidiscrimination laws require that all job vacancies be the subject of affirmative action, not merely certain jobs. The obvious effect of this AETC proposal would be to keep traditionally underrepresented groups out of management positions and forever at the lower levels of broadcasting.

Second, AETC's proposed engineer-training program, for only four student interns, from which permanent hiring of one would be attempted, was found by CITIZENS to be too narrow. Training in all job categories was suggested by CITIZENS, including management. It was also suggested that efforts to attract career-oriented persons, in addition to students, be undertaken.[82] CITIZENS found AETC's proposed commitment to hire only the "most qualified" individual for a job opening "unacceptable." This system is no better than the old system. Conceivably, a white individual of equal ability with a black or woman, but who would, due to the history of racial and gender-based exclusion of blacks and women, possess some prior broadcast experience, could easily be deemed most qualified.[83] There is, then, no component of affirmative action, as required by EEO rules,[84] and by federal law,[85] in AETC's proposal. In addition, it was pointed out that where a highly disproportionate representation of minority persons employed at a station is found, and where it can be found that no additional efforts, or insufficient efforts, are undertaken to recruit, employ, and promote minority employees, then administrative action to secure compliance with the FCC's rules is appropriate.[86] In other words, this AETC proposal is far afield from the requirements of the law.

Third, the reinstatement of the MCAC and disclosure of budget information were essential to an agreement. Obviously, if the MCAC could be terminated in such summary fashion, it would mean that no such group could ever serve its purpose, because as soon as it identified relevant problems, it would be unilaterally disbanded. Further, it is a matter of law that the financial budgetary information be disclosed.[87]

There were other issue areas, concerning communication between citizen advisory boards, minimal support for xeroxing and notice mailing, and disclosure of feedback solicited by AETC from its different citizens' committees. AETC chose to leave these issues ill-defined and therefore did not seem to approach them with positive results in mind.[88] Further, AETC refused to establish goals and timetables for its EEO program. This is a particularly troubling refusal; for, as the U.S. Commission on Civil Rights has itself posited, no effective EEO program can be carried out in their absence.[89]

It is hoped that negotiations to settle the controversy will prove fruitful. After nine years from the filing of the first complaints in 1972, four years from the license denial, and the expenditure of incalculable sums of money, where are we?

None of the stations originally the subjects of these comparative hearings—those in Birmingham, Montgomery, and Demopolis—has been granted to Alabama Citizens, after four years of procedural fights, community organization, arranging of financing, personal confrontations, or negotiations. Alabama Citizens has been able to pursue only one of the educational stations in the eight-station educational network of Alabama. AETC has been able to file anew for licenses for two of the originally contested stations, which it may or may not be granted. However, since there are, at this writing, no others competing for the stations and since the FCC did not permanently or temporarily disqualify AETC from reapplying, it seems certain to the author, that AETC will get its stations back. Further, there has been no FCC determination, prejudicial to AETC, that would bar its recoupment of the stations.

The FCC, on balance, has bogged down the hearings with procedure, instead of squarely facing the issues and removing from broadcasting a licensee found guilty of dereliction of its duties to the public.[90] There is much evidence to the effect that the same conditions and wrongs affecting the minority people of Alabama are continuing.[91]

There has been no formal designation, of any of the issues, requested by any of the public parties. There is little indication that negotiations will be concluded soon. In fact, just the opposite conclusion is apparent, if the history of this case can be used as an example of future actions.

There is, further, no indication that, even if Alabama Citizens should be unopposed in its application for the Birmingham station, the FCC will find it qualified and grant it the license.

Lastly, there is no indication that the FCC will ever take serious action against AETC or licensees like them, in light of its actions thus far. If the case is not settled amicably, the hearings will continue before the commission. How long it would take to resolve is anyone's guess. The WLBT case took more than 14 years, including two trips to the appeals court, and still has not terminated.

The message is clear: neither minorities, nor women, weigh heavily enough in broadcasting regulation.

NATIONAL BLACK MEDIA COALITION

Early Beginnings

The National Black Media Coalition (NBMC) was born in 1973, out of the now-defunct Black Efforts for Soul in Television (BEST).[92]

BEST was started and run by a former dental technician named William ("Bill") Wright. Wright, black and extremely concerned about the position of blacks in broadcasting, started BEST in an effort to give blacks an organization with which to achieve more responsivity from the media. He and his group were tireless. He gave speeches, wrote letters, and counseled citizens. They lobbied at the FCC and in Congress for changes they thought necessary to aid the cause of blacks.

BEST was the only organization which made the rights of blacks in broadcasting its top priority. After almost four years of relentless efforts, Wright left BEST. He went on to do research at Stanford University in California, under a grant from the National Science Foundation.

Since BEST was essentially out of business, some new organization was necessary to continue the work. James McCuller, executive director of a Rochester, New York group, Action for a Better Community, was the first chairman of NBMC. NBMC, with the assistance of Citizens Communications Center's attorneys, formalized the coalition. They prepared a 62-point petition for rulemaking. The petition requested the FCC to take specific enforceable action to redress many black grievances concerning their exclusion from the media.

Structure and Activities

Today, the National Black Media Coalition, is an organization with over 70 affiliates across the country, which has, as its purpose, that the communication industry provide basic access for blacks and other minorities.

NBMC holds workshops; assists its local affiliate groups with information and technical contributions; researches key communications areas and issues; participates in congressional hearings, and court and FCC proceedings; lobbies at the Corporation for Public Broadcasting; and distributes a newsletter of pertinent media events and dates.[93] In addition, NBMC aids in the negotiating of community-broadcaster agreements, such as the Gannett and Combined Communications Corporation merger, from which NBMC won many benefits for its affected affiliate members.

NBMC has received no funds, to date, from any foundation or other outside sources. It has survived through dues and contributions, and by holding receptions, discos, and other such events.[94] The organization does plan to submit proposals to several foundations in the near future.[95] There is a national board of directors, to whom policy matters are committed, and several paid support staff members in Washington. The day-to-day operations are under the control of the executive director.

NBMC has, since its inception, been concerned with greater minority ownership of broadcast facilities. In 1973, a request in its 62-point petition to the FCC was for establishment of a Minority Affairs Office within the commission, the purpose of which would have been to give assistance (both technical and financial) to minority entrepreneurs in the acquisition of broadcast properties. In addition, the office would have advised minorities on all related matters.

Citizens Communications Center v. FCC

The U.S. Court of Appeals for the District of Columbia, in 1971, had declared that it was in the public interest to assure a diversity of voices in the media:

> Since one very significant aspect of the "public interest, convenience and necessity" is the need for diverse and antagonistic sources of information, the Commission simply cannot make a valid public interest determination without considering the extent to which the ownership of the media will be concentrated or diversified by the grant of one or another of the applications before it.[96]

The court further explained that an effort to add more minority voices should be undertaken: "As new interest groups and hitherto silent minorities emerge in our society, they should be given some stake in and chance to broadcast on our radio and television frequencies."[97] Yet the court's admonitions were ignored by the commission.

TV-9, Inc. v. FCC

The issue of minority entrance into the field arose again in 1973. The Appellate Court reversed an FCC ruling denying the award of merit to a company having a number of minority owners seeking to win a license through a comparative hearing.

The court required the FCC to recognize and award merit for the superior worth of minority ownership and participation as a general principle:

> It is consistent with the primary objective of maximum diversification of ownership of mass communications media for the Commission in a comparative license proceeding to afford favorable consideration to an applicant who, not as a mere token but in good faith, as broadening community representation, gives a local minority group media entrepreneurship. . . .
>
> We hold only that when minority ownership is likely to increase diversity of content, especially on opinion and viewpoint, merit should be awarded.
>
> The fact that other applicants propose to present the views of such minority groups in their programming, although relevant, does not offset the fact that it is upon ownership that public policy places primary reliance with respect to diversification of content, and that historically has proved to be significantly influential with respect to editorial comment and the presentation of news.[98]

Still, no significant action, such as a rulemaking or change of policy, was forthcoming from the commission.

Garrett v. FCC

A second case soon came down wherein the value of minority ownership and participation was again recognized. In *Garrett v. FCC*, the appellate court fully embraced minority ownership: "Black ownership and participation together are themselves likely to bring about programming that is responsive to the needs of the Black citizenry. . . ."[99]

This new judicial recognition of long-espoused principles of NBMC and many others was very encouraging. The fight for greater minority ownership then took a new turn, opening up a new front.

The "Thaw"

In 1975, the FCC issued a rule which effectively "thawed" the freeze previously imposed on its AM-radio allocations,[100] thereby allowing power increases for existing stations, revised nighttime and frequency rules, new application standards, and other changes.

NBMC, through its counsel, CITIZENS, tried to stay the effective operation of the rule, and asked for reconsideration.[101] NBMC felt that with the new allocations of AM facilities and increases in power of existing stations, minorities would once again be left out unless some affirmative action on the airwaves was undertaken by the commission.

Essentially, said NBMC, minority owners can best combat negative, harmful stereotyping, the disparity in employment, training, and promotions, and the deeply resented exclusion of minorities from the airwaves.[102] Direct purchase and acquisition through comparative hearings were thought unworkable: prices ran into much more than blacks could readily finance at that time, and no one had ever won a license at a full comparative hearing (with the exception of the technically unique WHDH case in Boston).[103]

For these reasons, and for the public interest in diversity of ownership and program content, reasons embraced by the courts, NBMC requested the FCC to institute a program aimed at greater minority participation in ownership.

The request for a stay, and the petition were both denied. So, it was felt by minorities that the second opportunity for AM facilities had come, and again minorities were excluded from ownership en masse.

VHF Drop-Ins

In 1975 there came another opportunity for minority participation. The United Church of Christ had petitioned for a formal rulemaking on the issue of VHF drop-ins and the commission responded by requesting comments as to a continuance or conclusion of the inquiry.

Through improved technology, it was found to be possible to drop in added VHF television frequencies between those presently existing in many markets, without electrical interference. The White House Office of Telecommunications Policy had recommended 62 possible new channels while the FCC found a possible 29.[104] More channels meant more broadcasters.

NBMC told the commission several things. The public-interest benefits of maximizing diversity, of extending service to all of the people of the community, and of providing an equitable distribution of facilities were again obvious and required, argued NBMC. Further, since UHF no longer needed the 20-year-old protectionist barriers the FCC had placed around it in order to encourage its development, it was argued that the time was at hand to restructure

TV frequencies. Thus minority and other traditionally excluded groups would be allowed a chance to enter the mainstream of braodcasting. The commission, on reconsideration, stated it "was not insensitive to the 'affirmative action' issues raised by the Coalition," but it refused to adopt any such rules, preferring a case-by-case approach.

During this period, the U.S. Commission on Civil Rights rebuked the FCC for dragging its feet on minority ownership:

> Most valuable frequencies have already been assigned and, therefore, a minority applicant would be required to engage in a competitive proceeding to seek award of a license. FCC's rulings, however, tend to block new competition for licenses and preserve the status quo, thus continuing the exclusion of minority groups from ownership of communications media outlets.[105]

One can only speculate as to the reasons why the commision has not heeded the courts, the Communications Act, or the under-represented minorities and public at large, why it has not therefore moved to insure more minority ownership. NBMC noted that there might possibly be protectionist reasons for FCC truancy, and cited the trade paper, *Broadcasting* magazine, of October 29, 1973, to the effect that "the addition of new channels may be retarded due to reasons which are 'not so much technical as they are political and economic.'"[106]

A year later, NBMC again pressed for increased minority programming and employment, through ownership in the FCC's clear-channel proceeding.[107]

Clear Channel

In 1927, after a prior attempt to allocate radio frequencies had failed, a system of allocation was put in place by the Federal Radio Commission (the predecessor of the FCC).[108] Stations were divided into various classes based on certain discrete power limitations and operation-time limitations. The purposes of allocation were to eliminate the cacophony caused by allowing any station to broadcast on any frequency, to provide radio service over large areas of the country, and to provide service to the rural areas of the country.[109] This 52-year-old policy is still the basis of today's channel allocations.

The 1934 Communications Act, essentially the same act as that which authorized the 1927 Federal Radio Commission, was adopted. The act kept the "public interest, convenience and necessity"[110] as licensing standards, and it required frequency allocations to reflect "a fair, efficient and equitable distribution of radio service."[111]

The FCC, in 1938, finally adopted a plan allowing 24 clear channels that were given the exclusive right to operate at night in order to fulfill the goals of large-area coverage and rural coverage.[112]

In order to implement the policy to provide large-region coverage and to provide service to rural areas that had no primary nighttime service, other stations were required to close down operations at night. Naturally, clear-channel designation operators and the added nighttime protection given to clear channel operators caused an intraindustry conflict, which as yet goes unresolved. There were those who wanted to eliminate the clear channels and allow more local stations to come into existence, versus the clear-channel operators, who wanted even more power.

In 1961, after 16 years of controversy, hearings, and rulemakings, the FCC broke up (splintered) 13 clear channels and allowed a few new unlimited time stations to operate at night on those 13 duplicated channels. Through this action, the commission hoped to expand the primary nighttime service to those areas of the country having no primary nighttime service, and which had to rely on secondary service from a distant clear channel. The FCC reserved action on the others, saying that it wanted to conserve frequency space for future use.[113] In 1963, the commission changed its primary allocations goals drastically "to preserve the service areas of existing stations. . ."[114] In 1964, the commission completely froze its AM allocations, and subsequently received many waiver requests from license applicants—one of which even resulted in court recognition that the FCC's tight-fisted approach to frequency conservation was, in light of new technologies, perhaps too rigid.[115]

Finally, the commission opened yet another inquiry in 1976, saying it wanted to reconsider the issues of super power, splintering of clear channels, and the role of FM in rural broadcast service.[116]

NBMC Seeks More Minority Ownership

Amid this background of confused policy and uncertainty, NBMC, through its counsel, CITIZENS, entered its comments urging, among other objectives, a program for increasing minority ownership through a splintering of the clear channels.

Since the 1961 FCC policy to increase service had failed miserably (having increased delivery to only slightly more than 1 percent of the population),[117] NBMC urged a return to former FCC policies adopted prior to 1961. This action would eliminate the frequency-preservation priority adopted in 1961. The public interest demanded return to policies which would promote primary service to areas without primary service of their own, not secondary service from some distant high-power station; initial local service where none existed previously; and a multitude of rural service where possible.[118] All these goals were directly derived from the Communications Act of 1934.[119]

The false scarcity of frequencies that resulted from the existence of the clear-channel system would no longer be necessary. The clear-channel grants would no longer merit this special protection resulting in the exclusion, from broadcasting, of traditionally underrepresented groups such as minorities and women.

It was further argued that the clear-channel operators had trouble properly ascertaining and serving such large areas anyway, since their news and programming could not match very well with communities hundreds of miles away, which had not been properly ascertained in the first place.[120] In addition, local competition would increase, or a decrease in concentration of media would result, and the inflated prices of broadcast facilities caused by the false scarcity would shrink, thus allowing for easier entry of blacks and other minorities into the broadcast field. Again, NBMC based its arguments on the widely acknowledged public interest in diversity, on recent court decisions, and on the national affirmative action policies set forth in the U.S. rule changes implementing all of the above objectives; and more changes were proposed by NBMC. Despite all the above mentioned FCC confusion, and all the efforts of NBMC and other public-interest groups, the FCC has yet to approve substantial reformist ownership proposals. In addition, there is no time limit on such FCC proceedings. They could drag on for years, only to be concluded by a finding that the situation does not now require any such action. Federal agencies have that kind of broad discretion. So, the struggle for access continues.

The Congressional Black Caucus, the Office of Telecommunications Policy (OTP, presently reorganized into the National Telecommunication and Information Administration), and the United Church of Christ also filed petitions supporting increased minority ownership. The Congressional Black Caucus urged that new policies be adopted that would allow for sales of stations to groups with substantial minority participation (more than 50 percent)—

stations which had been run so inimically to the public interest that they were either designated for a hearing or were the subject of revocation proceedings. This "distress-sale" policy would be allowed to take place at reduced prices, as had been FCC policy in bankruptcy or other serious licensee-debilitating situations. OTP petitioned the FCC and proposed a general policy to procure greater ownership, recognizing "the unique importance of broadcasting to our democratic society."[121] OTP also relied on President Carter's then newly adopted policy of promoting minority business, including minority telecommunications.[122]

NBMC, through its counsel, CITIZENS, filed its supporting comments in that action. In addition to the grounds cited above, NBMC stated that the so-called racially neutral policies of the past would not serve to aid the interests of minorities in the future. One reason was the Catch 22 inherent in financing. NBMC cited the fact that many loans are denied potential minority broadcasters by lenders who say, "come back when you've developed some expertise and experience in the business." But unless you first own a station, from whence is that expertise to come?[123] After all these years of pushing for entry of minorities into the very nervous system of America, finally, the FCC organized a Minority Task Force and Conference to study the problems of ownership. Its report was released in 1978.

NBMC, the United Church of Christ, NOW, National Citizens Committee for Broadcasting (NCCB), the National Council of LaRaza, the NAACP, and others are continuing their efforts with respect to the ownership implications of the FCC's network inquiry and its top-50 market-policy inquiry.

Results

The Small Business Administration (SBA) has recently liberalized its financing of media-properties rules. It will now make direct loans up to $350,000 and will guarantee loans up to $500,000. Federal financing via MESBIC (Minority Enterprise Small Business Investment Corporation) is helpful; however, when the price of TV properties runs into the hundreds of millions of dollars, it is apparent that such financing is not sufficient to put a minority entrepreneur in the top markets without substantial infusions of capital from other sources.[124]

The National Association of Broadcasters (NAB) held its first broadcasting seminar for black-owned stations on September 21-23, 1976. The NAB recently formed a Task Force on Minority

Ownership, pledged to raise $37.5 million in cash and another $7.5 million in loan guarantees to help fund minority acquisitions. As of the writing, no funds have been raised.[125] It will be extremely interesting to see how much money is ultimately raised, how the fund will be administered, and what technical, managerial, and financial-packaging assistance will be forthcoming. The types of properties, locations, and liability of properties recommended will be of interest as well. The criteria for obtaining funds and the inevitable obligations and terms will bear close scrutiny. Minority owners have complained that only the "dog" stations are offered to them.[126]

To date, the FCC has issued only a policy statement on minority ownership, dated May 25, 1978.[126] A policy statement is just that. It is simply an expression by the FCC of what it intends to do in a given situation. It does not have the binding force of law behind it that a statute or agency rule would have. The commission has adopted a policy that, where a station is to be sold to parties with a "significant minority interest" (defined as over 50 percent control), the commission will examine the transaction prior to approval, and if it finds that "there is a substantial likelihood that diversity of programming will be increased," it will issue a tax certificate to the seller if it also finds that issuance would be "appropriate to advance its policy of increasing minority ownership."[127] "[T]o further encourage broadcasters to seek out minority purchasers," the FCC will allow stations designated for license revocation or renewal hearing, "on basic qualifications issues," to transfer their licenses to minority purchasers at distress-sale prices.

The congressional black caucus's petition proposing to establish a policy with objective rules for distress sales was not adopted. Although the commission endorsed their goals, it stated it preferred to perform a case-by-case review in order "to determine that the objectives of our policies will be met."[128]

The FCC has adopted a policy. The White House has come out in favor of promoting minority broadcasting. The SBA and NAB have also taken steps.

As of 1977, minorities had 51 percent or more control of only one TV station in the continental United States, a UHF commercial-television station located in Detroit. Two VHF-TV stations in the Virgin Islands make up the remaining black-owned television stations. Hispanics owned six UHF, and other minorities owned none.[129]

The pending transfer application for WHEC-TV in Rochester,

New York, may provide one exception to the exclusion of minorities from broadcasting. This chance at acquisition resulted from a broadcaster-community agreement situation (described below).

The question remains: How long will black, Hispanic, Native American, women and other traditionally underrepresented groups be excluded from the most viable marketplace of ideas?

NBMC Sparks Minority Ownership of WHEC-TV

The National Black Media Coalition has recently used the agreements process (described in the *UCC III* section above) to produce the first sale of a commercial VHF station in the continental United States to a minority controlled group and to produce significant assistance for minority entrepreneurs.

Background

In May of 1978, the proposed merger between two media giants, the Gannett Company and Combined Communications Corporation, was announced. The Gannett Company is the largest newspaper chain in the country, owning 78 newspapers. While Combined Communications, a diversified communications company, owns seven TV and 12 radio stations.[130]

Rochester, New York, is the cradle of the National Black Media Coalition and the present home of one of its founders, and first chairperson, Jim McCuller. WHEC-TV and the Gannett Company were no strangers to the NBMC, since WHEC-TV had been the subject of a petition to deny, based on the grounds of inadequate programming for the large black population in Rochester, and on employment grounds.[131] NBMC's efforts on this front had not met with much success, the FCC having refused to designate a hearing against WHEC-TV, despite the fact that its term-time employment figures fell outside the commission's own loosely defined equal-employment threshold test.[132] However, when the proposed merger announcement was made in May, McCuller immediately recognized that the NBMC had to move to closely scrutinize this merger, which would have implications and effects not only for Rochester blacks, but for all of the blacks in cities across the country where the Gannett-Combined Communications group had media outlets.

The Deal

Under present FCC multiple-ownership rules, the maximum number of VHF-TV stations that any one entity is allowed to own anywhere in the country is five.[133] Combined Communications already had its limit. Since Gannett owned WHEC-TV, a VHF station, the purchase of Combined Communications by Gannett would put it over the limit. It therefore had to rid itself of one of its VHFs in order to be in compliance with the FCC rules.

In license-transfer situations, the FCC must approve such transfers, and it must make an affirmative finding that the transfer would serve the "public interest, convenience and necessity,"[134] before any proposed transfer of a license from one entity to another can become legally operative. Therefore, even if the parties to a station sale agree on all terms, the license to operate does not change hands without express FCC approval. If, for any valid reasons, a third party intervenes and raises objections to the transfer, through a petition to deny the transfer—alleging that the transfer would not serve the public interest—the FCC would be presented with a situation where it might not be able to make the required public-interest finding and could therefore not approve the transfer. Thus, the deal would die. Even lengthy proceedings with a high chance of approval could kill a deal.

The proposed merger was to run into approximately $379 million. Furthermore, there were certain antitrust implications and concentration-of-control issues apparent in the proposed merger, the two companies being giants in the field even prior to the merger. NBMC had already challenged WHEC-TV's license once, and thereby established a record of past WHEC deficiencies. What was there, then, to recommend this sale?

NBMC fully understood the implications of the merger and its role in it. Negotiations were opened with Gannett and Combined Communications management. It was obvious that one of the VHF stations had to go. It was just as obvious that if NBMC were to file a petition to deny, the $379-million deal could be stopped in its tracks and thus might die. The fact that NBMC could step into the middle of this deal and legitimately raise certain public-interest issues, thus preventing the flow of the large sums of money pent up on either side, provided NBMC with the leverage it needed to win certain concessions for blacks from Gannett.[135] Approval from the FCC is slow enough in coming in the ordinary situation where transfer is uncontested. The prospect of dragging this out even longer was not very attractive to the two media companies.

On November 21, 1978, the National Black Media Coalition announced the conclusion of an agreement between itself and the Gannett Company, which went far to foster greater minority participation in broadcasting.[136] McCuller states that the agreement came about because of three reasons. First, Gannett was not naive about the pressure NBMC could have applied, using the issues at hand. Second, Gannett really took a close look at the media-concentration and newspaper/broadcast-concentration issues, among others, and decided that they were a possible source of problems. The limit on VHF ownership was, of course, obvious. Finally, in light of all of this, Gannett saw that the vote for approval at the commission might be close.[137] It therefore needed something to recommend this transfer—some public-interest benefits upon which the commission could make its affirmative finding necessary for approval. The benefits to minorities flowing from the agreement provided a good basis upon which to approve the transfer.

Terms of the Agreement

Broadcast Enterprises Network, Inc. the buyer, is the largest black-owned broadcast group in the country. It has six radio stations and is about to buy its first TV station, for $27 million.[138] Ragan Henry, a very successful, self-made black capitalist, and a Harvard Law School graduate, is president of the company.[139]

WHEC-TV is the first VHF station (out of 755 VHF stations) in broadcasting history to be sold to a predominately black company. Only 62 of the 8,500 radio stations in the country are black owned. Only 16 are owned by Latinos.[140] The implications are, of course, profound. Direct FCC intervention was not the cause of WHEC sale; the cause was, rather, a combination of FCC presence and grassroots black persistence in pursuing the goal of greater minority ownership of broadcast properties. Although a very unique set of circumstances converged to produce the sale, it is clear that such sales can be accomplished. One black-owned VHF TV station, out of 755, represents a very small percentage. Neither the FCC, the industry, nor the public should be at all proud of a record like this, after over 60 years of absolute minority exclusion. The sale is simply a beginning. If minorities and women are to be represented among the ranks of broadcast owners, there is still much to be done to correct the substantial underrepresentation of these two groups.

The widely accepted goal of furthering diversity of the content of programming, through diversity of ownership has been accomplished with this sale. Minorities are the best possible groups to promote their own views and images. This cannot be done by proxy, as the present system presumes.

> The fact that other applicants propose to present the view of . . . minority groups in their programming, although relevant, does not offset the fact that it is upon ownership that public policy places primary reliance with respect to diversification of content; and that historically has proven to be significantly influential with respect to editorial comment and the presentation of news.[141]

Ownership of a VHF station helps to bring minorities more fully into the economic mainstream of America, which itself tends to decrease the disparities which fuel the racism so prevalent in America. Management and ownership expertise flow from purchases such as this. This in turn increases the probability and possibility of future purchases by minorities.

Aside from the sale, other steps have been taken in the agreement to assist minority entrepreneurship. Four of these provisions follow.

First, when a media property is offered for sale to Gannett, and if Gannett decides that it is not interested in purchasing it, "Gannett will notify prospective minority purchasers of which it is aware of the availability of the property for sale," provided the seller has agreed.[142]

Second, "if Gannett does decide to sell any of its media properties and pursuant to that decision lists the property with a broker, Gannett will instruct the broker to contact prospective minority purchasers and will provide the broker with a list of prospective minority purchasers."[143]

Third, "Gannett will make available without charge its management expertise on a consulting basis in areas such as financial management and planning, property evaluation and engineering and systems planning."[144]

Fourth, "Gannett will assist in arranging for contributions of up to $10,000 per year for three years toward the financing of training seminars for minority and potential minority media owners."[145]

There are other provisions in the agreement, allowing for improvements in equal employment opportunity, minority membership on the Gannett board of directors, and the distribution of a media consumer guidebook that will explain how to get more media consumer messages on the air through Combined Communications media outlets.

Although implementation of the sale and agreement is dependent upon FCC approval, it would appear that approval will be forthcoming, thereby fixing a broadcasting milestone.

NOTES

1. United Church of Christ, *History and Program*, 2d rev. ed. (New York: United Church Press, 1974), p. 47.

2. Ibid.

3. Interview with Ralph Jennings, March 13, 1979, New York; Office of Communications, United Church of Christ, *How to Protect Citizen Rights in Television and Radio*, (New York, 1968), p. 3.

4. United Church of Christ, *History and Program*, op. cit.

5. Ibid.

6. Ibid.

7. Office of Communication, United Church of Christ Report to the Ford Foundation, "A Program to Combat Racial Discrimination in Broadcasting" grant number 680-0203D, October 9, 1973.

8. Ibid.

9. Ibid.

10. Office of Communication, United Church of Christ Report to the Ford Foundation, "A Program to Combat Racial Discrimination in Broadcasting," grant number 680-0203A, March 26, 1971, p. 2.

11. Ibid.

12. Ibid.

13. *See*, Communications Act of 1934, 42 USC s. 307 (b); *Ascertainment of Community Problems by Broadcast Applicants*, 41 Fed. Reg. 1372 (1976); William K. Jones, *Electronic Mass Media* (Mineola, N.Y.: Foundation Press, 1976), p. 15.

14. Ibid.

15. Office of Communication, United Church of Christ Report to the Ford Foundation, "A Program to Combat Racial Discrimination in Broadcasting," grant number 680-0203B, December 31, 1971, p. 15.

16. *See, In re Petition of Office of Communication, Board of Homeland Ministries and Committee for Racial Justice Now of the United Church of Christ For changes in rules*, April 21, 1967.

17. "Proposed Rule: Part 73, subparts A,B,C, and E of the Commission's Rules should be amended by adding thereto the following: 'No license shall be granted to any station which engages in discrimination in employment practices on the basis of race, color, religion, or national origin. Evidence of compliance with this section shall be furnished with each application for a license and annually during the term of each license upon prescribed forms.'"

18. See, Ralp Jennings interview, op. cit. (note #3).

19. *FCC's Proposed Policy Statement and Notice of Proposed Rulemaking re: Agreements Between Broadcast Licensees and the Public*, June 10, 1975, No. 20495. Office of Communication of the United Church of Christ, comments, July 25, 1975. The proceeding was initiated by the FCC to set its policy on citizen-broadcaster agreements, such as the one concluded in the KTAL-TV case. Comments are formal statements tendered by any interested party in an agency proceeding which set out the party's position on the issue which is the subject of agency proceedings.

20. Office of Communication of the United Church of Christ, *In re Petition for Rulemaking to Amend Television Table of Assignment to Add New VHF Stations in the Top 100 Markets and to Insure that the New Stations Maximize Diversity of Ownership, Control, and Programming*, March 26, 1974. The Office of Communication also entered its comments once the FCC formally opened the proceeding. See *Comments of Petitioners* in the above cited petition December 18, 1975.

21. *In re: Petitions of the Aspen Institute Program on Communications and Society and CBS, Inc., for Revision or Clarification of Commission Rulings under Section 315 (a) (2) and 315 (a) (4), 35 RR 2d 49, 1975.*

22. 47 U.S.C. 315.

23. *See*, Brief for Intervenors, Office of Communication et al., *The Honorable Shirley Chisholm, et al., v. FCC*, Nos. 75-1951 and 75-1994, October 28, 1975.

24. *See*, HR 13015, Communications Act of 1978, "A Summary of the Hearings and Comments," prepared by the Telecommunications Consumer Coalition, December 18, 1978.

25. Office of Communication, United Church of Christ Report to the Ford Foundation, "A Program to Combat Racial Discrimination in Broadcasting," Grant number 680-0203E, January 7, 1976, p. 2.

26. Sydney W. Head, *Broadcasting in America*, 3d ed., (Boston: Houghton Mifflin Co., 1976) p. 445; interview with Ralph Jennings, March 13, 1979, New York.

27. United Church of Christ I, 359 F2d. at 998 (1966).

28. *Office of Communication of United Church of Christ v. F.C.C.*, 425 F. 2d 543, 548 (1969) (hereinafter United Church of Christ II).

29. *United Church of Christ I*, 359 F2d. at 998 U966.

30. Interview with Jennings, March 13, 1979.

31. "The Commission's denial of standing to appellants was based on the theory that, absent a potential direct, substantial injury or adverse effect from the administrative action under consideration, a petitioner had no standing before the Commission and that the only harms sufficient to support standing are economic injury and electrical interference. The FCC asserted its traditional position that to allow the listening public at large to have standing would pose great administrative burdens on it. See, *United Church of Christ I*, 359 F2d at 1000 (1966).

32. "We cannot believe that the Congressional mandate of public participation which the Commission says it seeks to fulfill was meant to be limited to writing letters to the Commission, to inspection of records, to the Commission's grace in considering listener claims, or to mere non-participating appearance at hearings. "See *United Church of Christ I*, 359 F2d at 1003-4 (1966).

33. "The theory that the Commission can always effectively represent the listener interests in a renewal proceeding without the aid and participation of legitimate listener representatives fulfilling the role of private attorneys generally is one of those assumptions we collectively try to work with so long as they are reasonably adequate. When it becomes clear, as it does now, that it is no longer a valid assumption which stands up under the realities of actual experience, neither we nor the Commission can continue to rely on it." *See*, *United Church of Christ I*, 359 F2d at 1003-4 (1966).

34. 47 USC s. 307 (a).

35. *See*, *United Church of Christ I*, 359 F. 2d at 1005 (1966).

36. "We cannot fail to note that the long history of complaints against WLBT beginning in 1955 had left the Commission virtually unmoved in the subsequent renewal proceedings, and it seems not unlikely that the 1964 renewal application might well have been routinely granted except for the determined and sustained efforts of Appellants at no small expense to themselves. Such beneficial contribution as these Appellants, or some of them can make, must not be left to the grace of the Commission." *See*, *UCC I* at 1004 (1966).

37. *See*, *Petition for Reconsideration of NBMC, "Affirmative Action on the Airwaves," in re Amendment of Part 73 of the Commission's Rules Regarding AM Station Assignment Standards*, No. 20265, p. 6.

38. FCC Figures reveal that from 1972 through 1977, the commission has

renewed over 98 percent of AM radio licenses, over 99 percent of FM radio licenses, and over 97 percent of TV licenses. *See*, Deirdre Carmody, "Challenging Media Monopolies," *New York Times Magazine*, July 31, 1977, p. 22.

39. *See, United Church of Christ II*, 425 F2d. 543 (1969).

40. "When the matter was again before the Commission on our remand, therefore, it was in a posture that the *licensee* had yet to demonstrate that it was in the public interest for the license to be renewed." *See, United Church of Christ II*, 425 F. 2d. at 545 (1969). Yet the FCC had wrongly placed the burden on the public intervenors. "[M]oreover, the practical effect of the Commission's action was to place on the Public Intervenors the entire burden of showing that the licensee was not qualified to be granted a renewal." *See, United Church of Christ II*, 425 F. 2d. at 545 (1969).

41. "We did not intend that intervenors representing a public interest be treated as interlopers. Rather, if analogues can be useful, a "Public Intervenor" who is seeking no license or private right is, in this context, more nearly like a complaining witness who presents evidence to police or a prosecutor whose duty it is to conduct an affirmative and objective investigation of all the facts and to pursue his prosecutorial or regulatory function if there is probable cause to believe a violation has occurred." *See, United Church of Christ II*, 425 F2d. at 546 (1969).

42. Ibid. at 547 (1969).

43. *See*, Ibid., at 548 (1969).

44. "The record now before us leaves us with a profound concern over the entire handling of this case following the remand to the Commission. The impatience with the Public Intervenors, the hostility toward their efforts to satisfy a surprisingly strict standard of proof, plain errors in rulings and findings lead us, albeit reluctantly, to the conclusion that it will serve no useful purpose to ask the Commission to reconsider the Examiner's actions and its own Decision and Order under a correct allocation of the burden on proof. The administrative conduct reflected in this record is beyond repair." *See, Ibid.*, at 550 (1969).

45. Head, *Broadcasting in America*, p. 452.

46. Office of Communication, United Church of Christ Report to the Ford Foundation, "A Program to Combat Racial Discrimination in Broadcasting," grant number 680-0203A, March 26, 1971, p. 2;.

47. *See, NAACP v. FPC*, 425 US 662, 670 n. 7 (1976).

48. *See, KCMC, Inc.*, 19 FCC 2d 109 (1969).

49. Office of Communication, United Church of Christ Report to the Ford Foundation, "A Program to Combat Racial Discrimination in Broadcasting," grant number 680-230, November 7, 1964, p. 2.

50. In re *KCMC, Inc.*, 25 FCC 2d 603, 604 (1970).

51. Ibid.

52. Ibid. at 605-6.

53. Ibid. at 527.

54. Ibid.

55. *United Church of Christ III*, 465 F2d. 579 (1972).

56. In re *KCMC, Inc.*, 35 FCC 2d 24O (1972).

57. *See, e.g.*: "As we view the record the [Hearing] Examiner tended to impede the exploration of the very issues which we would reasonably expect the Commission itself would have initiated; an ally (the Public Intervenor) was regarded as an opponent." *UCC II* at 549, 1969. *See also*: "The Examiner and the Commission exhibited at best a reluctant tolerance of the Court's mandate [in *UCC I*] and at worst a profound hostility to the participation of the Public Intervenor and their efforts." *UCC II* at 549-550, 1969; *see also*, Office of Communication, United Church

of Christ, "FCC Rulemakings and Policy Changes," September 1, 1976. The UCC posits that over the 3-4 years running to 1976, the FCC has attempted to deregulate broadcasting in favor of the industry.

The authors of "Citizen Action and Broadcasters' Interests: The Record of the FCC," state that the FCC is biased in favor of the broadcast industry, neglecting its duty to the public in the process. See, Oscar Gandy, Timothy Haight, Jorge Reina Schement, Esteban Soriano, and Felix F. Gutierrez, "Citizen Action and Broadcasters' Interests: the record of the FCC," April, 1976, p. 7.

58. See, In re Applications by *Bob Jones University, Inc.*, 32 FCC 2d 781 (1971); In re Application of RKO General Inc. and *Heftel Broadcasting—Boston, INC.*, 42 FCC 2d 1076 (1973) *recon. denied as moot*, 29 R.R. 2d 396 (1974), reversed, *BCMC Minority Caucus v. FCC*, 32 R.R. 2d 599 (D.C. Cir. 1975).

59. *Final Report and Order in the Matter of Agreement Between Broadcast Licensees and the Public*, (December 19, 1975).

60. *Final Report and Order in the Matter of Agreement Between Broadcast Licensees and the Public*, (December 19, 1975).

61. *Final Report and Order in the Notice of Inquiry and Proposed Rulemaking in the Matter of Reimbursement for Legitimate and Prudent Expenses of a Public Interest Group for a Consultancy to a Broadcaster in Certain Instances*, FCC 76-5 (January 9, 1976).

62. See, Joseph A. Grundfest, *Citizen Participation in Broadcast Licensing Before the FCC*, (March 1976).

63. See, Agreement between the Post Corporation, the RBMC and Actions for a Better Community, August 19, 1977.

64. See, Chuck Shepard and Larry Dickter, "Washington's Citizens Communications Center: Tower of Strength in Media Reform", *access*, October 1, 1976, Issue 42 p. 6. Also, Deirdre Carmody's "Challenging Media Monopolies" N.Y. Times Magazine, July 31, 1977, p. 22.

65. Barry Cole and Mal Oettinger, *The Reluctant Regulators, the FCC and the Broadcast Audience* (Reading, Massachusetts, Addison-Wesley Publishing Co., 1978), p. 66.

66. Perhaps the first formal "Radio council" was created in 1922. The members, DePaul University, Northwestern University, The University of Chicago, the Rockefeller Foundation, The Carnegie Corporation, Rapid Stations WLS, WJJD, and WIND, and NBC, CBS and the Mutual Network came together to found the University Broadcasting Council. Its goal was to develop educational and cultural programming and to conduct research in educational radio.

67. Ibid., Sheppard and Dickter article.

68. Deirdre Carmody, "Challenging Media Monopolies, "*New York Times Magazine*, July 31, 1977, p. 22.

69. Citizens Communications Center, "Projects in Progress"—1978, p. 2.

70. *In re: Application of Alabama Educational Television Commission for Renewal of License*, 50 F.C.C. 2d 484, 485 (1973)

71. Bernard Rubin, *Media, Politics, & Democracy*, (New York, 1977), p. 102.

72. Ibid., p. 103.

73. Ibid.

74. Ibid., p. 103-104.

75. Ibid., p. 104.

76. Ibid.

77. See, Federal Communications Commission's *Report on Minority Ownership in Broadcasting*, May 17, 1978, p. i of the Summary.

78. See, letter from Ed Hayes, Jr., Esq., to Marvin J. Diamond, Esq., February 1,

1979. (Hayes & White is counsel for Alabama Citizens; Hogan & Hartson is counsel for AETC).

79. U.S. Commission on Civil Rights report, *Window Dressing on the Set: Women and Minorities in Television*, August 1977, p. 151.

80. Letter from Wilhelmina Reuben Cooke, Esq. to Marvin J. Diamond, Esq., February 12, 1979. (Wilhelmina Reuben Cooke is the attorney within CITIZENS assigned to this case.).

81. See, letter from Wilhelmina Reuben Cooke, Esq. to Gardner F. Gillespie, Esq., March 16, 1979.

82. Ibid., p. 2.

83. See, Letter from Wilhemina Reuben Cooke, Esq. to Gardner F. Gillespie, Esq., March 16, 1979. (Mr. Gillespie is an attorney at Hogan & Hartson, AETC's counsel.).

84. FCC Rules, § 73.125, 73.301, 73.599, 73.680, 73.783, 73.311.

85. Title VII of Civil Rights Act of 1964; 42 U.S.C. Section 1983 (1964).

86. See, C.F.R. § 73.2080; *Rust Communications Group*, Inc., 53 F.C.C. 2d 355 (1975).

87. See, MCAC petition.

88. See, Letter from Wilhemina Reuben Cooke, Esq. to Gardner F. Gillespie, Esq., March 16, 1979, p. 4-5. (Mr. Gillespie is an attorney at Hogan & Hartson, AETC's counsel).

89 See generally, U.S. Commission on Civil Rights Report, *Window Dressing on the Set: Women and Minorities in Television*, August, 1977, p. 74-152.

90. Memorandum Opinion and Order, Alabama Citizens for Responsive Public Television, FCC 78-507, p. 10 (July 28, 1978).

91. See generally, MCAC Petition.

92. "NBMC at 22 (Months): Maturing, Optimistic", *access*, September 22, 1975, p. 18.

93. See, *NBMC Brief for Intervenors, Office of Communication of United Church of Christ, et al., v. FCC*, FCC No. 76-4187, November 1, 1976; *NBMC News Summary*, Vol. II, #14, January, 1976, p. 1.

94. NBMC News Summary, Vol. II, #14, January, 1976, p. 1.

95. Interview with David Honig, March 18, 1979, Ocean Pines, Maryland.

96. *Citizens Communications Center v. FCC*, 447 F2d 1201, 1201, 1213, n. 36 (1971).

97. *Citizens Communications Center v. FCC*, 447 F2d 1201, 1201, 1213, n. 36 (1917).

98. *In re TV 9, Inc. v. FCC*, 495 F2d 929 at 937—938 (D.C. Cir. 1973), *cert. denied*, 418 U.S. 986 (1974).

99. *Garrett v. FCC*, 513 F2d 1056, 1063 (D.C. Cir. 1975) (footnote omitted).

100. *In re: Amendment of Part 73 of the Commission's Rules Regarding AM Station Standards, Report and Order*, Dkt. 20265, (1975); Or *Report and Order, AM Station Assignment Standards*, FCC 75-769, p. 34 R.R. 2d 603, released July 14, 1975.

101. NBMC *Petition for Reconsideration, in re Amendment of Part 73 of the Commissions' Rules Regarding AM Stations Assignment Standards*, Dkt. 20265, Aug. 13, 1975.

102. Ibid., p. 57.

103. NBMC Comments *in re: Clear Channel Broadcasting in the Standard Broadcast Band*, Dkt. 20642, 1976, exhibit 2, p. 7; see also, n. i.

104. NBMC Comments on *VHF-Drop-Ins*, December 1975, Dkt. 20418, p. 12.

105. U.S. Commission on Civil Rights, *The Federal Civil Rights Enforcement Effort*—1974, Vol. I, p. 49.

106. NBMC Comments, *VHF-Drop-Ins*, December 1975, Dkt. 20418, p. 14-15, citing *Broadcasting*, October 29, 1973.

107. In re: *Clear Channel Broadcasting in the Standard Broadcast Band*, Dkt. 20462.

108. FRC General Order #40, T-9-10.

109. See *NBMC Comments, in re: Clear Channel Broadcasting in the Standard Broadcast Band*, Docket No. 20.

110. 47 U.S.C. § 307 (a).

111. 47 U.S.C. § 307 (b).

112. *See generally*, AM Station Assignment Standards, 25 R.R. 1615, 1626 (1963) (Notice of Proposed Rulemaking, Docket 15084).

113. Clear Channel Broadcasting in the Standard Broadcast Band, 31 FCC 565, 21 R.R. 1808 (1961), reconsideration denied, 24 R.R. 1595 (1962).

114. *AM Station Assignment Standards*, 5 R.R. 1615, 1626 (1963).

115. *WAIT Radio v. FCC*, 459 F. 2d 1203, 1210 (D.C. Cir. 1972).

116. *Notice of Inquiry and Proposed Rule Making, in re: Clear Channel Broadcasting in the Standard Broadcast Band*.

117. See, *Notice of Inquiry and Proposed Rule Making in re: Clear Channel Broadcasting in the Standard Broadcast Band*.

118. See, NBMC Comments *in re: Clear Channel Broadcasting in the Standard Broadcast Band*, Docket 20642, 1976, p. 16.

119. 47 U.S.C. § 151; 47 U.S.C. § 151; 47 U.S.C. § 307 (b).

120. See, *Rust Communications Group*, 53 F.C.C. 2d 355 (1975) (where the clear channel station was designated for a hearing on improper ascertainment of its substantial Black audience of Rochester, New York).

121. *Office of Telecommunications Policy and the Department of Commerce's Petition for Issuance of Policy Statement or for Notice of Inquiry*, 1977.

122. White House memorandum, issued September 17, 1977, transmit a statement by the dated September 12, 1977.

123. NBMC Comments on *Congressional Black Caucus' Petition to Formulate a New Policy to Promote Minority Ownership of Broadcast Properties*, February 2, 1977, p. 11.

124. See, FCC report on *Minority Ownership in Broadcasting*, May 17, 1978, p. 8, 23.

125. See, *Broadcasting*, January 1, 1979, February 19, 1979, p. 64.

126. See, FCC Report on *Minority Ownership in Broadcasting*, May 17, 1978, p. 9, n 23.

127. See, *F.C.C. Statement of Policy on Minority Ownership of Broadcasting Facilities*, Federal Communications Commission "Public Notice," May 25, 1978.

128. FCC, "Statement of Policy on Minority Ownership of Broadcasting Facilities," Public Notice, May 25, 1974, p. 7.

129. *Id.*, p. 8.

130. Broadcast Summary Statistics for U.S. Office of Telecommunications Policy, September 13, 1977.

131. "National Black Media Coalition Wins Landmark Agreement with Gannett Covering Broadcasting, Newspapers," *Access* 62 (December 4, 1978):4.

132. *WHEC, Inc.*, 52 FCC 2d 1079 (1975).

133. *Id.*, at 1089.

134. William K. Jones, *Electronic Mass Media*, (Mineola, New York, Foundation Press, Inc., 1976), p. 9.

135. 47 U.S.C. § 310 (d).

136. Interview with James McCuller, April 15, 1979, Rochester, New York.

137. NBMC Press Release, November 21, 1978.

138. Interview with Jim McCuller, April 15, 1979, Rochester, New York.

139. Jacqueline Trescott, "Ragan Henry: Matter-of-Fact Broadcast Pioneer," Washington Post, November 24, 1978, p. 10.

140. Mr. Ragan Henry grew up in Sadieville, Kentucky, the son of a family of tabacco sharecroppers. He practised financial, Corporate law and did some trial work in his present hometown of Philadelphia, prior to becomming involved with broadcasting. In 1970, he invested in the newly formed Sheridan Broadcasting and by 1973 Mr. Henry was pursuing his own stations. He put up $28,000 of his savings, used his salary to pay for his feasibility studies and raised another $3.5 million from friends, banks and venture capital companies in order to close his first radio station deal in Atlanta. Mr. Henry now presides over the largest Black-owned broadcast group in the country.

141. See, Note 2 above; and U.S. Office of Telecommunications Policy Broadcast Summary Statistics, Minority Ownership Table, September 13, 1977.

142. In re *TV 9, Inc. v. FCC*, 495 F. 2d 929, 938 (D.C. Cir. 1973), cert. denied, 419 U.S. 986 (1974).

143. Gannett Co., Inc. Public Interest Proposals and Policies, p. 22.

144. Gannett Co., Inc. Public Interest Proposals and Policies, p. 23.

145. Ibid.

146. Ibid.

ABOUT THE EDITOR AND CONTRIBUTORS

BERNARD RUBIN is the Director of the Institute for Democratic Communication at Boston University's School of Public Communication and a professor there and in the Graduate School. He earned the Ph.D. in Political Science from New York University. Before joining the Boston University faculty in 1959 he taught at Brooklyn College, Skidmore College and Rutgers University. He has also been a visiting Professor at the Naval War College.

He has been a consultant to the Agency for International Development, the United States Air Force and other government departments. Dr. Rubin was Chief of Research Design at the United States Information Agency in the late 1960's. He has recently served, on two extended visits, as advisor to the Malaysian government MARA Institute of Technology (1974 and 1975) where he worked on middle management training of Malaysians in the communications professions. In 1978 he was a member of the American delegation to the "International News Media and World Development" conference in Cairo, Egypt. Numerous other research trips have taken him to France, Great Britain and the Federal Republic of Germany.

During 1979 he lectured at San Francisco State University, and the University of Denver. Also, he lectured in Southeast Asia (India, Philippines, Sri Lanka and Thailand) on international information subjects for the United States International Communication Agency (present name of the former U.S.I.A.).

Dr. Rubin is the author of numerous articles in the areas of mass communications, public policy and administration and politics. His books include: *Public Relations and the Empire State* (1957); *Political Television* (1967); *Propaganda and Public Opinion* (1972); *Media Politics and Democracy* (1977); *Big Business and the Mass Media* (1977); *Questioning Media Ethics* (1978).

CARYL RIVERS is associate Professor of Journalism at the School of Public Communication at Boston University. She is the author of "Aphrodite at Midcentury: Growing Up Female and Catholic in Postwar America" (Doubleday, 1973) and co-author of "Beyond Sugar and Spice" (Putnam's, 1979). The latter is a comprehensive look at research on feminine development and was selected as a Book-of-the-Month Club selection for fall, 1979. The book's co-authors are psychologists Grace Baruch and Rosalind Barnett, both of Brandeis.

Professor Rivers writes frequently for newspapers and national magazines. She was Writer-in-Residence at the Washington Star in 1976, writes regularly for the syndicated column "One Woman's Voice" and for The Boston Phoenix. A story she wrote for New Times Magazine, "The Nightmare of Hugh Rivers Jr."—about the chaos in America's Mental Health system—is currently being produced as a made-for-television movie. Her articles have appeared in The New York Times Magazine, Ms., New Times, The Nation, Saturday Review, Mother Jones, Rolling Stone, Redbook, McCalls and others. She was a finalist in the national competition for excellence in magazine journalism sponsored by the University of Missouri and the J.C. Penney Co. for 1978. She was cited for an article written for Womensports magazine, "The Girls of Summer." She also received the 1978 award as outstanding magazine writer for the New England area given by the New England Women's Press Club.

During her five years as a Washington correspondent for a number of papers and magazines across the country, Prof. Rivers covered Capitol Hill and the White House. She has also been a television commentator. She holds a Masters degree in Journalism from the Columbia University Graduate School of Journalism and an A.B. in History from Trinity College, Washington D.C.

EVERETTE E. DENNIS is professor of journalism and mass communication at the University of Minnesota, Minneapolis where he is director of graduate studies in mass communication and a member of the faculty of American Studies. He was liberal arts fellow in law at Harvard Law School in 1978-79. His book credits include *The Media Society, Evidence About Mass Communication in America, Justice Hugo Black and the First Amendment,* and *Enduring Issues in Mass Communication* (all 1978), *New Strategies for Public Affairs Reporting* (1976), *Other Voices: The New Journalism in America* (1974) and *The Magic Writing Machine* (1971). He is also a frequent contributor to professional journals and law reviews. Dennis has taught at Minnesota, the University of Oregon, Northwestern University and Kansas State University. At Minnesota he was director of the WCCO Minorities in Broadcasting Program for four years. His graduate degrees are from Syracuse University (M.A.) and the University of Minnesota

(Ph.D.). He has worked as a reporter, information officer and communication consultant.

JOHN TAYLOR WILLIAMS is a practicing attorney specializing in publishing, First Amendment, and copyright law, with a long involvement in civil rights. His clients include authors and creators of intellectual properties as well as publishers, museums, and television and radio stations.

He is currently the chairman of the American Bar Association's Committee on Authors, and cochairman of the Boston Bar Association's Committee on Legal Services to the Indigent. He is director of Boston's Lawyers Committee on Civil Rights, the Massachusetts Prison Legal Services Corporation, the Institute of Contemporary Art, and the City of Cambridge Arts Council.

A graduate of Harvard College and the University of Pennsylvania Law School, he is a partner in the Boston firm of Haussermann, Davison & Shattuck.

MELVIN MEDERO MOORE, JR. is an associate producer at WGBH-TV, Boston. Since joining WGBH in 1974, he has been employed in the capacity of director of content development for Rebop, a national multicultural children's program; an associate producer for "Say Brother," a public affairs, third-world program; and is currently assisting WGBH's Department of Cultural Affairs in the development of a black dramatic series. Mr. Moore received the B.A. and M.A. degrees from Michigan State University and the Ph.D. in clinical psychology and public practice from Harvard University.

JOSEPH BOSKIN is a professor of History and Afro-American Studies, and serves as the codirector of the Urban Studies Program at Boston University. He is the author of numerous articles on images and stereotypes in American culture, and has authored and edited a series of books on racial, urban, and humor topics, including *Seasons of Revolt: Protest and Radicalism in Recent America* (1972); *Into Slavery: Racial Decisions in Colonial Virginia* (1976); and *Humor and Social Change in 20th Century America* (1976). His media connection involves three television series and one radio series. He was awarded an Emmy for writing and hosting the NBC series "The Negro in American Culture" (1968).

WILLIAM ALFRED HENRY III heads the broadcast department of The Boston Globe. He has won regional awards for news feature and editorial writing from Associated Press and United Press International, including 1977 AP prize for Best Story of the Year in New England.

His writings have appeared widely in Horizon, The New Republic and other magazines, and newspapers including The Washington Post and The New York Times. He has had his fiction and poetry published and is working on a novel. Other works of the fairly recent past include a history of Yale football and a commissioned screenplay.

He is a graduate of Yale University and was awarded the highest undergraduate, academic honor (Scholar of the House, B.S., 1971). At Yale he was the Executive Editor of the Yale Daily News and the yearbook.

JEAN C. REINHARD has a bachelor's degree in english literature from Trinity College, and a master of arts in speech and drama from Catholic University, both in Washington, D.C. She has a Master of Science degree in Communications from Boston University's School of Public Communication. Ms. Reinhard has worked in production in professional theater in New York and Washington, D.C. In New York she also worked as an assistant to Audrey Wood, an agent representing an elite group of Broadway playwrights. She spent three years in Germany, directing armed-forces shows for the U.S. Army. From 1963 to 75, she taught speech and communication arts at several colleges, including Mount Saint Mary College in Newburgh, N.Y.; Orange County Community College in Middletown, N.Y.; and Middlesex Community College in Bedford, Mass.

LAWRENCE M. MARTIN is an associate professor of journalism at Boston University's School of Public Communication. He received his doctor of international law degree, and an M.S. degree in journalism from Charles University, Prague. His teaching focuses on international press problems, history of journalism, and journalistic research methods. Before joining Boston University in 1971, he was research associate at the Fletcher School of Law and Diplomacy, Tufts University, Medford. He came to the United States in 1968 from Czechoslovakia, after a 14-year career in the Czechoslovak foreign service that had brought him to Korea, the Peoples Republic of China, the German Democratic Republic, the Federal Republic of Germany, Austria, and several other countries. He is the author of several books, among them: *The Chancellor Was the First to Die* (1968), and *The Deception Game* (1972).

EMIL WARD received his B.S. from Dickinson College, Carlisle, Pennsylvania (1970) and his J.D. from Northeastern University (1978). He has concentrated on communications and entertainment law. He interned with Citizens Communications Center, the public-interest communications law firm of Washington, D.C. There he drafted much of the brief for the National Black Media Coalition in a key case involving the Federal Communications Commission's equal employment opportunity rules. He traveled extensively in East Asia from 1970 to 1972. He is now practicing law in Boston.